Key Concepts & Skills for Media Studies

Vivienne Clark
James Baker
Eileen Lewis

Hodder & Stoughton

A MEMBER OF THE HODDER HEADLINE GROUP

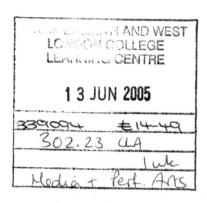
Orders: please contact Bookpoint Ltd, 130 Milton Park, Abingdon,
Oxon OX14 4SB. Telephone: (44) 01235 827720. Fax: (44) 01235 400454.
Lines are open from 9.00 – 6.00, Monday to Saturday, with a 24 hour
message answering service. You can also order through our website www.hodderheadline.co.uk

British Library Cataloguing in Publication Data
A catalogue record for this title is available from the British Library

ISBN 0 340 807849

First Published 2002

Impression number   10 9 8 7 6 5 4 3
Year   2007 2006 2005 2004

Typeset and produced by Gray Publishing, Tunbridge Wells, Kent
Printed in Malta for Hodder & Stoughton Educational,
a division of Hodder Headline, 338 Euston Road, London NW1 3BH.

Contents

Preface: to the student   **vii**

Preface: to the subject tutor   **ix**

Acknowledgements   **xi**

Chapter 1   **Key concepts and skills**   **1**

Defining communication processes and media forms   1

The key concepts of Media Studies   3

Ways of studying media texts and products   8

Media studies skills   11

Media production skills   13

Chapter 2   **Analytical skills**   **15**

How to study a media text   15

Studying genre   15

Part 1: analysing audio-visual media language   18

Focus genre: action/adventure films   25

An exemplar textual analysis of *Raiders of the Lost Ark*   28

Part 2: analysing print-based media language   30

Focus genres: lifestyle magazines and tabloid newspapers   33

An exemplar textual analysis of the front cover of *Sugar* (October 2001)   37

An exemplar textual analysis of the front page of *The Mirror* (Tuesday 4 September October 2001)   43

Part 3: analysing ICT-based media language   44

Common theoretical approaches to textual analysis   52

Studying narrative   55

Chapter 3   Case studies **59**

Case study 1: studying documentary forms   59
Castaway: an analyis of a documentary text   72
Case study 2: studying gender representation in television   75
TV situation comedy   79
TV soap opera   86
Case study 3: studying new media technologies   92
Digital television   99
Case study 4: studying media ownership and institutions   109
AOL Time Warner   116

Chapter 4   Being creative: production skills **123**

Approaches to practical production and evaluation   123
Part 1: how to write an evaluation   125
Part 2: general advice and production principles   130
Part 3: video production   134
Part 4: print production   153
Part 5: audio production   159
Part 6: ICT-based production   167

Chapter 5   Improving your study skills **173**

Introduction   173
Note-making   174
Making notes from moving image media texts   178
Essay writing   179
Research and reading   182
Revision   185

Appendix **191**

Bibliography and recommended reading   191
Useful websites   195
Student guidence   196
Resources and contacts for tutors   197

Glossary **199**

Index **203**

Preface: to the student

We wrote this book to support you in preparation for your Media Studies assessment. It is meant to be a practical companion to use while you're studying and revising (whether at home, school or college) and we've tried to design it so that it is easy to find what you are looking for, quickly.

We cannot claim to have included everything you need to know here in such a small space, as the subject is very wide-ranging, but the main aim of the book was to produce something that would give you the basic key concepts and skills you need to get started.

Media Studies is a demanding subject. You are required to be a know-it-all about new technology, current affairs and new topics, on the one hand, and you're asked to be a graphic designer or a film director for your practical project, on the other. In addition, someone, somewhere (usually a self-appointed guardian of the nation's educational standards or a jaded newspaper editor), will tell you that this subject is a soft option!

We do not believe that Media Studies is an easy option and this book aims to provide you with definitions and examples of the **key concepts** and **skills** that you will have to learn; the essential 'what', 'how' and 'why' of studying the media. We also provide you with demonstrations of **textual analysis** of a variety of media texts as examples to show you the application of key concepts and skills in action.

How the book is arranged

The book has the following features to help you to find your way around:

- ☐ **Key terms:** these are important terms with their definitions. They are provided near to their use in the relevant chapter and are included in the index, so that you can look up other references to them.
- ☐ **Activities:** these offer you opportunities to engage with some of the ideas in the book. They are numbered to help you and your tutors to identify them quickly.
- ☐ **Examiners' tips:** these are some points of advice from our experience as GCSE and A-level Media Studies examiners, to help you to prepare for your assessments.
- ☐ **Extend your knowledge:** this gives you some suggestions for more advanced research, especially if you are continuing this subject to the

second year of A-level, to SQA Advanced Higher level, to AVCE or preparing to start an undergraduate course in a media-related subject.

We are pleased to have included photographs of some of our own students at work, with some examples of their media production projects, to show you how they have approached their work.

What level are you studying for?

The book is ideal for **AS-level Media Studies** and has been written for students following the Media Studies specifications of **OCR**, **AQA** and **WJEC** awarding bodies alike. However, it has been designed with students on other courses in mind, such as **GNVQ**, **AVCE**, **BTech** and **Scottish Higher** courses. It will also be very useful to you if you have not studied Media Studies at A-level, but are starting as an undergraduate on a **media-related degree** course.

Chapter 5, **Improving your study skills,** aims to help you to prepare for the range of assessments you are likely to encounter. It also anticipates some of the types of study you will progress to in the second year of an A-level course or on an undergraduate course, such as research.

In the Appendix, the sections on **Bibliography and recommended reading** and **Useful websites** contain lists of books and sites that you might find helpful for your studies. Within this section is **Student guidance**, which contains sources that offer you guidance on choosing a media-related degree course or on career routes if you are considering taking your studies further in this field.

The authors have many years' experience of teaching GCSE and A-level Media Studies to hundreds of students, many of whom, we are pleased to say, went on to study a media-related degree course and are currently working successfully in various parts of media industries.

Whatever path you choose to follow, we hope that you find the book useful and we would be pleased to hear from you about anything you liked or think that we have missed out. You can contact us at mailto:info@screenstudies.com when you have a moment.

Vivienne Clark, James Baker and Eileen Lewis

Preface: to the subject tutor

Given that exam specifications tend to change frequently, we decided to produce a book that dealt with the essential foundation of Media Studies, namely the **key concepts** and the **skills** of analysis, research, exam preparation, student media production and evaluation.

Even though new topics and texts may be introduced and technology changes, this common conceptual foundation for studying media texts and products remains, and will probably remain, essentially the same. This foundation is shared by most Media Studies courses at all levels and so it is our intention that this book is a versatile, accessible and, in times of restricted budgets, fairly timeless resource.

In such a space as this, there will inevitably be omissions and a lack of detail (for example, we have not addressed Key skills, but these are comprehensively referenced in every awarding body's specification). But given the wide-ranging nature of this subject, and the tendency of other textbooks on the market to pack a bit of everything in, we decided to emphasize the basic key concepts and skills that you need to cover with your students.

Levels of study

This book is ideal for **AS-level Media Studies** and has been written for students and tutors following the Media Studies specifications of **OCR**, **AQA** and **WJEC** awarding bodies alike. These three specifications essentially share the same **conceptual framework**, even if the nomenclature or emphases may differ slightly. They also have much in common in terms of topics and methods of assessment and we have focused on these common areas, namely textual analysis, preparing for unseen media text examinations, student media production and key topics.

This book was in production while the first cycle of the new A-level specifications was in progress and what was quite apparent to us from our teaching was that there was quite a jump in the level of demand required between AS- and A2-level. While it is clear that not much theory is needed to succeed at AS-level, students are certainly required to demon-strate much more theoretical understanding at A2-level. Therefore, we have included some examples of using theory and make references to exten-sion or research activities to help students (and tutors) to anticipate this jump, identified as **Extend your knowledge**.

This book has been designed with students on other courses in mind, such as **GNVQ**, **AVCE** and **BTech** and **Scottish Higher** courses. It will also be very useful for anyone who has not studied Media Studies at A-level, but who is starting as an undergraduate on a **media-related degree** course.

How this book is arranged

The book has been designed to be used by the student for independent learning as well as by the tutor in class or small group work.

See the preface for students earlier (page vii) for a guide to the book's features.

CONTINUING PROFESSIONAL DEVELOPMENT AND RESOURCES

The increasing number of students opting to take Media Studies at A-level as an option in our schools and colleges has inevitably resulted in an increase in demand for numbers of tutors to deliver the course. From our work with awarding bodies and for various professional development agencies, the authors are well aware that many tutors find themselves 'in at the deep end' at the start of September, many not having taught the subject before and with no prospect of training. This book has also been written with you firmly in mind.

In the Appendix we have included a section, **Resources and contacts for tutors**, that includes contact details of most of the key networking, continuing professional development and resources agencies, at the time of publication.

Please feel free to contact us at info@screenstudies.com if you have any feedback on our book.

Vivienne Clark, James Baker and Eileen Lewis

Acknowledgements

The authors and publisher would like to thank the following for permission to use copyright material in this book:

Routledge and the author for extract from Paul Levinson, *The Soft Edge*; Routledge and the author for extract from John Fiske, *Television Culture*; M.U.P. and the author for extracts from Richard Kilborn and John Izod, *An Introduction to Television Documentary: Confronting Reality*; Ebury Press and the author for extracts from Mark McCrum, *Castaway: The Full Inside Story of the Major BBC Series*. BBC Radio 4 and the presenter, Paul Lewis, for the script extract from *Moneybox* (16 September, 2001). Canterbury Christ Church University College, Kent, UK for stills from *What Women Want* and for the script extract from the radio play *Beans Means Fines*. Film Education and Aardman Animations for the synopsis and script extract from *Chicken Run*. Arnold and the authors for material on websites in David Gauntlett and David Silver, *Web Studies*, Arnold, 2000. OCR, AQA, WJEC, Ed-Excel and SQA awarding bodies, for references to their post-16 qualifications specifications.

The authors and publisher would like to thank the following for permission to use copyright illustrative material in this book: AOL Time Warner page 118; BBC page 73; British Film Institute/Sight & Sound page 120; Colombia Pictures pages 50 (right), 140; Corbis pages 54, © Underwood & Underwood page 23; Disney Pixar page 50 (left); Eyevine, © Amanda Searle page 59; Robert Flaherty/Pathé Exchange Inc. page 62; Gaumont-British Picture Corporation Ltd. page 27 (left); © Granada Television pages 67, 91; Ronald Grant Archive/Paramount Pictures/Lucasfilm page 29; Robert Gray/Gray Publishing page 32; © Hachette Filipacchi Ltd. page 36; Lawrence of Mar pages 124, 126, 151, 165; Mersey Television page 89; Mirrorpix pages 40 (above), 43, 56, 148; NBC page 83; New Line Cinema page 49 (left and right); Arch Oboler/United Artists page 95; Paramount Pictures pages 25, 186; Paramount Pictures/Lucasfilm page 27 (right); Quentin Tarantino/Miramax page 110; Times Newspapers Limited, London pages 39, 40 (below); Touchstone Pictures page 50 (middle); Working Title Films page 182.

Special mention is due to Nina Welling and to Laurence of Mar for their excellent photographs of students at work and to the students of Hurtwood

House, Ravens Wood and Maidstone Boys' Grammar themselves for allowing us to feature their work, which bring all the theories alive.

Every effort has been made to trace and acknowledge ownership of copyright. The publishers will be glad to make suitable arrangements with any copyright holders whom it has not been possible to contact.

Thanks

The authors would like to thank our many students, past and present, for their enthusiasm, creativity and commitment to their studies, as well as the staff at Ravens Wood School, Maidstone Grammar School for Boys and Hurtwood House, respectively, for their support.

We would also like to thank our long-suffering families for their support and encouragement.

We are very grateful to Lesley Riddle and Alexia Chan at Hodder Arnold, for their helpful guidance and enthusiasm for the project. Thanks are also due to Lesley Gray and the team at Gray Publishing for all their hard work.

CHAPTER 1

Key concepts and skills

Defining communication processes and media forms

- What is your personal style of inter-personal communication?
- Ask a friend or family member what typifies how you communicate with family, friends and others.
- If it is difficult to think objectively about yourself, try asking a friend for their opinions or make a video recording of yourself when you are talking to friends and directly to the camera. Watch yourself on the recording.
- What can you observe about your voice, gestures, body language and vocabulary?

It is an obvious point to remind you here that communication is an essential part of the human experience, but it is worth pausing for a moment to consider how methods of communication have evolved from what we might term as **inter-personal** to those communicated via mass media forms. This book is concerned with **media communication**, but in many cases these forms are essentially the result of centuries of creative and technological evolution from basic forms of inter-personal communication.

Diagram 1.1 outlines the basic ways in which humans communicate on an inter-personal basis. However, there are other forms of communication, which are neither inter-personal nor strictly media forms, in the contemporary sense of the word, which are very closely related to the areas that we will be studying and which contribute a great deal to collective and individual identities, cultures and self-expression. For example:

- ☐ art, sculpture and architecture
- ☐ literature (including poetry, plays and novels)
- ☐ theatre, music concerts and dance
- ☐ fashion
- ☐ hobbies and crafts, including sport.

MAIN MEDIA FORMS

Throughout this book we have grouped the various forms of media communication into **three study areas**, for ease of reference:

- ☐ **audio-visual media forms** comprise moving image media (film and television), which use moving images and sound, and audio forms
- ☐ **print media forms** which use still images and words
- ☐ **ICT-based media forms** combine elements from both moving image and print media.

Diagram 1.1   The main forms of inter-personal communication.

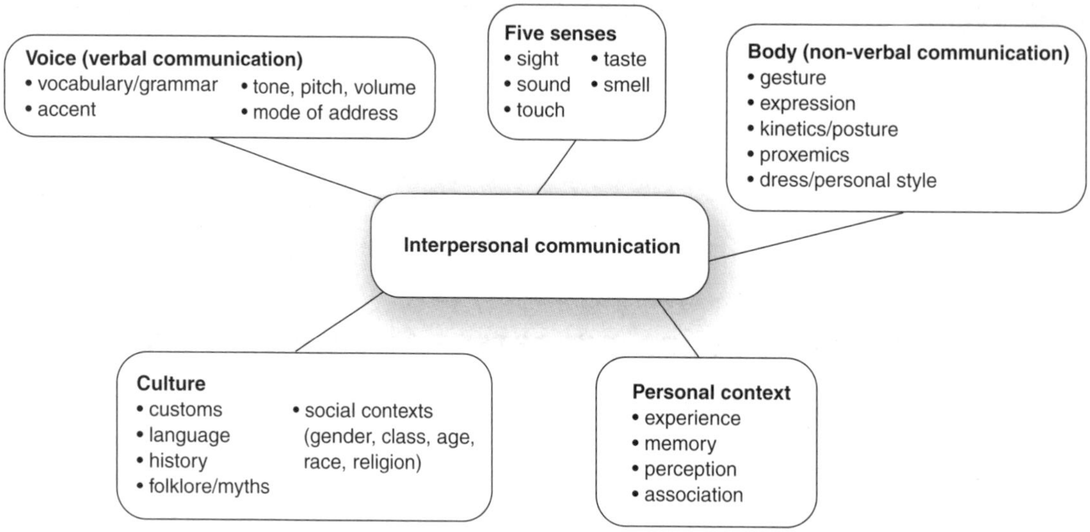

Voice (verbal communication)
- vocabulary/grammar
- accent
- tone, pitch, volume
- mode of address

Five senses
- sight
- taste
- sound
- smell
- touch

Body (non-verbal communication)
- gesture
- expression
- kinetics/posture
- proxemics
- dress/personal style

Interpersonal communication

Culture
- customs
- language
- history
- folklore/myths
- social contexts (gender, class, age, race, religion)

Personal context
- experience
- memory
- perception
- association

ctivity 1.2

- Using the information above about these forms of communication, consider the various ways in which you communicate your identity and opinions to other people.
- What forms of communication do you enjoy, other than media forms?

In this book we will be referring to the objects of our media study as either:

☐ **media texts**, if we are studying their content and meaning or
☐ **media products**, if we are studying them as the outcome of a production process and in an institutional and audience context.

You might find that this distinction is useful to you in your own writing.

xtend your knowledge

- Communication Studies is a discipline related to Media Studies and looks at a wide range of communication, including linguistics, psychology and sociology as well as media forms.

- Have a look at some textbooks on Communication Studies to consider the relationship between Media Studies and Communication Studies.

ctivity 1.3

Keep a diary of what you watch, read and listen to for one week. What patterns emerge about:
- Favourite choices?
- Times of day? When do you access different media forms?
- Duration? How long do you do this activity for?

- Location? Where do you access these forms?
- Activity and company? What else are you doing when you are watching/reading/listening? Who else is with you? What impact do they have on your experience/enjoyment?

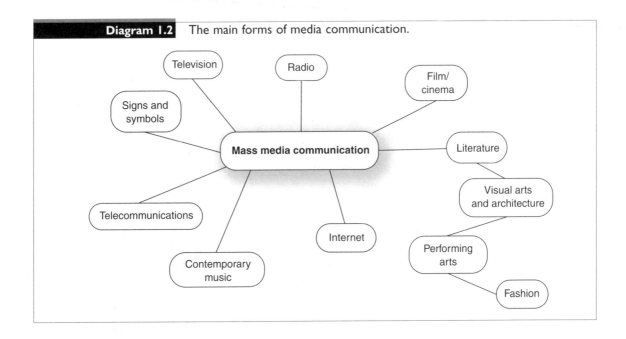

Diagram 1.2 The main forms of media communication.

The key concepts of Media Studies

We don't need an explicit understanding of key concepts to understand how to read a newspaper or enjoy a film, as these are skills that we have developed along with other competencies we use in our daily lives. Nor does a film-maker necessarily analyse the representation of female characters in a film, but they will nevertheless be influenced by ideas, decisions and processes that we study as the concept of **representation**, in the casting of a particular actor or the design of a costume, for example.

You will also be introduced to a number of **media theories** in what follows below. But it is important to understand that these have been developed over time, by a wide variety of writers and academics to explain the **effects** and **processes** of media texts and industries, rather than to provide rules to which media producers adhere.

These key concepts make **explicit** that which is **implicitly understood** by us all, when we watch a television programme or see a billboard campaign, but more importantly, they can direct us to levels of knowledge and understanding that are not immediately apparent to us.

The key concepts of Media Studies are those that have been gathered together to form the academic study of the media, and, together with various skills referred to below, you will need to demonstrate your competence in them in order to be successful in your Media Studies assessments. Furthermore, what you will learn from these various perspectives will undoubtedly deepen your enjoyment of media products and might encourage you to be creative yourself.

A concept is abstract, an idea or way of thinking about something. Over the years, several key conceptual areas have been assembled from a variety of other disciplines (such as linguistics, literary studies, politics, history, economics, sociology, aesthetics, psychology and anthropology) about how to study the media. These **concepts** are considered to be of essential, or **key**, importance because they unlock ways of understanding media texts and products that we may not have considered before. A stone arch contains a key stone, the most important one, as it holds the whole arch together, by supporting the weight of the other stones. So a key concept is one which supports the structure, or conceptual framework, of Media Studies.

Without these key concepts, Media Studies would be a chaotic and haphazard subject. There are so many media texts and products to study and they keep changing on a regular basis, with new films being released, news events occurring by the minute and new technologies being invented and superseded on a daily basis, that it would be impossible to learn everything about everything!

This is one of the features that makes Media Studies such an exciting subject, for students and tutors alike. But, armed with an understanding of the key concepts and skills associated with this subject, you can transfer them to any topic or text without much difficulty. This is the intention of this book.

Every awarding body (exam board) that offers a qualification in Media Studies has its own conceptual framework and assessment objectives, as well as different areas and topics of study. We have tried to assemble the elements that are common to most of these qualifications post-16 and while there are slight differences in the terms used by different awarding bodies in their specifications, we have tried to make it as easy as possible for you to follow.

It is important to point out here that there is a variety of terms used for a variety of purposes and that Media Studies combines two specialist languages that you will have to learn and apply:

- ☐ the first is the **technical language** of media production processes
- ☐ the second is the **critical language** of media analysis and theory.

The key concept areas of Media Studies comprise main groups of related concepts and we have outlined them below as sets of basic questions that you can apply to texts in order to analyse them more closely. The outcomes of applying these key questions are what you will be assessed on, so keep referring back to them occasionally.

MEDIA LANGUAGE

Media language, sometimes termed **mediation**, refers to the languages used by audio-visual, print and ICT-based media to produce meaning.

Picture 1.1 Students use the language of film promotion in their own media production, for example, this poster for the film *The Painting* by Jonathan Prout and Daniel Harris (poster by Jonathan Prout).

The key questions to ask here are:

- [ ] What is this text called and what associations do we have with this title/name?
- [ ] What is this text about? What does this text 'say'?
- [ ] How does it 'say' it?
- [ ] What are its languages (print, moving images, sounds) and style? How do they create meaning?
- [ ] How are these languages put together, or constructed, to make this text?
- [ ] What languages do we need to consider and use when making our own media text?

FORMS AND CONVENTIONS

The concept area of **forms and conventions** refer to the forms, categories and conventions used to organize and structure the languages of media products.

The key questions to ask here are:

- [ ] What category, or genre, of text is it? How can you identify this?
- [ ] What can we learn from this text from its opening minutes or front cover?
- [ ] What codes and conventions does it follow or disobey?
- [ ] What categories and conventions do we need to consider and use when making our own media text?

AUDIENCES AND INSTITUTIONS

The concept area of **audiences and institutions** refers to the participants with roles in the media production process, the institutions they represent, how they are financed and generate profit, and the processes of media production themselves.

It also concerns the relationship between the media and audiences and a look at the audiences themselves, made up from individuals and social/cultural groups, and are involved in the consumption of media texts and their responses to them.

The key questions to ask here are:

- [ ] How was the text produced (production processes)?
- [ ] By whom (company, individual, team) and why (entertainment/information) was it produced? What else have they made?
- [ ] Who is in it? What else have they produced/appeared in?
- [ ] How does this effect our understanding of this text?
- [ ] When and where was it produced and how did this influence its production?
- [ ] What is it similar to? Why might this be relevant?
- [ ] What was/is its competition/market?
- [ ] For whom was it produced (target audience)?

Picture 1.2   Students use the codes and conventions of charity advertisements to create their own media products – Daniel MacNamara (top left), Joel Simons (top right) and Tim O'Neill (bottom).

- [ ] Who actually watches/reads/listens to it? How do we know?
- [ ] How was it financed and by whom? How much profit did it make?
- [ ] How did it reach its audience?
- [ ] How/where/when was it advertised? Where is it shown, sold or available?
- [ ] How do audiences respond to or interpret/make use of the text?
- [ ] What expectations and pleasures do audiences have in response to the text? What effects does it have on them? How do we know this?
- [ ] What have other people said about this text (critics, academics, etc.)?
- [ ] How do you respond to this text and why?
- [ ] What aspects of audiences and institutions do we need to consider when producing our own media text?

REPRESENTATION AND IDEOLOGY

The conceptual area of **representation** and **ideology** considers the relationships between people, places, events, ideas, values and beliefs and their representations in the media; and the issues and debates arising from their representations.

This includes how we might choose to create representations of ourselves, our families and surroundings. We also look at how we make sense of the meanings of media texts and how these meanings contribute to the ways in which our society and communities function.

The key questions to ask here are:

- [ ] Whose interests does the text serve?
- [ ] Who is present in this text? Who is absent from this text?
- [ ] Who or what can it be said to represent?
- [ ] What does the text tell us about who made it and when and where they made it?
- [ ] Has its meaning changed over the years and in what ways?
- [ ] What judgements do you make about the truth, accuracy or effect of this text?
- [ ] What judgements might other people or groups make about it?
- [ ] What values are offered, either directly or indirectly, by the text?
- [ ] What conclusions can we draw from it, what issues does it raise?
- [ ] What do we need to consider when making a media text?
- [ ] What messages and values are we using in our decision-making?

Key terms

Representation: the process of making meaning in still or moving images and words/sounds. In its simplest form, it means to present/show someone or something. However, as a concept for debate, it is used to describe the processes by which an image etc. may be used to represent/stand for someone or something, for example a place or an idea.
Ideology: often referred to as the system of **ideas, values** and **beliefs** which an individual, group or society holds to be true or important; these are shared by a culture/society, or groups therein, about how individuals/society should function.

Ways of studying media texts and products

One of the challenges of Media Studies is the number of media forms that could be studied in a 1- or 2-year course. You will usually have to study **three** media forms and several media texts/products as case studies within these forms. Therefore, the potential scope of what you could study would be almost infinite.

| Picture 1.3 | Two video covers for the student short film *The Painting* by Jonathan Prout (bottom) and Daniel Harris (top). |

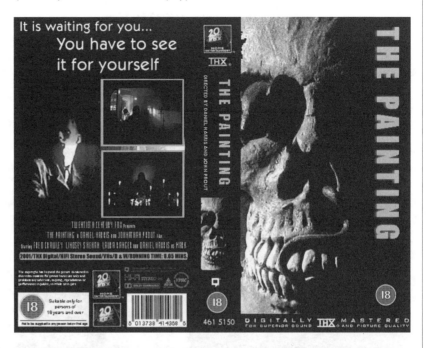

Picture 1.4 A student example of an exercise in self-representation by Daniel MacNamara.

Thankfully, as with all academic subjects, the main method of assessment in Media Studies is via sets of **assessment objectives** that assess the key concepts and skills, rather than your knowledge of *every* media form. The details of the specification that you are studying will show details of the assessment objectives that are linked to each module or unit exam that you will sit.

It could be that your tutor will provide you with the assessment objectives and assessment criteria (in the form of mark schemes) before you start work on a module or unit, which would be useful. Examination specifications are public documents and if you would like to see the content of the specification you are following, you can access it on the website of your awarding body (see the **Appendix** for **Awarding body contacts**).

The assessment objectives for each module/unit will show you which key concept or skill is being assessed on which occasion and they act as a focus or emphasis for your study of a particular media text/product. Diagram 1.3 shows you the range of key concepts and skills as applied to the medium of film. As you can see, you would need a great deal of time to study even one text from all of these different perspectives.

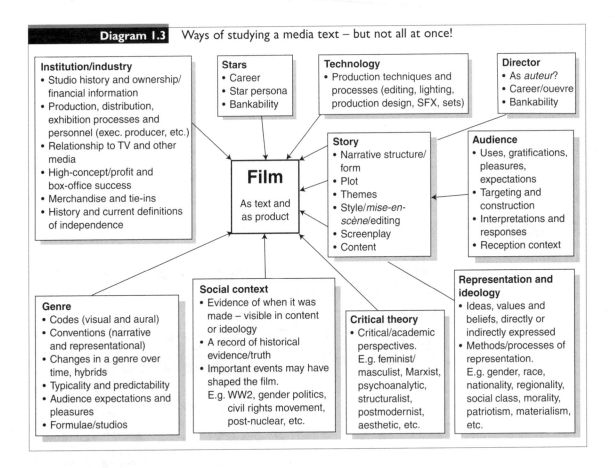

Diagram 1.3   Ways of studying a media text – but not all at once!

Institution/industry
- Studio history and ownership/financial information
- Production, distribution, exhibition processes and personnel (exec. producer, etc.)
- Relationship to TV and other media
- High-concept/profit and box-office success
- Merchandise and tie-ins
- History and current definitions of independence

Stars
- Career
- Star persona
- Bankability

Technology
- Production techniques and processes (editing, lighting, production design, SFX, sets)

Director
- As *auteur*?
- Career/ouevre
- Bankability

Film
As text and as product

Story
- Narrative structure/form
- Plot
- Themes
- Style/*mise-en-scène*/editing
- Screenplay
- Content

Audience
- Uses, gratifications, pleasures, expectations
- Targeting and construction
- Interpretations and responses
- Reception context

Genre
- Codes (visual and aural)
- Conventions (narrative and representational)
- Changes in a genre over time, hybrids
- Typicality and predictability
- Audience expectations and pleasures
- Formulae/studios

Social context
- Evidence of when it was made – visible in content or ideology
- A record of historical evidence/truth
- Important events may have shaped the film. E.g. WW2, gender politics, civil rights movement, post-nuclear, etc.

Critical theory
- Critical/academic perspectives. E.g. feminist/masculist, Marxist, psychoanalytic, structuralist, postmodernist, aesthetic, etc.

Representation and ideology
- Ideas, values and beliefs, directly or indirectly expressed
- Methods/processes of representation. E.g. gender, race, nationality, regionality, social class, morality, patriotism, materialism, etc.

Media studies skills

ANALYTICAL SKILLS

Some people are of the opinion that analysis, or **deconstruction** (effectively taking something apart to see how it was made), is anti-creative and the opposite of the ways in which we really engage with media products. However, it is fair to say that we almost cannot resist some kind of analysis or evaluation of media products in our daily lives, as we regularly exclaim that a particular film or television programme was 'rubbish' or point out mistakes.

Analysis is, however, an essentially critical activity undertaken for academic purposes. The closest activity to detailed analysis of media texts and products that you have already encountered (if you did not study GCSE Media Studies) is likely to be the study of literary texts for GCSE English or English Literature.

Media Studies goes beyond the current state of literary study, as it updates the study of stories, for that is essentially what all media texts deal with, and extends it to encompass the economic, social and cultural contexts of these stories.

See Chapter 2 for detailed advice on:

☐ analysing audio-visual media
☐ analysing print-based media
☐ analysing ICT-based media.

| **Picture 1.5** | Early storyboard ideas (by Daniel Harris) and screen grabs from the final student short film *The Painting* by Jonathan Prout and Daniel Harris. |

See Chapter 3 for case study examples of:

☐ studying documentary forms
☐ studying gender representation in television
☐ studying new media technologies
☐ studying media ownership and institutions.

Media production skills

This aspect of the subject is probably what attracted you to Media Studies in the first place, as it is an opportunity to experiment with technology and your own ideas; some of you might have already decided that a job in a media industry is something you want to progress to. Hands on experience with media production techniques is very much a part of this subject, but it does not qualify you for a job in media production, nor can most schools compete with industry facilities or tutors compete with the knowledge and skills of media professionals.

However, the purpose of practical production work in 16–19 Media Studies courses is two-fold:

☐ to offer you a chance to be creative and learn new skills
☐ to give you contexts in which to explore the relationships between media theory/analysis and media practice.

See Chapter 4 for detailed advice on practical skills in:

☐ video production
☐ print production
☐ audio production
☐ ICT-based production.

EVALUATIVE SKILLS

You will find that there is always a written activity that accompanies any media production exercise. This is because it forms an essential part of the assessment of your skills in the production and analysis of media products. The ability to evaluate your own work with objectivity and detailed reference to key concepts and technical terms is a difficult one and it is important that you develop it to complete your assessment successfully.

See Chapter 4 for detailed advice on how to write an evaluation.

See Chapter 5 for advice on how to improve your study skills in preparation for your exams.

| Picture 1.6 | Evaluation of your own media product can involve detailed textual analysis – *The Painting*, Jonathan Prout and Daniel Harris. Analysis by Jonathan Prout. |

of the bars in a prison cell: in this case, our main character's forthcoming entrapment in the painting.

Venetian blinds are used as a stylistic reference to film noir as in these three examples. Clockwise from top left: Harrison Ford in *Blade Runner* (Dir. Ridley Scott, USA, 1982), Fred MacMurray in *Double Indemnity* (Dir. Billy Wilder, USA, 1944) and Dan in our film.

The music in the dining room sequence is an unused piece of music from the film *The Exorcist* (Dir. William Freidkin, USA, 1973). This music is used to add suspense to the scene. The editing in the scene starts off slowly and gets quicker as the scene progresses, another device to increase the tension in the scene.

Page 11 of 18

Analytical skills

How to study a media text

We will look at different approaches to textual analysis applied to a range of media texts, divided into the following three media areas:

- ☐ **audio-visual media**: film, television, radio and music
- ☐ **print-based media**: magazines, newspapers, comics, photography, advertisements, posters, flyers, VHS, DVD and CD covers
- ☐ **ICT-based media**: video games, CD-ROMs, DVDs, interactive communications technology, the internet and websites.

The skills of textual analysis underpin the whole of your Media Studies course, including the analysis of your own media production. It is essential that you have a basic understanding of the key concepts: **forms and conventions**, **representation and ideology**, and **audiences and institutions** before you start (see Chapter 1), so, you need to keep referring back the key questions to ask of media texts in that chapter.

The main purpose of the textual analysis you undertake for assessment may vary; for example, to compare representation of two television characters or to analyse editing technique in film, so make sure you are clear which concepts are being tested by each unit of your particular course.

Studying genre

The term **genre** comes from the Latin word 'genus', meaning 'category' or 'type'. This basic meaning is useful for us, as it is a reminder that genre is the classification of any media text into a category or type.

Identifying and analysing genre is a continually changing process, as genres change over time and in response to social change and economic need. **Hybrids**, combinations of more than one genre, develop as ways of keeping these narrative 'formulae' interesting to both audiences and producers alike.

GENRE THEORY

As a critical term for Media Studies, the term 'genre' has been debated since the mid-1960s and is difficult to define precisely. Genre theory can be defined as an attempt to provide a framework of **structuring patterns,** which can be applied to different groups of texts. A good starting point is to consider genre as a set of relationships between the **institution** that produces the text, the **audience** that consumes it, and the **text** itself.

☐ A text will have certain elements which help to place it in a particular genre.
☐ Audiences recognize and have expectations of particular genres.
☐ The institution which produces the text will use the idea of genre in order to market their product to audiences.

IDENTIFYING GENRES

A genre text, such as a television soap opera, will be easily understood by audiences, as it will contain a **repertoire of elements** which are familiar conventions and expectations, including:

ctivity 2.1

Look at how the codes and conventions of a particular genre are used to market books, music, films and TV programmes.

☐ **points of interaction**, such as the pub, club or café
☐ **stock characters,** or **archetypes,** like the matriarch and the gossip
☐ a **multi-diegetic** (as many as 12 plotlines) or **multi-strand** plot
☐ a **cliff-hanger** to hook the audience into watching the next episode.

These elements form a pattern that helps us to identify the genre. It is also this recognizable pattern that creates **audience pleasure**; the recognition of familiar conventions together with the addition of a number of changes or differences. This aspect of genre is known as **repetition** and **difference** and again reinforces the notion that genres are not fixed, but change and are part of a continuous process of **redefinition**.

It is also important for media industries to identify genres, as an important way of making sure that the intended audience finds its products.

The audience's generic expectations are fulfilled, deferred or disrupted according to how far the conventions of a text are similar to the conventions of other texts of that genre, and how far they are different. Note that the conventions do not just concern plotlines, but also stylistic features, such as camerawork and lighting, characters and similarities in themes, or controlling ideas.

ICONOGRAPHY

Film theorists in particular have used the concept of **iconography**, or familiar stylistic features to attempt to define genre. However, this is

Activity 2.2

Choose two of your favourite soaps.
• Identify the following key generic elements in both of them.
• How similar are the elements?

Elements	Soap 1:	Soap 2:
Three character types		
Two points of interaction/ meeting places		
Three issues which are being covered in the plotlines		
Three typical camera shots		
Three regular props		
Typical codes of dress/costume for two characters		
Catch phrases or typical statements of two characters		
Two cliff-hangers		
A significant change; e.g. the introduction of a new character		
The theme tune: is it identical to the tune in the first episode of your soap?		

Activity 2.3

Select two films for each of the following genres:
• Science fiction, action/adventure, teen horror and historical epic.
• List their main contents under these headings: themes, characters and iconography.
• Compare the conventions to see how similar they are.

complicated by the fact that different theorists have offered different definitions of iconography. Ed Buscombe (1970) argued that because film was a visual medium, recurrent visual images such as codes of dress, settings and props should be used to define genre, rather than narrative structure. In a western, iconography would include a dusty landscape, a frontier town, horses and saddles, chuck wagons, rifles and six shooters, Stetson hats and so on.

Colin McArthur (1972) also claimed the importance of iconography in his study of gangster/thrillers. He drew attention to the importance of the cultural knowledge and expectations of the audience in recognizing the iconic conventions. Tom Ryall (1978) argued that themes, characters and iconography need to be considered when analysing genres.

However, Stephen Neale (1980) argued against too much reliance on iconography, and stated that genre should be anchored by the narrative. In addition, defining genre through iconography alone means that important details of visual style, such as camerawork, editing and lighting are not considered.

So we can see that examining iconography is another useful technique for identifying genre, but that it does need to be used together with other techniques, which include narrative and the technical aspects of film-making.

An understanding of genre is important not just for film, but for all media forms, as we shall see in the sections on print- and ICT-based media.

Part 1: analysing audio-visual media language

This area of study includes film, television, radio and music.

TECHNICAL TERMS FOR ANALYSING THE MOVING IMAGE

At some point in your course you are likely to be tested on your ability to analyse the **forms** and **conventions** of the moving image. As this could be based on television or film this section covers both media, including sound and music. You need to know the key terms for each technical aspect and they are listed below.

Where the **technical terms** are specific to either film or television, this has been indicated to help you identify differences. For ease of reference, the terms are divided into five sections:

(1) camerawork
(2) editing
(3) sound
(4) special effects
(5) *mise-en-scène*.

(1) Camerawork

☐ **Establishing shot**: a shot (usually wide or long), often used at the start of a programme or film, a new section of a programme, or at the start of a new scene to establish the relationship between the set/ location and the characters and to show the whole view.

☐ **Master shot**: a shot that a director will cut from and return to. For example, this might be a two-shot of two characters from which the director will get the editor to cut to reaction shots and to which they will return. This establishes clear spatial (space) and temporal (time) relationships.

☐ **Close-up (and variations)**: close-ups, including extreme, big and medium close-ups, are used to draw the viewer closer and to involve them in what is happening; they are also used to observe reactions and emotions, such as happiness, elation or tension. These shots are often used to privilege the protagonist over other characters and position the audience to identify with him or her.

☐ **Long shot**: this is often used for an establishing shot of a set or location.

☐ **Wide shot**: this can used as an establishing shot of a set or location or to show a large crowd of people. It can also emphasize the isolation of a single figure.

☐ **Two-shot**: of two people, usually a medium close-up or medium shot. The shot shows the spatial relationship of the two people, who are often in conversation. This is commonly used in television soaps.

☐ **High angle**: to provide a view from above the subject(s), often making the subject look vulnerable, isolated or powerless. This is sometimes combined with a crane shot into a closer shot of the subject(s).

☐ **Low angle**: used to provide a view looking up at the subject(s). Low angle shots can emphasize power, strength and importance.

☐ **Aerial shot**: a view from directly overhead to afford a clear view – sometimes used to emphasize a spectacle. Again, a crane shot is usually necessary to achieve this (sometimes called a bird's-eye shot).

Picture 2.1 Camera shots and angles.

Wide Shot

Long Shot

Mid Shot

Medium Close Up

Close Up

Extreme Close Up

High Angle Shot

Low Angle Shot

Activity 2.4

Analysing camerawork in film
- Watch an action sequence from a film.
- Identify the different camera shots used, using the list.
- How is the importance of the setting and action emphasized by the camera movement?
- What is the effect of the choice of camera shots?

Activity 2.5

Analysing camerawork in television documentary
- Watch a 5-minute sequence of a recent documentary.
- Identify the different camera shots which are used, using the glossary given earlier.
- Does the camerawork add to the authenticity of the documentary?
- Does the documentary draw your attention to the presence of the camera operator or does it attempt to conceal it?

☐ **Point of view shot**: generally used either directly before or after a shot of the protagonist looking at the object or character who features in the point of view shot.

☐ **Cutaway**: a shot of an object, detail or gesture which can be included at any point without breaking the continuity of the main action.

☐ **Reaction shot**: a shot of a person responding to an action, for example, by nodding their head at what someone is saying. These shots are often used in television interviews to help to maintain continuity and are termed **noddies**.

☐ **Pan**: originally 'panorama', meaning a view; a pan shot is a horizontal movement left or right by the camera on a fixed axis (of variable speed depending on the desired effect). It affords a more extensive view of a set or location and makes spatial relationships clear to the audience.

☐ **Crane**: this shot is from a camera on a crane, which can move horizontally, vertically or diagonally from a high to a low position to afford a variety of views. It can be used to draw the audience right into the centre of the action.

☐ **Tilt**: a movement of the camera either up or down on a fixed axis to afford a high or low view by movement.

☐ **Tracking/dolly shot**: the movement of a camera on a dolly (tripod on wheels, usually on a track) which affords the smooth following of a character.

☐ **Zoom/reverse zoom**: the camera is fixed and a zoom lens is used to move in closer (at variable speed), or out, further away, from the subject(s). This is used to involve the audience or to focus on the expression of a character, by zooming into a close-up to heighten suspense.

☐ **Framing**: the control of visual elements within the camera frame.

☐ **Composition**: the arrangement of visual elements within the frame, for clarity, balance or aesthetic judgement.

☐ **Depth of field**: the range of objects in focus, of particular importance in film.

☐ **Hand-held**: the use of a camera without a tripod to produce a 'shaky' effect, to convey immediacy and excitement.

☐ **Ciné-vérité**: often used in documentaries which claim to get as close to the subject as possible; often hand-held, with a low budget look.

☐ **Steadicam**: a camera that is on a lightweight counterbalance, harnessed to the camera operator, producing a smooth, flowing shot which can follow action.

(2) Editing (sound and vision)

☐ **Cut**: the instantaneous change of one camera shot to another. This is used when the action is continuous; when there needs to be a change of impact, or when there is a change of information or location.

☐ **Fade**: a gradual fade (in or out) of the picture to black or white suggests a passage of time, usually of hours or to the next day. It can also

Activity 2.6

Analysing editing in film
- Watch the opening sequence of *A Bout de Souffle* (Godard, 1959) up to the point where the policeman is shot.
- How far does the editing conform to the conventions of continuity editing?
- If the conventions are broken, identify the exact points where this happens by drawing the shots on a storyboard.
- What is the effect of the unconventional editing?

Activity 2.7

Analysing editing in television
- Watch the first 5-minutes of an edition of *The Naked Chef: Happy Days* (BBC, 2001).
- Identify the editing techniques used.
- Note the changes in the pace of the editing.
- Note any points where the sequence does not conform to the conventions of continuity editing.
- What is the effect of the editing?

be used at the beginning or end of a programme or film. It is sometimes used for flashbacks in a narrative.

☐ **Dissolve**: also known as the mix, this is the transition from one shot to another with the two images being overlapped, so that near the end of one shot, the next shot becomes gradually more visible. This is used for changes in time and location, for slowing down time, or for flashbacks.

☐ **Wipe**: a type of mix, this is the replacement of one image with another, by means of a horizontal, vertical or diagonal line, which wipes the image off the screen to be replaced by another.

☐ **Editing**: the selection of shots (or sounds), linked as a continuous sequence.

☐ **Continuity editing**: the dominant approach to editing which makes the editing appear seamless and disguises the text's construction.

☐ **Action match**: when a character or vehicle leaves the frame on the left, the same character enters the next shot on the right to maintain continuity.

☐ **Cross-cutting/parallel action**: a cut from one shot in one location to a second shot in a different location and then a cut back to the first. This suggests to the audience that the events in the two different locations are happening simultaneously.

☐ **Jump cut**: increasingly used in television advertisements, the jump cut occurs when two shots are shot from approximately the same position, and one immediately follows another when the text is edited. It appears to the audience that part of the action is missing. The jump cut can be used to create excitement and tension.

☐ **Long take**: each time a shot is recorded it is called a take. A long take is one that is allowed to remain for a long duration before it is cut.

☐ **Superimpose**: the appearance of writing/symbols or images on top of an image so that both are visible at once, increasing the amount of information a viewer has in one shot.

☐ **Slow motion**: used in the editing process to slow down the action for emotional or comic effect.

(3) Sound

☐ **Soundtrack**: in film, all the combined sound recordings used throughout the film are dubbed onto one final soundtrack. This includes music, dialogue, sound FX, ambient sound.

☐ **Diegetic/non-diegetic sound**: diegetic sound refers to sound which is either recorded synchronously with the image or added later in post-production to give the audience the impression that is part of the world of the text. Non-diegetic sound, for example, could include incidental music.

☐ **Theme**: a key passage of music linked to the subject matter/style of the film or programme or film, which helps to create the mood.

Activity 2.8

Analysing sound in film
- Listen to the first 3 minutes of any film without looking at the images
- Write down what you think is happening.

- Watch the first 3 minutes with the sound muted.
- Now watch the film and listen to the soundtrack.
- How important is the soundtrack to your understanding and reading of the film?

Activity 2.9

Analysing sound in television documentary
- Watch a 5-minute sequence of *The Blue Planet* (BBC, 2000) or *Walking with Beasts* (BBC 2001) with the sound muted
- Now watch the same sequence with the soundtrack
- How does voice-over add to our understanding of the images?
- How do the sound FX and the especially composed music affect our reading of the documentary?

☐ **Tune**: a melody used, particularly in television, for the theme tune and throughout the programme to reinforce its identity.

☐ **Incidental music**: the use of music to punctuate a specific event or action, or to provide a sound background.

☐ **FX**: sound effects, such as explosions or doors slamming.

☐ **Ambient sound**: naturally occurring sound, available from a specific location.

☐ **Atmos/Wildtrack**: recorded soundtrack of background sound.

☐ **Dialogue**: that which is spoken by actors/presenters.

☐ **Voice-over**: the use of a voice, over images, perhaps as an introduction, a linking narrative device or to comment on action. Often used in documentary.

☐ **Mode of address/direct address**: (mainly for television), the style of delivery used by presenters/interviewers. In particular; this is a key factor in establishing the mood and tone of a programme, for example, by being friendly, authoritative, and fun as appropriate.

(4) Special effects

Activity 2.10

Analysing special FX in film
- Watch a sequence from *Lara Croft: Tomb Raider* (West, 2001).
- Make a note of all the special FX used, including stunts.
- How important do you think the special FX are to the film's success?

☐ **Animation**: creating a moving image with a series of varying still images. Can be used to design graphics and effects, which bring something, such as a cartoon figure or title, to life, mostly by **CGI**.

☐ **Back projection**: the use of a projected background image (still or moving) behind actors to simulate a real setting.

☐ **Captions**: superimposed words/numbers over the image on screen.

☐ **Chromakey**: an effect which allows the superimposing of a secondary video image over the original camera shot when the main subject of the original shot is in front of a blue background. Used for weathercasters on television and to make Superman fly.

☐ **Computer-generated images (CGI)**: used to design graphics and effects not achievable using conventional means.

☐ **Graphics**: the use of design for words (typography), symbols or images specifically appropriate to a programme or film, such as in the title sequence.

ctivity 2.11

Analysing special FX in television drama
- Watch an episode of *Ally McBeal* (Twentieth Century Fox, 2001).
- Make a note of the scenes where special FX are used.
- How far do you think the FX add to the humour of the programme?

☐ **Models**: the construction of models to represent real vehicles/ buildings/objects, etc. which stand for the real thing.
☐ **Pyrotechnics**: the spectacular use of explosions/fire.
☐ **Stunts**: the use of spectacular action sequences and difficult/dangerous actions.

ctivity 2.12

Analysing lighting in film
- Watch the sequence where the audience first meets the main protagonist, Rick (Humphrey Bogart) in *Casablanca* (Curtiz, 1942).

- What does the lighting suggest about Rick's character?
- What is the effect of the shadows in the bar?

Picture 2.2   Rick's character is suggested through the low-key lighting of *film noir* in *Casablanca* (Curtiz, 1942).

(5) *Mise-en-scène*: that which is placed, or put, in the scene or frame

- ☐ **Location**: the place where the film or programme is shot, outside a studio.
- ☐ **Production design**: the overall design of the film or programme.
- ☐ **Studio/set design**: this tends to be designed in keeping with the subject matter, theme or style of the programme or film; there will be a clear design concept or aesthetic.
- ☐ **Costume**: the selection of costume for actors and presenters will be deliberate, in keeping with their character or persona on the one hand and the design concept for the text as a whole.
- ☐ **Properties**: 'props' for short; these are used to dress the set in a way appropriate to its subject matter, style and theme.
- ☐ **Ambient lighting**: using the source of available lighting (e.g. outdoors).
- ☐ **Artificial lighting**: the use of **high** or **low key** lighting for desired effects, including colour, shadows and lighting design.
- ☐ **Key light**: the main light source in a film set-up, normally placed near the camera.
- ☐ **Back light**: used for three-point lighting. The light is placed behind the subject and emphasizes its depth and shape.
- ☐ **Fill light**: often a soft light which is diffused, this is usually placed on the other side from the key light, but lower down to fill in shadows.

FORMS AND CONVENTIONS OF THE MOVING IMAGE

We have looked at the constituent parts of a moving image text, but without **form**, they are meaningless. It is best to think of form as the overall structure or shape of the text, the order in which its constituents are arranged. The structure of a text can be determined by its **narrative** or its **genre**.

Generic codes and **conventions** can be defined as the unwritten rules which have become established as accepted ways of communicating meaning. For example, television news conforms to the presentational convention of using a live on-screen presenter, while a typical narrative convention of a science fiction film is an invasion of Earth by extraterrestrial beings. We can often recognize a villain by his codes of dress, or the presence of sinister chords in the musical score.

Focus genre: action adventure films

Films in this genre often incorporate a whole range of other genres. *The Terminator* (Cameron, 1984) and *Terminator II* (Cameron, 1991) could both be classed as science fiction, the *Lethal Weapon* series as 'cop' movies, and *Gladiator* (Scott, 2000) as a historical epic. Nevertheless, all these films have elements of the action/adventure film:

- ☐ fast-paced action
- ☐ chases
- ☐ spectacular fights
- ☐ stunts
- ☐ special effects
- ☐ heroes and villains
- ☐ hero's love interest.

ctivity 2.15

A Female Terminator?
- *Terminator III* (Cameron, 2002) has a female terminator.
- To what extent is this character a progression from the other female representations?

The term action/adventure was used from the early days of Hollywood, often to describe historical fiction films like *King Solomon's Mines* (Stevenson, 1937) or 'swashbuckling' pirate films with stars like Douglas Fairbanks and Errol Flynn.

Saturday afternoon serials with strong male heroes like Flash Gordon, Buck Rogers and Zorro were produced from the 1930s to the 1950s. They offered escapist, entertaining adventures with fantasy worlds, clear-cut villains and heroines in distress. In the 1960s the Bond films were classified as action/adventure. In the 1980s and 1990s the term was used to cover a wide range of films, including the *Rambo* films, *Batman* (Burton, 1989) and *Clear and Present Danger* (Noyce, 1994).

| Picture 2.3 | *Lara Croft: Tomb Raider.* |

The dominance of the male hero in this genre was challenged by Sigourney Weaver's Ripley in *Alien* (Scott, 1979), followed by Linda Hamilton's Sarah Connor in *The Terminator* in 1984 and Angelina Jolie in *Lara Croft: Tomb Raider* (West, 2001). However, media theorists have debated the extent of this challenge, as in some cases these characters are helped by males rather than taking on the full extent of the role of the isolated central male leader.

THE ADVENTURER ABROAD: *RAIDERS OF THE LOST ARK*

ctivity 2.17

Identifying the conventions of the action adventure film

- Watch *Lethal Weapon* (Donner, 1987) and identify as many action adventure conventions that you can.
- Watch *Clear and Present Danger* (Noyce, 1994) and identify as many action adventure conventions that you can.
- Compare the two films. Would you argue that both could be placed in the genre of action adventure?

A sub-genre of action/adventure films has its roots in nineteenth-century adventure novels, such as *King Solomon's Mines* by Rider Haggard (1886). This sub-genre includes Spielberg's *Indiana Jones* trilogy (1981, 1984, 1993), *Romancing the Stone* (Zemeckis, 1984) and *The Jewel of The Nile* (Teague, 1985) and features international travel and exploration.

Raiders of The Lost Ark borrows heavily from the Saturday afternoon cinema Republic serials of the 1930s and 1940s, retaining the generic elements of clear-cut villains and heroes. George Lucas (one of the three scriptwriters of the film, together with Spielberg and Lawrence Kasdan) stated: 'We were back to good guys beating bad guys' (*Rolling Stone*, 25 April 1981). However, while the functions of the characters are clear, there is some ambiguity and weakness in the central male hero of Indiana Jones, as we shall see in the sample textual analysis below.

Raiders of the Lost Ark references the 1937 and the 1950 film versions of *King Solomon's Mines*, as well as the book by Rider Haggard. The hero of *King Solomon's Mines* is Allan Quatermain, a rugged, respected 'gentleman adventurer', very similar to archaeologist Indiana Jones, played by Harrison Ford, already known to audiences as the rebellious but tough Han Solo in *Star Wars* (Lucas, 1977).

Both Indiana and Quatermain have a firm belief in their moral superiority and in 'the spirit of adventure'. Both are white, male, Western heroes whose courage is tested away from home – in Quatermain's case in the British Empire.

Many mainstream films use formal relationships, between characters and/or themes, which structure the meanings of the film. This is especially so in action/adventure films, where there are usually clear representations

ey terms

Stereotype: an assumption about a person, place or issue that does not allow for flexibility or detail.
Archetype: a stock character, which is frequently copied in literature,

television, radio, film, etc. The hero, for example.
Protagonist: the leading character in a text.

| Picture 2.4 | The rugged, adventuring archetype of 'the gentleman adventurer' in *King Solomon's Mines* (Stevenson, 1937) is followed by the character of Indiana Jones in Spielberg's trilogy. |

Activity 2.17

Representations of gender in the action adventure film

- Watch *Terminator II* (Cameron, 1991). Examine the representation of Sarah Connor.
- How far would you argue that Sarah Connor is the hero of the film?
- Whose set of values are we encouraged to respect?
- What function does the terminator play?

of good and bad, civilised and uncivilised, moral right and wrong. Increasingly in recent films, these opposing qualities and characters are not so clearly defined and we see heroes whose actions are not always beyond moral reproach. This could be a reflection of the morally ambiguous nature of modern society.

This **archetype**, or model of a character such as a hero, has been used many times as one of the conventions of the action adventure film in characters like James Bond and Ethan Hunt in the *Mission Impossible* films.

As well as retaining the elements of the Saturday serials, Spielberg also retained many of the values; there is little or no challenge to the serials' representations of race, or gender. The Nazi leader, Toht (Ronald Lacey), is a **stereotypical** comic-book villain, with steel-rimmed glasses, whose menace is limited by the comedy. At one point he is given a vicious-looking weapon by his Nazi henchman to use against Marion. He deftly puts it together to form a coat hanger, turning menace into ridicule.

The female protagonist, Marion (Karen Allen), is first seen in the film as an independent, hard-drinking woman in trousers who owns her own bar. But her role quickly deteriorates into the 'heroine in distress' of the Saturday serials when she is captured by French villain Belloq and inevitably rescued by Indiana. Is this a clue to the film's 1980s context?

xtend your knowledge

The Theories of Claude Lévi-Strauss

Key Text: *The Raw and The Cooked* (vol. I of *Mythologies*, London, Cape, 1970).

Social anthropologist Lévi-Strauss studied the myths of tribal cultures and revealed

underlying recurring themes in the myths which he expressed as **binary oppositions**, such as darkness/light and good/evil. Lévi-Strauss's work has been **adapted by media theorists to reveal underlying themes and symbolic oppositions in media texts**.

An exemplar textual analysis of *Raiders of the Lost Ark*

While this example of textual analysis skills is focused specifically on *Raiders of the Lost Ark*, we have included it to help you with any moving image analysis. The sample refers to the first 3 minutes of the film.

The film opens with the Paramount studio logo that reassures the audience that this film is part of a long-established tradition of film-making, as the studio opened in 1914. The design of the mountain peak with the 24 stars symbolizes the peak of excellence and the American pioneer spirit of adventure.

The camera slowly zooms out and the shot of the Paramount logo dissolves almost imperceptibly into a long shot of a mountain of similar shape and size, but with bleaker, harsher landscape on either side. This highly effective and amusing dissolve suggests that some of the audience pleasure in this film will come from a recognition of technical effects like these and from references to other film texts of the past, possibly parodying other action/adventure films. As the dissolve takes place, audiences see a brief glimpse of the 24 stars of the logo being superimposed over the 'real' mountain. This symbolizes US values being transferred to another land, which we later find out is South America. The opening titles are then superimposed over the landscape, reinforcing this point.

The music begins quietly during the zoom out, creating an unsettling mood with discordant notes, mainly played by horn, trombone and drums. The nose flute suggests that the unknown land is South America. The music is mixed with what we assume to be animal sounds of the jungle, including chattering monkeys, which sound as though they are mocking the adventurers. The soundtrack helps to create

a sense of menace and mystery that emanates from the jungle, or the unknown. It could be argued that the jungle takes on the function of the villain at this point, with its potential threat to the hero.

Throughout the zoom out and for a few seconds after it ends, the landscape is empty, as if waiting for the American hero to fill the space. The audience sees a rear view mid-body shot of Indiana Jones (although they are not certain of his identity at this point) as he moves into the frame from the left, obscuring the mountain entirely. This again suggests that American values will dominate other cultures' values.

As Indiana strides towards the mountain, his face away from the camera, he stands with his arms at his sides, reminiscent of a gunfighter's pose in a western film. His codes of dress: a big cowboy-style hat, and long leather jacket have connotations of the western genre but the whip and the leather explorer's bag also remind audiences of the colonialist explorers like Allan Quatermain in *King Solomon's Mines*. His independent stance, looking forward, emphasizes his voluntary isolation, dominance and sense of purpose, referencing the heroes of the Saturday afternoon serials.

At this point, the title 'A Steven Spielberg Film' appears in the frame. This will suggest action and excitement to those audiences who know Spielberg's work. The audience who may ask questions such as: 'Who is he?'; 'What does he look like?'; and 'Why is he here?' as the two Peruvian porters and two tired and untrustworthy looking guides follow Indiana as he strides confidently towards the unknown. This designates Indiana very clearly as the leader of the expedition and is an example of one of the conventions of the hero in a mainstream text.

The title 'Harrison Ford' appears on the screen, reminding audiences of the unconventional heroes Ford has played in the past, such as Han Solo in *Star Wars* (Lucas, 1977) and in *The Empire Strikes Back* (Lucas, 1980). The opening shot is a very complex one and has lasted for about 40 seconds, gratifying a cinema literate audience who can guess just how difficult a shot like this is to set up.

In the following four tracking shots, Indiana leads the expedition confidently into the jungle. The rear-view shot of Indiana shows him leaving the others behind him, symbolizing his willingness to be set apart from the rest. This recalls the isolation of the action adventure heroes of the Saturday serials and of heroes like James Bond who have a duty to their country and are prepared to be different from the crowd.

The American hero Indiana Jones in *Raiders of the Lost Ark* (Spielberg, 1981).

The mist in the trees and the tracking movement of the camera suggest again the menace of the jungle; it is as if the jungle is watching the expedition. The darkness of the jungle is associated with primaeval fears and suggests the symbolic opposition of darkness/light and 'primitiveness'/civilization, reinforcing ideological attitudes about the dangers in store for the 'civilized' Westerner as he encounters 'primitive' people.

The low-angle of the first two shots emphasizes Indiana's superiority, as does the comparison with the other four men on the expedition who are all struggling. The two Peruvian porters are bowed down by their packs, and the two guides have dishevelled and dirty codes of dress: their jackets and hats are torn. At the close of the first shot, both the guides looked behind, suggesting the possibility of betrayal, while Indiana only looks ahead throughout this sequence.

A rear-view long shot of the expedition penetrating into the jungle shows the audience that one of the porters is now leading the expedition, usurping Indiana's role as leader. The audience may question this, but their concerns are quickly dealt with as the porter is punished in the following three shots. A close-up 1-second shot places the audience in the position of the statue that marks the way to the ancient temple. As the leaves are hacked away by the porter, there is a suggestion that this is a violation of ancient beliefs and traditions, therefore questioning Indiana's role as a hero as he is a part of this 'raid'.

The next shot is a reverse close-up of the statue revealed by the porter, dominating the frame as it dominates the porter, who screams in a strangled high-pitched voice as birds fly out of the statue's eyes and mouth. This recalls the conventions of the horror genre, that is often associated with action/adventure. There are also elements of parody of the horror genre as the porter throws up his hands in terror and runs off screaming.

This helps to defuse any fear the audience might experience and also emphasizes Indiana's function as the hero again, as he walks casually into the frame from the left to replace the porter and approaches the statue without fear. As all this happens within one shot, it offers the audience a strong contrast between the porter's susceptibility to superstition and fear and Indiana's supposedly superior education as an archaeologist, who is able to use the statue as a pointer to show that he is on the correct route for the temple.

Extend your knowledge

Read some lively professional analyses from *Sight & Sound* magazine writers on a wide variety of major action/adventure films. (See Arroyo, J. in the Film section of the Bibliography.)

Part 2: analysing print-based media language

This area of study includes newspapers, magazines, comics, photographs, advertisements, posters/flyers, VHS, DVD and CD covers. This section of the chapter focuses mainly on the analysis of magazines, but will offer you a range of theories and techniques which will help you to analyse any print text.

TECHNICAL TERMS FOR ANALYSING PRINT

- ☐ **Advertorial**: an advertisement which is disguised as part of the editorial content of the newspaper or magazine.
- ☐ **Banner**: front page headline which goes across the full width of the page.
- ☐ **Brand identity**: that which distinguishes one magazine or newspaper from another and enables the target audience to recognize it easily.
- ☐ **Byline**: the name of the journalist who has written the article or feature.
- ☐ **Caption**: written text under a photograph or drawing to anchor the image.
- ☐ **Circulation**: the number of copies sold or distributed to audiences.
- ☐ **Copy**: the basic written material before it is incorporated into the magazine or newspaper.
- ☐ **Cover lines**: summaries of the most enticing features and articles which are inside a magazine.
- ☐ **Cropping**: cutting off parts of an image to emphasize a particular aspect.
- ☐ **Editorial**: a statement or comment by the editor of a magazine or newspaper (often placed near the front pages of a magazine).
- ☐ **Editorial**: news and features written by the journalists (not advertising).
- ☐ **Exclusive**: the story is promoted to the audience as *only* available in this newspaper or magazine.
- ☐ **Feature**: longer than a news story, with more background information and a more individual viewpoint (newspaper); article with some research and depth (magazine).
- ☐ **Graphics**: the use of design for words, symbols or images.
- ☐ **Gutter**: space between pages in centre spread; sometimes used to describe space between two columns.
- ☐ **Headline**: the main heading with the biggest font which relates to the main story.

- [ ] **House style**: rules for a particular newspaper or magazine, on spelling, punctuation and abbreviation.
- [ ] **Hybrid**: a mixture of genres.
- [ ] **Layout**: the design of a page.
- [ ] **Lure**: a small section of a story is printed on the front page and the full story or interview is advertised as continuing inside.
- [ ] **Masthead**: the title at the top of the front cover or front page which identifies the newspaper or magazine.
- [ ] **Mass market product/audience**: a product aimed at a wide range of the population, possibly spanning age, gender and class (such as one of the television listings magazines).
- [ ] **Mode of address**: the way a magazine or newspaper speaks to its audience.
- [ ] **Niche product/audience**: a product aimed at a specific interest group.
- [ ] **Sans-serif**: a typeface without a bar or 'foot'.
- [ ] **Serif**: the little bars added to the ends of letters in a typeface.
- [ ] **Standfirst**: the introductory paragraph before the main article.
- [ ] **Strapline**: headline in smaller font appearing over main headline.
- [ ] **Typeface**: a set of text and symbols with a consistent design. Also called 'font', when used on computer.

FORMS AND CONVENTIONS OF MAGAZINES

We can identify a number of different genres within the larger print category of magazines, newspapers or comics. The magazine group is very wide and fragmented, catering for a **mass** or a **niche** (specialist) audience. The mass sector includes **teenage lifestyle** magazines, such as *Sugar*, **music** magazines, such as *NME* and **listings** magazines, such as *What's On TV*, while the niche sector includes magazines which focus on hobbies like skateboarding, surfing or sailing. Just as we looked at hybrid genres in the section on film, there are **hybrid** magazines (containing a mixture of genres), such as *The Big Issue*, which includes articles on politics and entertainment, listings and jobs.

Magazines target specific audiences, with particular hobbies and interests. Most newspapers have sections which also target specific audiences, such as *FeMail* in *The Daily Mail* and *Guardian Education* in *The Guardian*. They also offer lifestyle magazines, usually in their weekend editions. However, newspapers are not so clearly targeted at a specific audience; they are more likely to appeal to audiences because of their political stance and their **news values** (the factors which journalists use to select stories for publication and to decide how important they are – see below for details).

Advertising is essential to both magazines and newspapers, although most magazines aim to make a profit from both advertising and the **cover price** (as shown on the cover), while most newspapers only expect to make a profit or cover their costs from the advertising revenue.

| Picture 2.6 | Mass and niche (specialist) market magazines. |

FRONT COVERS: THE HOOK

Magazines have to compete with each other in order to attract their target audiences. One estimate states that 70% of magazines are bought on impulse and there are over 7000 magazines on the market in Britain. The front cover is one of the most important techniques for promoting the magazine, as it is the first thing we see. The cover aims to **hook** (attract and maintain the interest) the reader through glossy images, often of stars and celebrities, vibrant colours, exciting **cover lines**, free gifts such as a lipstick for a woman's magazine or a CD for a music magazine and competitions with attractive prizes.

The layout of the front cover and the magazine as a whole is conventionally consistent for every issue, in order to establish **brand identity** and to fulfil the target audience's expectations of familiarity. The masthead is usually at the top of the page in a typeface style which reflects the tone and **mode of address** of the magazine.

A **strapline** often appears over the masthead, possibly advertising a free gift. An image of some kind usually fills most of the page and approximately 6–12 cover lines, summarizing the features, quizzes and competitions inside are overlaid over the image to further promote the magazine. The cover lines are displayed in a range of colours and typefaces, down the sides and at the bottom of the page. Clashing colours for the masthead and the cover lines are increasingly used to grab the audience's attention.

Focus genres: lifestyle magazines and tabloid newspapers

Even though they may be aimed at very different audiences, lifestyle magazines tend to include the following elements as appropriate: feature articles on celebrities, competitions, quizzes, letters pages, opinion columns, fashion, product and entertainment reviews.

This genre of magazine aims to produce a title that will complement the lifestyle of a particular readership, by basing its contents on such factors as age, gender, race and by including coverage of our hobbies, such as gardening, music, cooking, sport, fashion and holidays, often all in one magazine.

ctivity 2.19

- Try to list as many magazine titles as you can and organize them under different categories.
- Identify the common elements of lifestyle magazines and any exceptions.

MASLOW'S HIERARCHY OF NEEDS

According to sociologist Abraham Maslow's **hierarchy of needs** (1954), human behaviour reflects a range of needs, ranked in order from basic needs to higher aspirations. When one need has been fulfilled, the next need emerges. The unsatisfied needs are what motivate our behaviour. Lifestyle magazines and advertisements promise to fulfil many of our needs to be accepted into social groups and our need for self-esteem and self-respect and this theory offers a useful insight into the reasons why we are attracted to certain products and advertisements.

Maslow stated that the hierarchy was dynamic and reversible; the needs are not necessarily present in the same order in everyone. Maslow also acknowledged that behaviour can be influenced by a whole range of motivations and external pressures.

Diagram 2.1 Maslow's hierarchy of needs (1954).

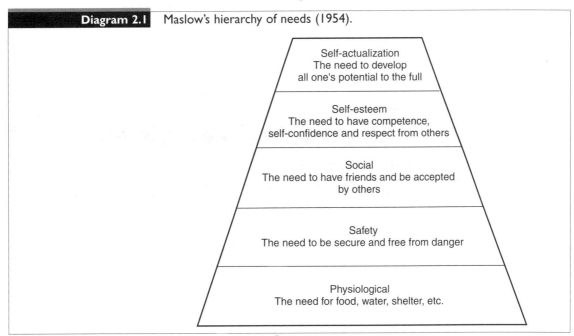

Self-actualization
The need to develop
all one's potential to the full

Self-esteem
The need to have competence,
self-confidence and respect from others

Social
The need to have friends and be accepted
by others

Safety
The need to be secure and free from danger

Physiological
The need for food, water, shelter, etc.

Select any fragrance advertisement from a magazine.
Using Maslow's hierarchy of needs, analyse how this advertisement appeals to its target audience.

THE USES AND GRATIFICATIONS THEORY

Another theory that we can use to analyse advertisements and lifestyle magazines is the **uses and gratifications** theory. This suggests that audiences actively use advertisements and magazines to meet some of the needs identified by Maslow. Magazines may be used by some members of their audience to compensate for a lack of self-esteem or social success, as in the example of the girls' teenage lifestyle magazines, which address their audience as a 'best friend', rather than as an authority figure.

McQuail, Blumler and Brown (1972) defined four major areas of need which the media in general seek to gratify:

- ☐ **diversion**: an escape from our routine and problems, an emotional release
- ☐ **personal relationships**: companionship, feeling part of a social group
- ☐ **personal identity**: exploring or reinforcing our own values, through comparison with others' values (this would include the values of the media producers and of celebrities)
- ☐ **surveillance**: the need for a constant supply of information about what is happening in the world.

Identifying ways in which magazines seek to gratify audiences' needs
- Select one magazine of your choice.
- Examine the front cover and the contents page.
- Try to match the articles and the regular features to some of the needs listed above.
- In what ways does your magazine attempt to meet the needs of its target audience? Or does it merely stimulate or create false needs?

MODE OF ADDRESS

Magazine journalists adopt a **mode of address** which is particular to that magazine and aimed to construct a bond between the magazine and its audience. For example, the front cover of *Sugar* (October 2001) includes the following cover lines: 'Will your name make you a star?', 'Boys Uncovered! Discover what he secretly thinks about you'. Such cover lines 'speak' to the audience and mean that they not only recognize that they are being spoken to but feel that they are members of an exclusive club.

This bond is further reinforced in girls' teenage lifestyle magazines such as *J17*, *Bliss* and *Sugar* by the house style of the magazines, using colloquial vocabulary such as as 'ickiest', 'gorge', 'crush ', 'snoggable' and 'celebs'. This mode of address is that of a best friend, or mate, rather than that of a distant authority figure telling the audience what to think.

 **ctivity** 2.22

Analysis of the editorial and contents pages of teenage lifestyle magazines

- In pairs, look at the contents pages and the editorials of a selection of teenage lifestyle magazines, such as *J17*, *Bliss* and *Sugar*.
- Examine the photographs of the editors and any other journalists on these pages. How are they represented?
- Analyse any written editorial or 'Meet the Team' written text. How do the producers of these magazines use particular modes of address to speak to their audiences?

xtend your knowledge

- The French theorist Louis Althusser discussed this way of 'hailing' or speaking to the audience in his work on **interpellation** (*Lenin and Philosophy*, New Left Books, 1971).
- Research Althusser's theories to look at this concept in greater detail.

Picture 2.7 The front cover of *Sugar*, October 2001.

An exemplar textual analysis of the front cover of *Sugar* (October 2001)

Sugar, published by Attic Futura, falls into the category of teenage girls' lifestyle magazine. Competing with magazines like emap's *J17* and *Bliss*, the front cover has to stand out from the whole range of magazines in the shop and grab the audience's attention. The front cover of this edition attempts to attract its audience through clashing 'hot' colours of orange/pink and yellow; through the model used in the conventional photograph; through some 'shocking' personal interest stories and through its main cover line: 'Boys Uncovered'. This cover line, with its sexual connotations, suggests that the target audience is a little older than the target audience for *J17* and that the magazine may be offering some pin-up photographs of naked men, possibly in the style of *More* magazine, aimed at a late-teen market.

The word 'Boys' is presented in capitals in sans-serif font half-way down and to the right in the biggest typeface on the page (apart from the masthead) and in white against the model's dark red jumper so that it stands out clearly and will catch the audience's eye. The word 'Uncovered', also in capitals, is in a contrasting yellow in a slightly smaller font but still stands out clearly as it stretches across the whole width of the page.

However, if the audience looks carefully at the three starred sub-headings under 'Boys Uncovered', which are presented in white in much smaller lower case, it is clear that the word 'Uncovered' has been used metaphorically: 'Discover what he secretly thinks about you'. It is possible that the audience might feel cheated by the magazine after the promise of nudity, but more likely that they will gain pleasure from enjoying a joke with the magazine, as if it is a friend.

The direct mode of address with the use of the word 'you' helps the target audience to recognize that they are being spoken to. The next sub-heading: 'Drive your dream boy wild – we show you how. Grrrr!' adopts the mode of address of an older, slightly more experienced sister who is there to empower the less-experienced audience to flirt effectively with boys. In the feature, the audience discover that it is celebrity popstar Samantha Mumba who suggests seven 'Flirt Factors' to turn boys' heads.

This reinforces the 'older sister' role of the magazine, as Samantha is likely to be a role model for many of the target audience and is referred to as 'Sam' as if she is close to the audience. It also fulfils the needs for personal relationships and personal identity, offering the audience the companionship and advice of a celebrity (McQuail, Blumler and Brown, 1972). The use of the exclamation 'Grrrr!' has connotations of 'girl power', such as 'Go Girl!' and female empowerment over men, emphasizing the 'female territory' of girls' magazines as discussed by Janice Winship (1992).

The up-to-date, youthful style of the magazine is reinforced by the design of one of the cover lines to make it look like an orange sticker, with yellow and white written text advertising 'Poster spesh, R'n'B Boy Babes. (Phwoar!)' The audience's eye is drawn to the 'sticker' as it is positioned centrally at the top of the page, just under the masthead. The word 'spesh' is part of the language of the teenage lifestyle girls' magazines: a shortened, slang and exclusive version of the word 'special'. The audience is invited to objectify the male R'n'B stars (most of whom are presented in a medium shot, fully clothed) as 'babes', a term which at one time was used only for the objectification of women.

Like the 'Drive your dream boy wild' article, this is the induction of the younger teenage girl into the 'world of personal life, of emotions and relationships, clearly involving men and heterosexuality' (Winship). The brackets around the word 'Phwoar!' further reinforce the notion that the younger teenage girl is being invited into a select club, where others will share her needs and desires and understand her. The needs for personal relationships and personal identity are again being met here.

The cover lines positioned at the top left of the page offer 'Shocking real life stories', appealing to the audience's need for diversion from their own problems: 'My mum was murdered', 'I caught my boyfriend wearing my bra!' and 'My illness made me kiss cars'. As cover lines, the last two stories have entertainment as well as shock value, partly through the use of alliteration, again reinforcing the bond that the magazine constructs with its audience through the 'joke'.

One cover line, in white and yellow lower case, connoting informality and familiarity, refers to an interview with Destiny's Child who, despite their celebrity status, are constructed to share the interests of the target audience: 'on fame, fashion and fingernails', again fulfilling the audience's need for companionship. At the same time, this article fulfils their need for surveillance, as detailed information is given about this world famous group.

The masthead, *Sugar*, is in lower-case sans-serif orange, connoting fun and unconventionality. It is positioned so that it appears half-hidden behind the model's head, reinforcing the audience's willingness to feel part of an élite group, or club, that recognizes the magazine without the need to see the more conventional full magazine title of its counterparts. The free offer: 'Free! Tommy Color Lippie for every reader!' in yellow and orange capitals is positioned as a strapline above the masthead and overlaid over the model's blonde hair.

The image of the model is conventional for this genre of magazines; she is slightly older than the target audience (13–16), making her a potential role model. She looks straight out at the audience in a confident manner, with her head slightly dropped to her right and smiles at the audience in a friendly, rather than provocative or aloof way, reinforcing the notion that the magazine is a 'friend'. She wears an informal dark red ribbed t-shirt which provides a good contrast background for the yellow, white and orange cover lines. She has a lightly made-up look, with a clear complexion, freckles, and a 'natural looking' pink lipstick, providing an idealized version of the audience, but one that is not too unobtainable and that the audience can identify with.

TECHNICAL TERMS FOR ANALYSING NEWSPAPERS (IN ADDITION TO THE GENERAL PRINT TERMS GIVEN EARLIER)

- [ ] **Caption**: the written text that anchors a photograph or image.
- [ ] **Gatekeeping**: process of selecting some news stories and rejecting others.
- [ ] **Nag**: news at a glance, often used on the front cover of a broadsheet newspaper to quickly update the reader.
- [ ] **Newsgathering**: the processes, such as press releases, news agencies, which are used in constructing news.
- [ ] **News values**: the factors that influence journalists and editors in their selection and rejection of stories for publication and in deciding on their importance.
- [ ] **Nib**: news in brief.
- [ ] **Puff**: small sections on the front page, often with coloured images, which advertise features inside the newspaper.
- [ ] **Splash**: lead news story on the front page of a newspaper.
- [ ] **Strapline**: a headline in smaller font that precedes the headline and gives more information.

FORMS AND CONVENTIONS OF NEWSPAPERS

Newspapers can be divided into two categories according to their size: **broadsheets** (60 × 37 cm) and **tabloids** (30 × 37 cm). According to their style of **layout**, mode of address and content, national daily newspapers can be divided into three categories:

- [ ] the **red-top tabloids**: *The Sun, The Mirror* and *The Daily* Star
- [ ] the **mid-market tabloids**: *The Daily Express* and *The Daily Mail*
- [ ] the **broadsheets**: *The Daily Telegraph, The Times, The Independent, The Guardian,* and *The Financial Times.*

However, increased competition in the newspaper industry has meant that recent changes have taken place which can make it more difficult to distinguish between the content and the style of the three categories.

BRAND IDENTITY

Each newspaper works to establish its own brand identity through the front page. The front page generally uses the conventions of a **masthead, splash** (main news story), colour **photograph** with **caption, headline, puffs** (advertisements for features inside the paper), **publishing information** and the newspaper's **website address**.

Other common conventions are: a **logo**, which acts as a symbol for the paper, a **strapline** (a headline in smaller font which precedes the

Picture 2.8 The front page of *The Times* annotated to demonstrate points given above.

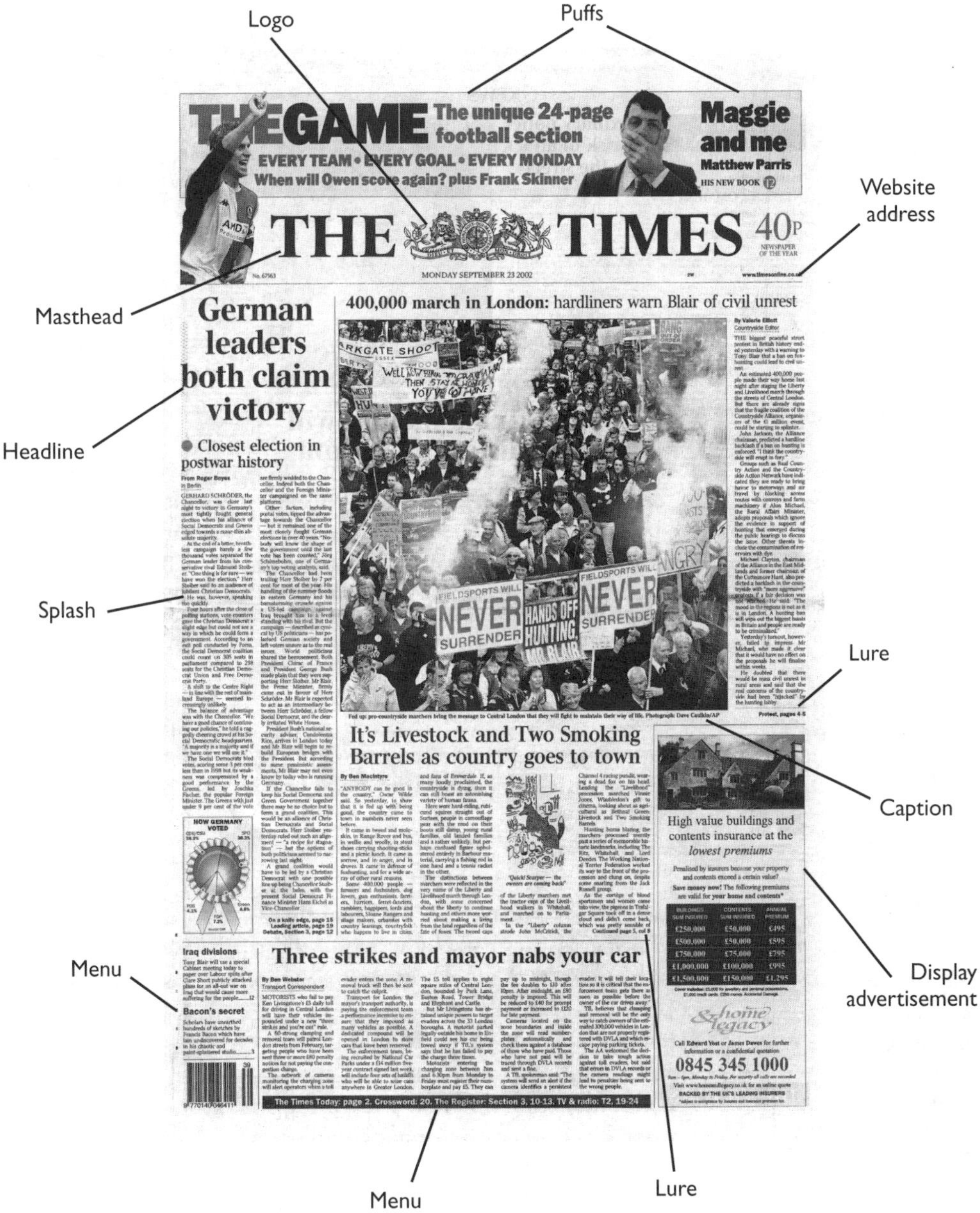

Logo

Puffs

Website address

Masthead

Headline

Splash

Lure

Caption

Display advertisement

Menu

Lure

Menu

THE GAME
The unique 24-page football section
EVERY TEAM • EVERY GOAL • EVERY MONDAY
When will Owen score again? plus Frank Skinner

Maggie and me
Matthew Parris
HIS NEW BOOK

THE TIMES 40P
NEWSPAPER OF THE YEAR

MONDAY SEPTEMBER 23 2002

www.thetimesonline.co.uk

400,000 march in London: hardliners warn Blair of civil unrest

German leaders both claim victory

● Closest election in postwar history

It's Livestock and Two Smoking Barrels as country goes to town

High value buildings and contents insurance at the *lowest premiums*

Three strikes and mayor nabs your car

Iraq divisions

Bacon's secret

Picture 2.9 Mastheads from *The Times* and *The Mirror*.

Activity 2.23

Close analysis of daily newspapers' mastheads
- In pairs, analyse the mastheads and logos of the national daily newspapers.
- How different are they from one another?
- What values does each newspaper attempt to convey through the masthead and the logo?

headline and gives more information), **menu** (an index of other stories inside the newspaper), a **lure** (the opening of a story which then continues inside) and **display advertisements**. All these conventions help to make up the newspaper's mode of address.

Newspapers aim to create **brand differentiation** through distinctive layouts and fonts. The red-top tabloids use a **sans-serif** typeface, which connotes an up-to-date, no-nonsense mode of address. The broadsheets and the mid-market tabloids mostly use a **serif** typeface, connoting tradition and authority.

NEWS VALUES

Activity 2.24

Identifying news values
- Compare the front pages of a broadsheet newspaper and a red-top tabloid of the same day.
- Identify the news values for each newspaper using Galtung and Ruge's list.
- Place the news values in order of priority for each newspaper by looking at the splash, the photographs and the puffs.
- How different are the news values for each newspaper?

Galtung and Ruge (1981) defined a set of news values to explain how journalists and editors decided that certain stories and photographs were accepted as newsworthy, while others were not.

This list is adapted from their work:

- ☐ **Immediacy**: has it happened recently?
- ☐ **Familiarity**: is it culturally close to us in Britain?
- ☐ **Amplitude**: is it a big event or one which involves large numbers of people?
- ☐ **Frequency**: did the event happen fairly quickly?
- ☐ **Unambiguity**: is it clear and definite?
- ☐ **Predictability**: did we expect it to happen?
- ☐ **Surprise**: is it a rare or unexpected event?
- ☐ **Continuity**: has this story already been defined as news?
- ☐ **Elite nations and people**: which country has the event happened in? Does the story concern well-known people, such as celebrities?
- ☐ **Personalisation**: Is it a human interest story?
- ☐ **Negativity**: is it bad news?
- ☐ **Balance**: the story may be selected to balance other news, such as a human survival story to balance a number of stories concerning death.

NEWSPAPER LANGUAGE

As news stories have to fit the space available, the language selected reflects this. The tabloids have less space than the broadsheets and use shorter headlines and fewer words. All categories of newspapers use alliteration in their headlines, but the red-top tabloids are far more likely to use puns than the broadsheets. 'NICE ONE SUN' was *The Sun*'s punning headline after the England/Germany match on 3 September 2001, referring to another pun on advertisement boards on the football pitch: 'SVEN GORAN ERIKSUN', displayed in the front-page colour photograph. The mode of address is colloquial, while the headline both congratulates Michael Owen on his hat-trick and promotes the newspaper itself at the same time.

The Independent's headline on the same day read 'England fans soak up a famous victory, leaving Germany to lick its wounds.' The mode of address is formal, uses a compound sentence and two metaphors and is aimed at an educated audience.

NEWS PHOTOGRAPHS

All newspapers carry colour photographs on the front page. The photographs often stand as a news story in their own right in the tabloids. The front page of *The Mirror* on 3 September 2001 consisted of the image of a pair of Adidas gloves in flames against a black background. The gloves were supposedly similar to those worn by German goalkeeper Oliver Kahn and the story referenced the origin of the cricket Ashes in 1882.

The rest of the front page consisted of the masthead, a lure for the souvenir football pages inside and the xenophobic statement written in italic font: 'In affectionate remembrance of arrogant, clinical, penalty scoring, and downright bloody irritating German football, which died at the Olympia-stadion, Munich, on 1st September, 2001. Deeply unlamented by a large circle of English football fans, RIP.' The mode of address is different from the usual friendly and direct tone, as it is a parody of a serious obituary and therefore adopts a mock-serious tone. It is an example of triumphalism which the journalists believe will speak effectively to its audience.

CELEBRITY AND THE TABLOID PRESS

Photographs of celebrities are increasingly used to sell all categories of newspapers. Some of the reasons for the success of the use of the celebrity as a **commodity** (an object to be bought and sold) in magazines and newspapers can be understood by looking at research into audience needs.

A particularly helpful approach comes from the research of McQuail, Blumler and Brown (1972) into audience needs (see page 33). The researchers defined four major areas of need which the media seek to gratify and these theories can be used to examine a current obsession with celebrities:

- ☐ diversion
- ☐ personal relationships
- ☐ personal identity
- ☐ surveillance.

The focus on celebrities and stars in lifestyle magazines is one way in which audiences can escape from routine boredom and problems, and the increasing interest in this area in both magazines and newspapers suggests that the need for **diversion** is one of the most dominant needs of audiences in the early twenty-first century.

The need for **surveillance** is compensated by the proliferation of media products, particularly with the development of new technologies such as the internet. This need also helps to explain why newspapers and magazines promote themselves through increasing amounts of information about celebrities.

Audiences can explore their own values and **personal identity** through comparison with celebrities' views in interviews. This particular need and use of the media helps to explain why criticisms are often levelled at public figures and celebrities who are seen as role models, particularly for young people. Geri Haliwell's dramatic weight loss in the summer of 2001 was reported in countless magazines and newspapers, broadsheet as well as tabloid. This caused debate throughout the media because of criticisms that as a role model she could be encouraging girls to become anorexic.

Like stars, celebrities can be seen as **commodities**, objects to be bought and sold in a capitalist market. The fact that newspaper sales are going down and that there is such fierce competition to raise **circulation** figures helps to explain why celebrities have become the staple fare of both tabloid and broadsheet newspapers.

Princess Diana was constructed by both tabloids and broadsheets as a glamorous star and a fairytale princess. Her image was seen as so important for the sale of newspapers that the tabloids employed photographers whose sole job was to take photographs of her. Some theorists have argued that her death in a Paris car crash meant that a whole range of minor celebrities were constructed in order to fill her role, with Victoria and David Beckham and Madonna and Guy Ritchie, among others, being referred to as the 'new royalty'.

The role of the celebrity can be constructed around anyone whose image is circulated regularly in television, film, magazines and newspapers. It can include popstars, DJs, actors, chefs, footballers, astrologers, gardening experts and presenters. Celebrities depend on the media for their celebrity and there are some people 'who are famous for being famous'.

Both the media and celebrities have a mutual dependency on each other, which sometimes breaks down when the press are seen as infringing a celebrity's privacy, as numerous court cases can testify.

ctivity 2.25

What is a celebrity?

- Look through two tabloid newspapers and two mid-market tabloids. Identify six celebrities who appear in each newspaper.
- List the reasons for their fame, e.g. actor, singer, Royal family, boyfriend of actor, etc.
- How positively are they represented by each newspaper?

Picture 2.10

Front page of *The Mirror* 4 September 2001.

An exemplar textual analysis of the front page of *The Mirror* (Tuesday 4 September 2001)

The front page of *The Mirror* of 4 September 2001 is devoted almost exclusively to an attack on actor Kate Winslet's decision to separate from her husband.

The clean sans-serif font of the masthead and the headline give the newspaper a modern 'no frills' look, suggesting that the newspaper will get straight to the point. The white masthead stands out against its red background, so that the target audience can quickly differentiate it from broadsheet newspapers and mid-market tabloids. The single puff has a close-up of England football manager Sven Goran Eriksson looking with a rare smile towards the masthead, implying his approval of *The Mirror*. Through the use of capitals the mini-headline: 'SVEN the game we HAVE to win SEE PAGES 4 AND 5'

suggests an urgent importance attached to the game itself as part of the World Cup and an urgent need for the target audience to buy *The Mirror* to read the double-page feature inside.

The splash is introduced as: 'SHOWBIZ EXCLUSIVE', suggesting that only *The Mirror* has access to the details of the separation. The strapline in lower case is underlined for emphasis: 'She had a child, she lost weight now she leaves her husband'. The pronoun 'she' connotes disrespect while the change from past to present tense, emphasized by the word 'now', offers a narrative structure, suggesting a deliberate plan with a structured time sequence. The desired interpretation, or preferred reading, is that Kate Winslet has behaved irresponsibly.

The headline relies on the audience's familiarity with the celebrity status of Kate Winslet, which has been promoted and circulated by *The Mirror* (together with other media institutions). This is an example of the news value of continuity – that which has been defined as news will continue to be news. *The Mirror* readers will identify Kate Winslet easily from the image and from the weak pun on her name: 'KATE WINSPLIT', which further mocks her behaviour.

To the right of the strapline is an oval-framed photograph of Kate and her husband Jim Threapleton with their new-born baby. The framing is reminiscent of a family photo album and the image is tightly cropped to symbolize the closeness of the family group. Threapleton is holding his daughter and gazing down directly at her, connoting that he puts his family first, while Kate's future betrayal of the family group is suggested through her pose as she looks directly at the camera, rather than her family. The caption: 'TOGETHER: Kate and Jim after birth of daughter Mia' reinforces the connotation of the headline that Kate is the agent who has destroyed the 'happy family'.

However, the tone of the opening five paragraphs of the article is far more balanced. The article is positioned directly underneath the image and blocked on a white background so it is highly visible and easily read. The standfirst, in bold and a different font from the rest of the article, apparently contradicts the connotations of the strapline, headline and image as it suggests that both husband and wife have made the decision to separate: 'Actress Kate Winslet and husband Jim Threapleton are splitting up, they revealed last night'.

The fourth paragraph reveals the tabloid's excessive interest in the weight of female celebrities: 'And last month Kate showed off a new slimline shape after shedding four stone following a pregnancy in which she had reached $13\frac{1}{2}$ stone.' This weight loss had been formerly celebrated by *The Mirror*, but here Kate's weight loss is so closely linked with her separation from her husband that there is an implied criticism, almost as though her 'new slimline shape' were part of a ploy to attract other men. Yet in the same sentence the word 'reached' suggests that Kate's pregnancy weight of $13^1/_2$ stone was too high.

These details, not overtly relevant to the story, satisfy the audience's need for a constant supply of detail, identified by McQuail, Blumler and Brown (1972) as the need for surveillance. The article finishes on a lure: 'FULL STORY PAGE 7', encouraging the target audience to believe that their need for surveillance will not be fully satisfied until they have read more intimate details inside the newspaper.

The front page as a whole has no political content, satisfying the audience's need for diversion and demonstrating *The Mirror*'s news values of: personalization with a human interest story; élite people with celebrities like Kate Winslet and Sven Goran Eriksson and of negativity: the Kate Winslet story is bad news. This story was also the splash on the front page of the next day's *Mirror*, but since the attack on the World Trade Center on 11 September 2001, *The Mirror* has carried more political stories on its front pages.

Activity 2.26

- Track the progress of two celebrities through several weeks in two contrasting tabloid newspapers.

- Analyse their representation using the terms and examples given.

Part 3: analysing ICT-based media language

ICT stands for information communication technology. This area of study includes digital technologies, such as video games, CD-ROMs, DVDs and websites.

TECHNICAL TERMS FOR ANALYSING ICT

- ☐ **Access**: the possibility for an individual to become a consumer or a producer of a text.
- ☐ **Analogue**: analogue technology works by recording, storing or displaying information as a physical representation of the original, such as video tape.
- ☐ **Attachment**: when a document or graphics file is sent attached to an e-mail message.
- ☐ **Banner advertisement**: advertisements which appear on web pages, often across the top of the page. They may be animated or include games.
- ☐ **Bookmark**: a way of saving a **URL** to a site that has already been visited so that the user can return to that site at any time.
- ☐ **Browser**: software that enables the audience to view websites.
- ☐ **CD-ROM**: a way of storing large amounts of digital information on a compact disk.
- ☐ **Cookie**: a way of storing and recalling information a user has given to a website.

☐ **Default**: the original setting when your computer is first sold to you.

☐ **Digital**: data items that are stored, usually as binary data, represented by electronic or electromagnetic signals.

☐ **Digital camera**: cameras that store the information in a digital form, such as **JPEG**, allowing easy transfer to a computer.

☐ **DVD**: digital versatile disc, which can store large amounts of high-resolution audio-visual material, such as films and additional related material such as documentaries and interviews.

☐ **E-mail**: messages sent via the internet.

☐ **File**: information understood as one unit by a computer.

☐ **Flash**: animation format which can be used to create websites with interactive graphics and sound.

☐ **GIF**: graphics file which uses a limited number of colours.

☐ **Hard copy**: printed copy of a file or website.

☐ **Hard disk**: the permanent magnetic disk inside a computer's central processing unit, used to store data and run any programmes sent to its memory.

☐ **Hit**: the number of requests for a file. As each website is made up of one HTML file and a number of graphics files, visiting one web page might mean 10 hits and visiting one website might mean 50 or as many as 100 hits.

☐ **Homepage**: the 'front' page of a site, containing basic information and routes to other pages on the site.

☐ **HTML**: hypertext markup language – basic computer language which most web pages are written in.

☐ **Hyperlink**: an image, symbol or written phrase that will lead the reader to another webpage (on the same or another site) when clicked on.

☐ **Hypertext**: texts which allow the reader to read documents in any order, as they include shortcuts and links to other documents.

☐ **Internet**: a network of world-wide computers that can be used to transfer information.

☐ **ISP**: internet service provider – company providing access to the internet.

☐ **JPEG**: a compressed graphics file used for photographic images.

☐ **MP3**: audio file which provides good quality digital sound and can be quickly downloaded from the internet.

☐ **New media**: all forms of electronic media since television and radio, including video games, multimedia, CD-ROMs and the internet.

☐ **Plug-in**: extra software necessary to view a particular file, such as Flash.

☐ **Portal**: a website such as Yahoo! that acts as a gateway to the web, with news, e-mail and search facilities.

☐ **Program**: a set of instructions telling the computer what to do.

☐ **QuickTime**: a way of integrating video and digitized sound into programs and websites.

☐ **Scanner**: machine that will scan a photograph or an image and turn it into a file on the computer.

☐ **Search engine**: search facility like AltaVista or Google with huge database of catalogued subject matter.

☐ **Server**: computer that provides access to files as shared resources to a computer network.

☐ **URL**: Uniform Resource Locator – the address which can indicate the position of a file on a webserver anywhere in the world.

☐ **Webmaster**: the editor or producer of a site.

☐ **Webpage**: usually part of a website.

☐ **Website**: a collection of pages on the same theme.

☐ **Webzine**: electronic versions of magazines, which can be versions of existing print magazines or may exist only on the web.

☐ **World Wide Web**: the global network of pages which can be viewed using a browser and internet connection.

☐ **WYSIWYG**: what you see is what you get. WYSIWYG software programs like Dreamweaver allow website designers to design their pages on screen and to see what their web pages will look like.

(Compiled with acknowledgements to David Gauntlett and David Silver's glossary in *Web Studies*, Arnold, 2000.)

FORMS AND CONVENTIONS

As ICT is a fast growing and developing area, it has some new conventions. But although the technology in this area is new, ICT incorporates many of the traditional media forms, such as the moving image, audio and print. In order to appeal to audiences who enjoy these traditional forms, ICT producers use and combine many of the conventions with which we are already familiar.

This recognition and familiarity encourages and enables audiences to 'read' the texts. For example, the layouts of the homepages (the 'front' page of a site, containing basic information and routes to other pages on the site) of the online (on the internet) newspapers use many of the conventions of their traditional counterparts, such as banners, puffs and headlines (see the section on print production), as well as including moving images and hyperlinks to other pages, texts and sites.

NEWS ON THE NET

Online newspaper rivalry

Newspaper rivalry exists on the web just as it exists in the world of printed newspapers. Trinity Mirror re-launched its online version of *The Mirror* in October 2001 in direct competition with *The Sun*'s website. *The Sun* claimed 1.2 million users for the month of September, while *The Mirror* claims its site has gained 5% of users every week since its re-launch.

ctivity 2.27

Comparison of printed newspaper and its website
- Access the Guardian website (www.guardian.co.uk/) and obtain a copy of *The Guardian* newspaper of the same date.
- How is the electronic newspaper different from the printed version?
- Which conventions do they share?
- Make a note of the hyperlinks to other sites. How far are they likely to interest similar audiences?
- What do the advertisements tell you about the target audience?

ctivity 2.28

Compare the websites of *The Sun* and *The Mirror*
- Access the homepages of *The Sun* online: www.thesun.co.uk and *The Mirror*: www.mirror.co.uk.
- Compare the use of colour, fonts and layout.
- How easy is the site to navigate?
- What are the main news values of each site?
- What do the advertisements tell you about the target audience?

While much of the website content is similar to that of the printed newspapers, there are differences in the ways that audiences consume the texts. As the news can be constantly updated on the newspapers' websites, **breaking news** (being the first medium organization to report on an event and constantly relaying more information on that event) is one of the key ways that online newspapers aim to attract their audiences. *The Mirror*'s internet editor, Matt Kelly, said: 'the idea is to keep users coming back throughout the day'. (Source – *Media Guardian*, 2/10/01, 'Mirror Revamps Website' by Owen Gibson.)

New audiences

Newspapers can reach an entirely new audience through their websites. Pete Picton, editor of *The Sun*'s website, said: 'Part of our brief is to communicate with people who aren't regular newspaper buyers, such as the 16–24 age group'. Both *The Mirror*'s and *The Sun*'s online sites use a bold design with bright colours, confirming the idea that these websites are aimed at a youth audience.

Breaking news: the attack on the World Trade Center 2001

Research showed that the ability of being able to break news made the internet as important a source of information as radio during the reporting of the 11 September 2001 attacks on the World Trade Center in New York and the Pentagon in Washington (www.interactivepublishing.net/september/browse.php?co=BBC+Online%2FNews is an example of this). An NOP survey commissioned by the BBC found that 6% used the internet and 6% used the radio as their main source of information on the attacks and their aftermath. Unsurprisingly, 73% said television was their main source of news while 10% said newspapers. The figure of those who first looked at the news via the internet may have been affected by the fact that 92% of that group were at work when the news first broke, suggesting that the internet is still seen as a news source at work rather than at home.

Digital broadcasting

Since their first invention, television and radio have used analogue broadcasting, which means that signals are converted into waves that are then carried through the air by transmitters and received by television aerials. Digital broadcasting will change this, as it uses computer technology to convert sound and pictures into a series of digits.

For a detailed case study of digital television, see Chapter 3.

Digital versatile discs (DVD)

Progress in digital development is being made all the time. This means that new consumer products will continue to be developed. Some of the advantages of digital over analogue technology are:

- □ it takes up less space to store the same amount of information
- □ access to particular sequences or tracks is easier and almost immediate
- □ it provides a better quality recording
- □ it is more reliable.

DVDs can store large amounts of high-resolution audio-visual material, and are beginning to change the ways in which we view recorded films. Films are divided into 'chapters' and can be accessed by the viewer, almost instantaneously. Additional related material such as documentaries and interviews is now included as a matter of course on DVD versions of films and billed as **added value**.

Added value on DVDs

However, sometimes this added value material is disappointing. The DVD version of David Fincher's *Se7en* (1995) was first released in 1997 with one short documentary 'The Making of', the trailer and in letterbox format. Unluckily for those who had bought the first version, the DVD version was re-launched in 2000 with a far more interesting selection of extras, including deleted scenes and extended takes, alternate ending, production designs and stills. This shows how film companies can take advantage of DVD technology to re-launch and market their products effectively.

Some VHS versions of films have adopted a similar marketing approach, with *The Matrix* (Wachowski Brothers, 1999) offering a wide-screen version and three special 'Making of' documentaries called 'What is Bullet Time', 'Do you know Kung Fu?' and 'Government Lobby'. Whilst these documentaries only run to 14 minutes in all, they add to the marketability of the VHS. The documentary about the inventive approach to cinematography used for the fight scenes is of particular interest, as it can

| Picture 2.11 | The relaunched 2000 version of *Se7en* carried far more added value items than the first DVD version of 1997. |

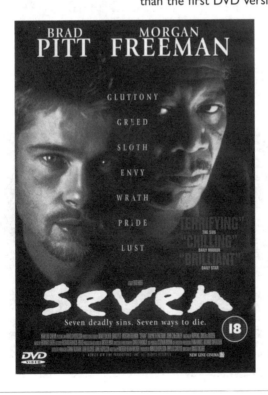

be argued that the special effects are the big selling point of the film. However, the DVD version of *The Matrix*, released in 2000, carried far more background material which would be of interest to fans of the film and those interested in the special effects.

How much added value do you really get from DVD?

- Compare the VHS version and the DVD version of a film of your choice.
- List all the extras available on the DVD.

- Analyse the extras in detail. Do they add extra insight or depth to your understanding of the film or do they merely act as an extended advertisement?

- Compare the quality of added value between several DVDs and work out which constitutes good value for money and which do not.
- Look at websites, such as Amazon or Blackstar, and see how important

DVDs are to the sites and how they are marketing in advance, with pre-release special offer prices.
- What other information do these sites give to entice film fans?

Picture 2.12   DVD offers new opportunities to sell us products several times over, as special collectors' editions often come out after an earlier basic DVD release.

The DVD of *Moulin Rouge* (Luhrmann, 2001) was released in March 2002, with approximately 6 hours of added value special features, including the facility to see sequences from multiple camera angles, which you could select like an editor. It could be argued that the theatrical release of a film is now, in effect, a trailer for the DVD or video game, which are far more lucrative commodities, with comparatively low overhead costs.

Interactivity

Perhaps the most significant development in this media area is the fact that the audience has the opportunity to **interact** with the text in a more developed way than with other media texts. It can be argued that the recent developments in interactive television have been driven by the audience's growing familiarity and interest in ICT.

Part of the success of Channel 4's three *Big Brother* series was due to the 24-hour access audiences had to *Big Brother*'s website. Constructed to appeal to a youth audience, who form the biggest group of consumers of the internet, the second and third series were also backed up by digital coverage on E4. This triple coverage strategy was copied by ITV's *Pop Idol* (2001–2) and contributed to its astonishing success as event television.

Despite the small developments in interactive television, such as the audience's individual choice of camera angles on Sky Sports Digital channel, the interactivity of the internet is far greater. The audience can:

- ☐ search for any websites which interest them.
- ☐ engage in instant communication with others; for example, in a chat room.
- ☐ purchase goods and services, from a car to a dinner party kit.
- ☐ invest in shares and check their bank balance.
- ☐ play games, either alone or with others across the globe.
- ☐ read a newspaper article and listen to a live report on the same issue.

ctivity 2.31

Research on the internet
- Access a search engine, such as AltaVista or Google. Type in the title of a television programme that you have been studying.
- Eliminating the sites that are irrelevant, explore as many of the relevant sites as you can.
- How many of these gave you useful information or other useful hyperlinks?

ctivity 2.32

Analyse a home page and two other pages of a film website of your choice
- Choose a film that is soon to be released. Access the website produced by the production/marketing company for the film.
- How effective do you think the site is as a marketing tool?
- Research the hyperlinks. How far do they interest you?
- What advantages are there in this form for (a) the audience and (b) the producer?

Essentially a website offers a combination of the languages of the moving image (with animated features or video clips), the still image (with thumbnail photographs or stills), journalistic, graphic design and layout principles from magazines, advertising and newspapers (in its copy content). Therefore when analysing websites, and to a large extent, video games, you need to make reference to the key terms and concepts (and theories) which relate to the 'original' medium.

Common theoretical approaches to textual analysis

Examiners' tips

- Remember that your tutors and examiners are more interested in your own ideas and how you apply the theory than in simply describing the details of the theory itself.

Media Studies has developed by applying the theories of linguists, anthropologists, psychoanalysts and sociologists. These theories offer you a range of different approaches to analysing texts. Once you have understood the different approaches, your task will be to select those that are most effective for the text you are analysing.

The theories have been developed by people who tried to put into words how and why language, ideas, images and culture make sense. We don't need media theories to understand and enjoy media texts, but they are sometimes useful to inform academic study of media texts.

SEMIOTICS

Each medium has its own media **language**, or set of **codes** and **conventions**. We have learned to read this media language by understanding the organizing rules of each medium, just as we learned to read books by understanding the rules which organize the written language. It is important to understand the basics of semiotics, as it forms the foundation of one of the main approaches to textual analysis in Media Studies. **Semiotics**, or semiology, is the study of how meaning is constructed through languages or codes.

The signifier and the signified

This approach uses the work of Swiss linguist Ferdinand de Saussure (1857–1913). Developing his theory of semiotics, Saussure argued that language was a structured system of meaning. He distinguished between the **signifier** – the physical appearance or form and the **signified** – an idea or concept associated with the form.

For example, the word 'bank' can have at least two different meanings: a place where we deposit money and a grassy slope. In the same way, one signifier can have two or more signifieds, depending on the interpretation of the reader.

Denotation and connotation

Our interpretations of media texts will also be influenced by the society and culture to which we belong. The French semiologist Roland Barthes (1913–1980), termed the straightforward description of a text **denotation**, and the adding of associated information, insights and values to a text (interpretation) **connotation**.

ENCODING AND DECODING

We understand the technical codes of different media because we have learned to read them. Meaning is **encoded,** or packaged, by those who produce films, television, radio, newspapers and other media texts, while it is **decoded,** or interpreted, by the readers of those texts.

Not all of the intended meanings of the **encoders**, or producers of the texts, will be shared or agreed with or even understood by the **decoders**, or readers of the texts. For example, there was a strong negative reaction from some journalists and audiences to Oliver Stone's film *Natural Born Killers* (1994). These critics decoded the film as one that glorified violence and therefore saw it as dangerous to society. Oliver Stone maintained that his encoded meaning was one of anti-violence. He argued that his film was a critique of the ways in which we react to and report on violence.

Our task when analysing media texts is to try to take apart, or **deconstruct** the ways in which the producers have encoded the text, and also to examine how readers, or audiences, have decoded it.

PREFERRED READINGS

Media theorist Stuart Hall (1981) argues that media texts are constructed so that they have an intended or **preferred reading**, which will come from the producers' own ideas and values. Hall suggest three ways in which audiences decode texts:

- [ ] we accept fully the preferred reading – the meaning which agrees with **dominant** (the most powerful and influential) social and cultural values
- [ ] we take a **negotiated** position – agreeing with some, but not all, of the preferred reading
- [ ] we take an **oppositional** position, where we understand the preferred reading but use alternative values to construct our own interpretations.

An additional position which was identified later is the **aberrant** position, where the audience does not understand the preferred reading.

CODES AND CONVENTIONS

Technical **codes** such as codes of dress, camerawork, lighting, and editing operate through the use of **conventions**, which are like unwritten rules which we recognize and which offer shared meanings.

For example, in the language of film, we understand that the editing technique of a fade to black followed by a fade up to the next scene usually signifies that time has passed or that the location has changed. Throughout *Pulp Fiction* (Tarantino, 1994), for example, director uses the following technique:

- ☐ fade to black
- ☐ fade up underlined white title on black background, such as <u>THE BONNIE SITUATION</u> or <u>THE GOLD WATCH</u>
- ☐ fade title to black
- ☐ fade up to the next scene.

This links what might otherwise appear to be a series of disconnected narratives.

Picture 2.13 Our knowledge of the language of the fade helps us to understand the fragmented narrative of *Pulp Fiction* (Tarantino, 1994).

At the same time, Tarantino breaks with convention by deliberately displacing the **classic narrative** sequence. He follows French New Wave film director Jean-Luc Godard's advice by including a beginning, middle and end, 'but not necessarily in that order'. However, the clear signalling of the different narratives through the editing technique discussed above helps the audience to work out the chronological order of the narrative as a whole once they have viewed the film.

Studying narrative

Deconstructing the **narrative form**, or **structure** of the text, offers a useful, if sometimes limited, approach to textual analysis. Conventional mainstream texts, such as *Independence Day* (Emmerich, 1996), usually adopt the traditional narrative form, linking events through cause and effect and offering a clear, satisfactory **closure** (ending) to the narrative.

SYNOPSIS OF *INDEPENDENCE DAY* IDENTIFIED AS THREE NARRATIVE SEQUENCES

Beginning: introduction

(1) The story begins on 2 July. A centre for extra-terrestrial research becomes aware of atmospheric interference.
(2) This turns out to be a large number of huge spacecraft on a collision course with Earth.
(3) The huge spacecraft are piloted by strange aliens, similar to those in H.G. Wells' *War of the Worlds*. Ex-scientist David Levinson, played by Jeff Goldblum, attempts to communicate with the aliens but instead finds out that the aliens are going to attack important sites all over the world the next day.

Middle: development

(4) On 3 July, the aliens destroy most of New York, Los Angeles, and Washington.
(5) The survivors, including President Whitmore, played by Bill Pullman, make for Area 51, a secret government area where there are rumours of the military capturing and hiding an alien spacecraft. There is an alien in the centre and an old spacecraft.
(6) The President, Levinson and Captain Hiller, played by Will Smith, work out a plan to attack the aliens.
(7) The plan is put into action on 4 July (symbolically important for the Americans as it is the anniversary of the Declaration of Independence).
(8) All other countries unite under the leadership of the Americans.

Picture 2.14 The mainstream narrative of *Independence Day* uses cause and effect and ends on an uplifting closure.

End: resolution

(9)   The intellectual ability of Levinson is combined with the bravery of Hiller to make the plan succeed.

(10)   The aliens are destroyed and the world rejoices on 'Independence day'.

The 10 narrative sequences reveal a very clear cause and effect relationship that links every section of the narrative. There is a kind of three-act

Activity 2.33

Sequencing narrative
- Select a mainstream film of your own choice with which you are familiar.
- Divide it into about 10 narrative sequences.
- Is there a clear cause and effect to all the narrative sequences?
- How far is the ending a satisfactory closure to your film?

Extend your knowledge

The theories of Tzvetan Todorov
Key text: *The Politics of Prose*
(Oxford, Blackwell, 1977)
Todorov identified the basis of narrative as 'movement between two equilibriums which are similar but not identical'

(p. 111 of *The Politics of Prose*). This basic structure can certainly be identified in mainstream texts and can be of use in identifying the key elements of the narrative.

structure, more commonly found in plays (Shakespeare's plays had five acts) – an introduction, a development and a resolution.

In films like *Independence Day*, identifying the hero and the villain is usually easy. Independent or alternative texts are more likely to experiment with narrative form, providing an unsettling or unclear ending to the narrative, such as that of *Crouching Tiger, Hidden Dragon* (Ang Lee, 2000). Here the narrative sequences are not always clearly linked, there are more threads to the narrative and the resolution is unclear.

Narrative theorists argue that there are underlying common structures to all narratives. The structures are often symbolic rather than obvious, so it is useful to learn a range of techniques in order to help us with this kind of textual analysis.

Constructing narratives around events is one of the most fundamental ways in which we make sense of the world. The ways in which media texts construct narratives will vary according to the medium, the time and the society in which the text is produced, the organizations which produce it and the audience it is produced for. This is why it is useful for us to be able to choose from a number of different approaches in our analysis of media texts.

As you progress to higher levels of study in this, you will find that there are many useful sources of theory and research that you can apply to the topics you are studying. There are many books listed in the **Bibliography** section in the Appendix that will be of use and they, in turn, have lots of useful references in their bibliographies and further reading sections.

Extend your knowledge

The key theories of Roland Barthes
Key text: *S/Z* (London, Cape, 1975).
- French theorist Roland Barthes' approach to narrative theory is a flexible one, both with regard to analysing alternative narratives and to

recognizing that meaning is created in the interaction between the audience and the text. He identified five interwoven narrative codes that are useful to apply to the study of media texts.

Extend your knowledge

The theories of Vladimir Propp
Key text: *The Morphology of The*
***Folktale* (Houston, TX, University of**
Texas Press, 1968).
• Propp identified a number of common
  narrative structures through his

classification of 100 Russian folktales in
1928; he also identified common
character roles. His work has been
adapted by media theorists to apply to
other texts, particularly film texts.

CHAPTER 3

Case studies

Case study 1: studying documentary forms

INTRODUCTION

The popular success of television shows such as *Big Brother* (Channel 4) and *Popstars* (ITV) suggests that we are as keen on watching real lives for entertainment today as audiences were at the beginning of the last century, when short films of people doing everyday tasks were popular side shows.

Documentary is an umbrella term that covers a multitude of different forms (both in film and television) and styles, all of which have at their heart some element of the presentation, or a visual document or record, of reality.

The controversy that surrounds recent programmes also suggests that we are not entirely comfortable with this mixture of real life and entertainment. Questions about the authenticity of documentary products, their

| Picture 3.1 | *Big Brother*: millions tuned in to watch people do mundane tasks, sleep and bicker in the first three series. |

purposes and their relationship to the audience have been asked for as long as we have recognized the form of documentary. One of the key points of debate has been about reaching an agreed definition of the documentary form.

John Grierson, a skilled and highly influential early maker of documentaries, offered this famous, if brief, definition in 1936: '... the creative treatment of actuality'.

It is a good starting point for us to unpick some of the debates and questions which surround this media form. Conventionally, documentary is associated with **objectivity**, **authenticity** and **truthfulness**. However, Grierson's definition seems to suggest an element to documentary that is almost the opposite of these ideas – **creativity**.

A BRIEF HISTORY OF DOCUMENTARY

The impulse to portray reality on film has existed as long as the technology of recording itself. The first public projection of moving pictures by the **Lumière Brothers** in the Salon de Paris in 1896 consisted of a series of short sequences displaying life in the capital; a train arriving at Ciotat station, employees leaving the Lumière factory at the end of the day, a wall being demolished by workmen (this last extract was then screened in reverse to the amazement of the audience, who watched the wall reconstructing itself). However, the intention of these sequences was not to reveal new or unusual aspects of life to their audience, but rather to impress them by showing that life as they saw it could be reproduced by the new invention of moving pictures.

The term *documentary* was first applied to the work of **Robert Flaherty**. Flaherty, a former gold prospector and explorer turned film-maker, specialized in recording the lives of the inhabitants of far-flung corners of the world, often focusing on individuals from tribal or developing societies.

His most famous films are *Nanook of the North* (1922), an account of a year in the life of an Inuit Eskimo as he hunts, trades and migrates in order to provide for his family, and *Moana* (1926), which looks at the daily life of a Polynesian tribe in Samoa and the coming of age of one of the young warriors of the tribe.

Flaherty's films borrowed heavily from their fictional equivalents. Nanook and Moana were not real people, but characters played by individuals from these regions. Reconstructions and reordering of their daily lives were common strategies used to create a more dramatic account of these peoples.

One of the most ardent supporters of Flaherty's work was a British film-maker, **John Grierson**. Grierson has often been called the father of documentary, since it is through his work that many of the techniques which we have come to associate with documentary were initiated and developed. Initially an academic, Grierson was appointed as head of a film unit for the Empire Marketing Board (EMB), who were interested in his ideas on the propaganda value of films.

Activity 3.1

Brainstorm the titles of as many documentaries as you can.

- What elements do they seem to have in common?
- What are the key differences between them?
- Using this information, can you come up with a more detailed definition of the term 'documentary'?

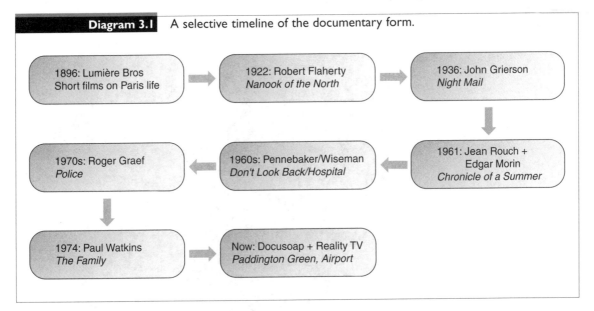

Diagram 3.1   A selective timeline of the documentary form.

1896: Lumière Bros
Short films on Paris life

1922: Robert Flaherty
Nanook of the North

1936: John Grierson
Night Mail

1961: Jean Rouch +
Edgar Morin
Chronicle of a Summer

1960s: Pennebaker/Wiseman
Don't Look Back/Hospital

1970s: Roger Graef
Police

1974: Paul Watkins
The Family

Now: Docusoap + Reality TV
Paddington Green, Airport

Inspired by the success of his first film *Drifters* (1929), the story of Scottish herring fishermen in the Western Isles, Grierson gathered a group of young, talented protégés, whose work he encouraged and supervised. When the EMB was disbanded in 1933, the group moved to the General Post Office, where they continued to make short films which examined or promoted aspects of British life rarely seen before on screen. Grierson's most famous film is *Night Mail* (1936), an account of the work of the Post Office, set to the poetry of W.H. Auden.

The effect of Grierson and his group's work was enormous and influenced a generation of documentary makers working throughout and in the aftermath of the second world war. However, the documentary was taken in new directions in the 1960s, as film-makers gained access to cheaper and more portable technology and began to react against the traditions of their predecessors.

Jean Rouch and **Edgar Morin** took to the streets of Paris in 1961's *Chronique d'un Eté* (*Chronicle of a Summer*) to allow the inhabitants of the city – including a refugee from Germany, an African student and a Renault factory worker – to tell their stories and to reveal their daily lives. Meanwhile, in the USA, film-makers such as **D.A. Pennebaker** and **Frederick Wiseman** turned their attention to subjects as diverse as the 1960s singer-songwriter Bob Dylan on tour to institutions such as high schools and hospitals.

In the past 30 years, television has become the dominant medium for documentary makers. In the 1970s, **Roger Graef** achieved success with his examinations of British institutions in series such as *Decisions* and *Police*. The latter programme on the BBC caused controversy with its depiction of the interrogation of an alleged victim of rape, eventually leading to a change in the procedures and law governing the treatment of victims.

Picture 3.2 *Nanook of the North* listens to a gramophone.

Extend your knowledge

John Grierson and the GPO Film Unit
Key text: *Night Mail* (1936)
• Look at the work of this unit in more detail.

• What do you think are the main similarities and differences between Grierson's work and modern television documentaries?

ey terms

Docusoap: a form of documentary, normally focusing on 'ordinary' people and their lives or occupations, in which a soap-opera-style approach is taken. In this, multiple characters and 'storylines' are interwoven with one another to create the impression of real-life unfolding before us, examples include *Paddington Green* (BBC) and *Airport* (BBC).

Reality TV: either (a) a format in which documentary footage is used for entertainment purposes, for example *Police, Camera, Action* (ITV1), *America's Dumbest Criminals* (Sky One) or (b) a format in which real people are placed into an artificially created situation for entertainment purposes, examples include *Shipwrecked* (Channel 4), *Big Brother* (Channel 4) and *Faking It* (Channel 4).

Paul Watkins is well known for his documentaries about family life such as *The Family* (BBC, 1994) and an Australian version *Sylvania Waters* (BBC, 1993). In many ways, the approach and subject matter which Watkins adopted have been highly influential in the development of the '**docusoap**' and **reality TV** genres which have proliferated in recent years.

In the 1990s, **Nick Broomfield** made a career out of being as well-known as his subjects, with such documentaries as *Kurt and Courtney* (1998). **Molly Dineen** received much acclaim for her television documentaries on the London Underground station, *The Angel*, on London Zoo, *The Ark*, and more recently with a documentary focusing on pop singer Geri Halliwell (2000).

Robbie Williams has added to the (allegedly) 'access all areas' genre of celebrity documentary as exemplified by Madonna's *In Bed with Madonna* (Keshishian, 1991) with *Nobody Someday* (Hill, 2001), both of which had a limited theatrical release.

There have been some highly successful film documentaries that are worthy of further research, for example, *Hoop Dreams* (James, 1994), the Oscar-winning *When We Were Kings* (Gast, 1996) and *The Buena Vista Social Club* (Wenders, 1999).

MODES OF DOCUMENTARY

As with all forms of the media it is possible to divide documentary into a number of different categories or genres. However, this is a largely academic exercise since the boundaries between these different categories are very blurred and it is not unusual for documentary texts to combine two or more different modes in order to achieve their effects.

Nevertheless, an awareness of these fundamental forms should help you to begin your analysis of an existing text or to help with preparation in your own production work. The categories used here are based on those identified by Kilborn and Izod (1997).

The expository documentary

The expository documentary uses a narrator to address the audience directly and to present an exposition, or explanation, interpreting what they are seeing on screen. During the 1930s and 1940s, technical limitations meant that it was easier to record the voice of the narrator off-screen, in post-production. Because of the disembodied nature of the narration, this form of documentary is sometimes known as the **voice-of-God** mode.

This is one of the oldest forms of documentary and one of the most established conventions. Programmes such as *Big Brother* and its follow-ups (Channel 4, 2000–2002) still use the voice-of-God narration, in the

form of voice-overs by one of the producers, in order to interpret the material we are watching.

Whether or not the narrator is represented visually, we are expected to trust the narration as a definitive interpretation of, or **anchor** for, the visual material and to accept it as authoritative on the subject matter. In order to make this kind of identification easier, the narrator will often represent the target audience for the programme (which frequently means a male, white, middle-class narration) and will address them as a group who share the implied values of the text.

On occasions, the narration of a documentary is shared between a number of people, as experts, witnesses or participants. This kind of narration is known as **talking heads** mode, describing the characteristic medium close-up shot which is used to frame the individual. This approach is often used in programmes such as *Emergency 999* or *Crimewatch* (BBC) where a number of different perspectives on a single incident are available.

The observational documentary

The observational documentary has its roots in two forms of cinema which were developed in the 1960s: **direct cinema** and *cinema verité*. Both of these forms were made possible by the introduction of lightweight 16 mm cameras and portable sound-recording systems.

Both terms also suggest that what we see is unimpeded by the makers and therefore, the truth. Philosophically speaking 'reality' and 'truth' are inevitably relative concepts – whose reality? Whose truth? These are key questions to consider when analysing a documentary text.

The observational documentary refuses the interpretative framework of a narrator, preferring to allow the visual material to 'tell its own story'. It creates the impression that events are unfolding 'naturally' in front of the camera and that the audience is being given unmediated access to the material.

In direct cinema, the film-makers attempt to remain invisible, observing but never interfering with the action. In *cinema verité* mode, the presence of a camera and crew is recognized by the participants, who may be asked to answer questions from the crew or to address the camera directly:

> *The direct cinema documentarist took his camera to a situation of tension and waited hopefully for a crisis;* cinema verité *tried to precipitate one. The direct cinema artist aspired to invisibility; the ...* cinema verité *was often an avowed participant. The direct cinema artist played the role of uninvolved bystander; the* cinema verité *artist [played] the* provocateur. *(Erik Barnouw cited in Kilborn and Izod, 1997: 70–71)*

As the conventions of the observational documentary were adapted in the work of television documentary makers in the 1970s, the mode was often referred to as **fly-on-the-wall**, emphasizing the privileged position of the audience. In other words, we are witnesses in a situation to which we would not normally have access.

The current trend for '**docusoaps**' is one illustration of the adaptation of *cinema verité* techniques for the medium of television. The participants of programmes such as *Airport* (BBC, 1996–2001) are filmed in their homes and workplaces as though they are carrying on with normal life. It is their 'normal' lives that we are interested in. Occasionally, the participants will acknowledge the presence of the crew by talking directly to the interviewer or camera, serving to give us public access to their private thoughts and viewpoints.

The reflexive documentary

The reflexive documentary is concerned not only with the subject matter covered, but the ways in which the programme itself achieves that coverage by reflecting on the production process itself. By constantly drawing attention to the processes of construction and by questioning the documentary's traditional claims to truth and authority, it refuses to offer a single viewpoint from which to make sense of the chosen material. This can be achieved by explicit acknowledgement of the camera and crew, by deliberate juxtaposition of contradictory viewpoints or ideals, or by juxtaposition of sound and image that seem to undermine one another.

Occasionally, the reflexive documentary works by introducing stylistic or reconstructed elements self-consciously borrowed from fictional film or television. In *The Thin Blue Line* (Morris, 1997), *film noir* style is used to suggest how our perceptions of the real world are distorted by the images and stereotypes that the media throws at us. This kind of documentary requires a sophisticated, media-literate audience to understand fully how the process of documentary is being called into question.

The first-person documentary

A product of the video age, the first-person documentary allows individuals to record their lifestyles and personal thoughts without the intervention of an interviewer or crew. The subject is able to set the camera up themselves and to choose what material is shot and when this occurs. The subject may or may not have control over the editing of the material recorded. Because of the individual nature of this enterprise it has tended to be used to cover subjects connected with the home, family or other aspects of our personal lives.

This mode of documentary is sometimes known as the **video diary** approach. In 1999, the BBC launched a nationwide project, *VideoNation*, in which dozens of ordinary people from a variety of backgrounds were invited to produce a 10-minute video diary for broadcast. The project was an attempt to create a sense of the diversity and cosmopolitan nature of the UK as it was about to enter the twenty-first century and to give access to voices which are rarely heard on our screens. Documentary series such as *Castaway* (BBC, 2000) use the video diary format to supplement and balance the fly-on-the-wall and expository modes which are used elsewhere in the programme.

Drama-documentary

Activity 3.2

- Choose a recent television documentary and watch it carefully.
- What category does it seem to fall into and what are your reasons for placing it there?
- Does it borrow elements from other categories?
- How do these fit in with one another?

This is one of the most controversial areas of documentary and one of the most difficult to define. This mode generally involves the dramatic reconstruction of real events, using actors (or occasionally the original participants) and employing the style and form of fictional film or television. It is generally used when there is no way of gaining access to original material or when there is a need to make that material more persuasive or more striking.

This mode can be used in small sequences to illustrate or support the wider concerns of the documentary (the dramatic reconstructions of *Crimewatch* or *999*, for example) or can constitute the whole programme. Drama-documentaries have always been controversial because of the ways in which they openly mix fact and fiction in order to gain an audience.

In 1980, a drama-documentary about the execution of a member of the Saudi royal family, *Death of a Princess* (Thomas, 1980) caused a breakdown in diplomatic relationships between the Saudi and British governments. More recently, Jimmy McGovern's account of the Hillsborough tragedy, *Hillsborough* (ITV, 1996), introduced sufficient new evidence into the debate for the government to call for a fresh inquiry into events.

A BRIEF NOTE ON REALISM

Debates about documentary are inevitably tied up with debates about truth and reality. In the next section, we will look at the techniques which documentary makers have tended to use to construct their versions of events and try to show that these share a surprising amount in common with fictional forms. This is not to say that all documentary makers are manipulating and deceiving their audiences, but rather that their depictions of real life represent a particular viewpoint or version of events, not the only one.

This notion that there is rarely a single 'truth' to be represented in a set of events, but rather different interpretations from different vantage points, is a difficult one to accept, but it is crucial in the understanding of the ways in which documentary works.

If we bear in mind this idea, we can see that judgements about whether a text is **realistic** or not are ultimately fruitless, since we are not likely to agree fully on what constitutes the 'real'. Our different values and beliefs,

Picture 3.3 A scene from the drama-documentary *Hillsborough*, which changed a police investigation.

xtend your knowledge

Realism in film and TV
Key texts: John Caughie (ed.)
Theories of Authorship
(Routledge/BFI 1981), Colin
McCabe 'Realism and the Cinema:
Notes on Some Brechtian Theses',
***Screen* Vol 15, No 2 1974.**

• Although difficult, it is worth having a look at the above work as it forms the basis of much of our current

understanding of how realism is created, which is especially useful for any detailed study of TV News, documentaries and TV soap operas, as well as in film.

• See if you can identify the main ideas explored by McCabe and Caughie and apply them to a contemporary media text.

ey terms

Realism: a combination of elements of form, style and content which has been constructed in order to create a particular sense of the real for the text's audience.
Mediation: the process through which the real world is reconstructed in order to make it understandable to the audience of a media text.

Examiners' tips

- When you are writing about a media text, particularly audio-visual texts, you should avoid passing judgement on how realistic they are. This kind of statement often suggests a simplistic engagement with the product and will rarely impress an examiner.
- On the other hand, if you are able to analyse the ways in which a text attempts to create realism for an audience – whether or not you think it is successful – you are likely to gain credit.

our different social experiences and our different exposure to various kinds of representations will all be obstacles to this process. However, we can debate the **realism** of a text as this is a *descriptive* term, not a *judgement*. It refers to the techniques chosen by the film-maker to create a sense of the real world for the audience. **Verisimilitude** is another term used to describe the imitation of reality. The following section will look at some of these techniques and the ways they are used.

DOCUMENTARY: FORM AND STYLE

The huge range and number of documentaries available make any attempt to generalize a little redundant. For every rule there are dozens of exceptions – that is partly what makes the genre such an exciting one to study. Nevertheless, some understanding of the general features should help us to see how documentary makers are able to create some sense of the real world in their work and how we may be able to analyse the kinds of ideas, beliefs and values which inform the text.

MISE-EN-SCÈNE

Although early documentary films such as Flaherty's *Nanook of the North* borrowed heavily from fictional features in order to provide a way of telling the stories that audiences would readily understand, it was not long before documentaries began to develop a style and a look of their own. As audiences became more sophisticated and film-literate, it was necessary for documentary makers to assert the truthfulness and accuracy of their work by differentiating it from the kind of Hollywood product which audiences associated with entertainment and artificiality.

Much of the film and television fiction that we watch is characterized by its 'transparent' style – sometimes known as **classic realism** – in which we are encouraged to believe that we are watching an untouched or **unmediated** piece of reality; it is almost as if the camera does not exist.

Paradoxically, documentary texts often attempt to construct a greater sense of the real by adopting the opposite approach. The presence of the

Key terms

Rule of thirds:
conventional *mise-en-scène*
of film and television
relies on the screen being
divided into three equal
sections, both
horizontally and vertically.
Using these as guides, the
framing appears 'natural'
and avoids being overly
symmetrical and artificial.
Whip pans: a very fast
pan between two or
more characters or
points of interest. It gives
the impression that the
camera has been
'surprised' by activity and
is used in the place of a
more conventional cut or
shot/reverse shot.

camera is recognized, but its use creates the impression that the events unfolding are doing so spontaneously and without any prior knowledge from the film-makers. This leads to some recognizable elements of *mise-en-scène*:

- [ ] Unsteady, handheld camera shots, rather than the steady fluent camerawork of fiction.
- [ ] Cramped, asymmetrical framing, rather than balanced composition and the **rule of thirds** is often ignored.
- [ ] The camera often appears 'surprised' by the action, causing sudden movements such as **whip pans**.
- [ ] 'Natural' lighting, using only those lighting sources available in the frame. This makes the shots look darker and less defined than the key lighting used in fiction.
- [ ] 'Natural' or ambient sound, which encompasses all sound sources within a location. This can create obscure sound or inaudible dialogue in contrast to the controlled and balanced sound used in fiction.

Of course, this way of filming is not exclusive to the documentary maker. Many fictional texts (including US television series such as *NYPD Blue* or UK drama such as *This Life* (BBC2) and *As If* (Channel 4)) have adopted the documentary 'look' in order to distinguish themselves from similar genre products and to create a greater sense of realism for themselves.

EDITING

Key terms

Transparency: in media
terms, used to describe a
text which does not draw
attention to its own
construction.
Convention: an element
whose repeated use in
any form of media has
become habitual or
unavoidable.
Continuity editing: the
system of editing which is
dominant in fiction TV
and Hollywood cinema. It
has been developed in
order to provide the
audience with a fluid and
seamless experience of
the text.

Fictional films and television tend to employ a set of editing conventions which audiences have accepted as a result of their familiarity and constant exposure to. Like the *mise-en-scène* of fiction, this editing style is characterized by its 'transparency'. In other words, if it is carried out correctly, we should not be overly conscious of the process and what we are watching should appear fluent and unconstructed. This system is sometimes known as **continuity editing**. One of the key functions of continuity editing is to position the audience in relation to the action, so that they understand the 'meanings' of the text.

The editing of documentary texts has the same function, although there are many different approaches to achieve this. Many observational documentaries rely on long takes – an absence of editing – to create a sense of realism. Others have chosen to break the rules of continuity editing, drawing attention to the construction process in order to create a paradoxical impression of openness and authenticity.

It is important to realize that all documentaries require editing and that editing enforces the selection of some material and the rejection of other material. Documentaries tend to demand a high degree of selectiveness in this process.

Many documentaries have a **shooting ratio** of 30:1 (in other words 30 minutes of footage have been shot for every minute which appears in the

Activity 3.3

- Using several short sequences that you have shot around your school or college, edit three different versions of a sequence to create three viewpoints about the institution you work in.
- Add voiceovers to anchor your preferred meaning.
- What is the effect of changing the voiceover?
- Try showing your work to different audiences and get their opinions about accuracy.

final edit); for some documentaries the ratio might be as high as 150:1. We have to ask ourselves what decisions have been made in deciding what material has been retained.

Sometimes this decision will be made for technical reasons – the footage is unwatchable or the soundtrack too obscured. Mostly, however, decisions will be made based upon which footage best fits the intentions of the documentary makers, and material which appears to undermine or contradict an argument is likely to be omitted.

Once decisions have been made about what material is to be used, further choices are needed to work out how that material is to be arranged or ordered. Just as in fiction cinema, these choices will have an effect on the audience's understanding and interpretation of events.

The juxtaposition of shots will create meanings that may not have been available in the original footage. A long shot of the arrival of the prime minister at a party conference followed by a medium close-up shot of his deputy frowning may easily create the impression of animosity between the two and help to build on evidence of splits and arguments within the party.

Similarly, the arrangement of sound and vision is an important tool in creating meaning. Often, sound will be used, particularly in the form of a voiceover or interview, to anchor particular meanings to the footage we are currently viewing. Occasionally, because of the tendency for audiences to privilege the visual over the aural, the reliability of a witness or interviewee can be called into question by juxtaposing their words with footage which undermines their claims or ideas.

NARRATIVE

Activity 3.4

- Choose a documentary which you have seen or studied.
- Is it possible to break the structure of the documentary into the five categories suggested by Todorov's model?
- What viewpoints and attitudes are revealed in this process?

It may seem strange to use a term which is so strongly associated with fiction when we are discussing the elements of documentary. However, we need to appreciate the role that narrative plays in our everyday understanding of the world. Take this definition of narrative:

> ... the ordering of events into a logical, cause and effect structure which helps us to understand the progression between those events and the purpose of that progression.

This definition applies equally well to the fairy tale narratives of Cinderella or Goldilocks as it does to the real world narratives of news, sport or our own interactions with others. We largely make sense of the world through narratives of one kind or another, so it should not surprise us that documentaries should adopt this kind of structure.

There are some surprising similarities between fiction texts and their documentary counterparts. Most importantly of all, the presence of narrative within the documentary also reveals the implied presence of a narrator (or narrators); in other words that events are being constructed from a particular point of view.

| Diagram 3.2 | A basic model of narrative structure. |

Equilibrium/normality established
or implied

↓

Application of 'force' which
disrupts equilibrium

↓

Disequilibrium or instability

↓

Application of new 'force'
to resolve disequilibrium

↓

Establishment of new equilibrium
though often different to before

Documentaries need to establish a very specific sense of place and time in order to guarantee their authenticity. Establishing shots (possibly including captions and/or voiceovers) fulfil a similar function to those in fictional texts by providing a backdrop against which a series of events or conflicts can be played out. Additionally, the initial establishment will generally provide a state of normality or equilibrium which we will be expected to recognize or identify with.

As mentioned in Chapter 2, Tzvetan Todorov famously identified a narrative structure which he believed underpinned many fictional stories. At its most basic level, this consisted of five stages, which we can still apply to the narrative structure of documentaries.

If we accept that documentary is as dependent on narrative structure as fiction, then it should be possible to perceive this structure in the way in which the documentary has been put together (even if the primary or restored equilibria are implied rather than specifically stated).

The reason that this is important is that it can reveal yet again the viewpoints from which the text is constructed. The establishment of equilibrium creates the sense of what is 'normal' for the viewers, even though

Activity 3.5

- Using a television listings magazine, try to identify how many hybrids there are of the documentary form today.
- What are the appeals of the genre and its many hybrids for
(a) producers and
(b) audiences?

this may not be a universally agreed state. Similarly, it is the documentary makers who identify the destabilizing forces within a situation, again creating a particular version of events. The analysis of the structure reveals a clear viewpoint or agenda which determines the decisions of the documentary makers in presenting their version of the situation.

Finally, the majority of fiction narratives require the presence of characters as agents for the development of the story. Is the same true for documentary narratives? One important difference between the two forms is that the fictional character is played by an actor who will attempt to bring out the inner persona of that individual through their dialogue, actions, costume, props, locations and so on. The documentary participant is a real person and is therefore likely to be less conscious of the need to 'create' themselves as a character.

Nevertheless, our familiarity with fictional forms will encourage us to understand the subjects of documentary in the same ways we do the fictional characters. The documentary makers will use this process as a way of constructing their subjects as economically as possible, given the constraints of time and resources. The appearance and situation of the subject will be chosen to help our understanding.

Let us now try to put some of these ideas into practice by looking at a recent example of a documentary.

Castaway: an analysis of a documentary text

Castaway was transmitted by the BBC throughout 2000. The series followed the lives of 36 people, chosen from hundreds of applicants, to live in an isolated community on the remote Scottish island of Taransay for a year. The documentary covered the initial selection of the participants, through the preparations and early days on the island, before offering viewers regular updates of the events on Taransay as the members of the community struggled to live with one another. The series ended in January 2001 as the inhabitants left the island and attempted to settle back into their 'real' lives.

The approach taken by the documentary makers was clearly influenced by the success of the **docusoap** format, in which real communities (either geographical, *Paddington Green* (BBC), *The Village* (ITV), or determined by profession, *Hotel* (BBC), *Airport* (BBC)) are represented in ways closely related to the narratives and characterizations of drama, particularly soap opera.

Another influence may well have been the interest in the *Big Brother* format, which had been very successful in other countries and which Channel 4 were about to bring to the UK in the summer of 2000. In this, a documentary approach is applied to a competitive situation artificially created and determined by the programme makers themselves – 10 strangers living with one another in a purpose-built studio/house and forced to vote each other off of the show. Although *Castaway* was not a competition, it was clear that the show would rely on the audience's voyeuristic pleasure of seeing ordinary people struggling in an extraordinary situation.

The executive producer of *Castaway*, Jeremy Mills, referred to the programme as an 'ongoing, interactive, narrative observational documentary series' and had some grand aspirations for the show:

I'd been wanting to do something that looks forwards. I knew a lot of people were making programmes about the end of the millennium and all that stuff. I wanted to do something about the new century ... I'd always been intrigued by social experiments. (Castaway: The Full Inside Story of the Major TV Series, Mark McCrum, Ebury Press, 2000)

In order to achieve his ambitions, Mills and the production company, Lion Television, chose to construct *Castaway* out of several different elements employed by other documentary formats. Although the content might have been new to audiences, the way in which it was presented would have been very familiar.

Picture 3.4 *Castaway* sparked off a series of several documentary/game show hybrids which pitted ordinary people against the elements and each other.

First and foremost, *Castaway* functions as an expository documentary. Our understanding of the programme and of the events we witness is guided by a voiceover, provided by the actor Robert Lindsay. His commentary is given authority by both his social status – he is a middle class, middle-aged male – and by his celebrity status – he is also a recognized and talented performer associated with quality drama and comedy programmes. The presence of Lindsay as a voice-of-God within the programme also helps to ensure that we view the programme as a serious and responsible work, not simply an exploitative and voyeuristic attempt to generate ratings.

As in most mainstream expository documentaries, the credibility of the narration is of the highest importance. Lindsay's commentary is never undermined or contradicted by the images which accompany his words. He provides a clear sense of narrative time and space by explaining where and when events are happening in relation to one another, so that continuity is maintained and so that drama and suspense can be built up.

When one of the castaways, Ray, decided to leave the project in its second month, audiences were shown his attempts to contact the mainland and to find transport off Taransay. Crosscuts were made to conversations between different groups of islanders, some of who wanted to persuade him to stay, while others felt that it was best for

the community if he left. The editing, anchored by the Lindsay's narration ('Meanwhile, in their pods ...'), encouraged us to view these events as simultaneous and helped to create a sense of tension between the different individuals and viewpoints.

One of the reasons which contributed to Ray's eventual departure from the island was his deteriorating relationship with the documentary film-maker, Tanya Cheadle. The programme's acknowledgement of this conflict was characteristic of the open way in which the role of the film-maker was treated throughout. Much like *cinema verité* documentaries, the programme used this transparency as a way of securing the audience's trust in its authenticity. The fact that Cheadle was both a member of the community and a recorder of the events raised some issues which are central to many observational documentaries.

As a film-maker you're meant to be objective, or at least as objective as any individual can be, but the problem is at six or seven o'clock I don't go home from work, I go and socialise with these people – so how can I spend a year not forming friendships with people, not becoming involved? (McCrum, 2000)

Cheadle was often at odds with other islanders because of her choices as a film-maker. Many believed that there was too much concentration on conflict and argument, rather than showing the positive achievements of the community. Cheadle herself admitted that she was in a difficult situation:

There are certain people in the community ... who feel that I'm not covering certain aspects. So when I filmed the children playing in the snow – because it was beautiful and should be filmed and it might not snow again here – I got a complaint the next day: why was I not filming people putting up fence posts? (McCrum, 2000)

This situation highlights the importance of selectivity within documentary and the need to question the reasons behind the selection process. The castaways felt that material which celebrated their success and progress as a community was most important, while Cheadle's agenda was to produce a 'good' television programme – drama, conflict, beauty and so on. Although both groups were part of the same environment, there could be no agreement as to the 'truth' of the *Castaway* experience.

Similar issues were raised about the ways in which the castaways themselves were represented by the programme. Like many television documentaries, *Castaway* had to present its audience with a large number of individuals in a way which is clear and understandable within a 30-minute programme. Clearly this involves a simplification of complex and multifaceted individuals. This is achieved by focusing on one or two personality **traits**, which seem to 'explain' the whole person. This is a process which is used in fiction and which often relies upon very conventional representations or stereotypes in order to communicate conveniently to the audience.

The process upset many of the islanders. Several of the scenes from early episodes juxtaposed the assertive style of leadership of Dez Monks, with the collaborative and relatively light-hearted approach of another castaway, Ben Fogle. Scenes of Monks arguing with and shouting at members of his team during an orienteering exercise were used to construct him as an overbearing, even bullying, character. The characterisation was strengthened further by the direct contrast made to scenes of Fogle discussing tactics with his team, while laughing and joking with them.

Voiceover and captions helped to make this distinction even clearer, strengthening the representations already on offer. Monks was described as 'a 35-year-old salesman', linking his behaviour to the stereotypical view of a pushy and ruthless profession. Fogle, on the other hand, benefited from the sensitive and artistic connotations of being 'a picture editor with *Tatler* magazine'. In a video diary, Monks' partner, Liz Cathrine picked up on the limited construction of Dez that had been offered to viewers:

You've only shown his nasty side and I know for a fact you've got loads of footage of him being the joker, messing around, being caring and things. So I haven't been very impressed about your integrity in terms of showing a balanced view of people. (McCrum, 2000)

The video diary is, of course, another element borrowed from the observational and first-person modes, in which castaways addressed their thoughts and comments directly to camera for broadcast. A specific space on the island was set up for this purpose and the community was encouraged to use the video diary as a form of confessional. However, the castaways had no control over the use of this material in the final edit of the programmes.

In a first-person documentary, the video diary will often function as a means of linking the audience to a particular person and temporarily allowing us to see the world from their viewpoint. Because we are allowed privileged access to their thoughts and beliefs, it is almost a celebration of subjectivity. It succeeds by opposing the expository or observational documentary's traditional claims to be objective.

In *Castaway*, the video diary serves a different purpose. The large numbers of individuals involved would lead to a confusing mixture of voices and viewpoints if, as viewers, we were allowed equal access to them. Instead, the video diaries are used to reinforce the interpretation of events which we have already been presented with through the images shown and the anchorage of the voiceover. As such, we are encouraged to trust and respect certain diaries and voices, while dismissing or treating with cynicism those of other individuals. The video diary becomes one more means through which the film-makers' preferred version of events can be offered to the audience.

Castaway was not only a documentary, but also a media event, fuelling stories in national newspapers and magazines for the duration of the year. Many of the tensions and worries on the island revolved around the community's fears about how they were being perceived in the real world.

Perhaps this should be seen as a positive sign of the heightened awareness of the power of documentary in a media-literate culture. Certainly, the Inuit Indian whose experiences formed the basis for *Nanook of the North* would have had little idea how Flaherty would reconstruct his life. On the other hand, many of the elements which Flaherty brought to bear on Nanook's life – narrative, characterization, exposition – are still present in *Castaway* and many of the other documentaries which fill the television schedules.

Case study 2: studying gender representation in television

INTRODUCTION

It is probably fair to say that we take television for granted. Our sets sit in the corners of our living rooms, kitchens and bedrooms like any other piece of furniture.

We tend to treat television as part of a routine, automatically switching on when we come home from work or school, or when we enter a room, and allowing it to broadcast while we carry on with all sorts of other tasks: reading, studying, cooking, talking and so on. Of course, there are lots of programmes which grab our attention or which we have set aside time to watch. However, there are equally as many which we watch simply because we do not want to switch off the 'box'.

These elements in the viewing of television immediately suggest the influence of television's closest media relations: the cinema and the radio. These two media are respectively good examples of what we can call **primary** and **secondary** media. Cinema is a primary medium because it demands our attention and our concentration while being consumed. The experience of cinema is an 'event'; we make a conscious decision to attend and go through various preparatory rituals, such as buying drinks and popcorn. The darkened auditorium of the cinema is designed to encourage our focus on the film, with the minimum of distraction elsewhere.

We become easily annoyed by other people talking or moving about while we are trying to watch the film. The beginning and the end of the experience is clearly demarcated, often by the turning off and on of the house lights or by the curtains opening and closing.

Radio, on the other hand, exhibits many of the features of a secondary medium. It is generally played in the background of our lives, accompanying us while we are carrying on with other more important tasks. Radio is on in our homes as we rush to get ready in the mornings, or in our cars as we are driving, even perhaps in our workplaces.

Radio rarely demands our full attention, unless there is a particular song that we want to hear or a particular programme that we do not want to miss. In addition, radio is continuous. We experience the medium as a **flow** of sound, so that even when individual programmes finish, they are quickly replaced with the next set of shows. Radio broadcasts continuously and the audience is encouraged to dip in and out of this flow as it wishes.

Television, then, has the potential to act as a primary medium. It can demand our attention and keep us from wanting to do anything else. It can provide an 'event' for its audience (this might be a regular event, like an episode of your favourite soap opera, or a special event such as the broadcast of an international football match). However, television is often treated as a secondary medium, whose use is out of habit, rather than specific decision or effort.

ctivity 3.6

Are the following media primary or secondary? Explain the reasons for your decisions:
- newspapers
- websites
- CDs
- billboard advertising
- console games
- DVDs.

ey terms

Flow: a concept first used by Raymond Williams to describe the experience of watching television. In this and related media, products are not consumed as separate or discrete items, but as a continuous progression of sounds and images.

In most industrialized nations of the world, more than 95% of homes have a television and the majority of these have more than one set. In the UK, recent statistics suggest that there is an average of more than one television set for every person watching.

In the 1990s, audiences in the UK were watching television for between 27 and 30 hours a week or more than 1500 hours every year. Only sleeping and working accounted for more time in the average person's life cycle. In the past few years or so, the amount of time people spend watching television has dropped to around 24–25 hours per week as audiences have begun to turn to other forms of home entertainment such as computers, games consoles, DVDs and so on. However, there is no doubt that television remains the most widely consumed medium and arguably one of the most influential.

In this section, we will look at the power of television to construct and promote particular versions or **representations** of the real world to its audiences. We will also look in detail at two of its most popular genres – the **situation comedy** and the **soap opera** – in order to examine how representations of gender are used and circulated through the medium.

TELEVISION AND ITS REPRESENTATIONS

ey terms

NVLA: The National Viewers and Listeners Association is an organization which campaigns for stricter controls for material broadcast on television and radio. It is most strongly associated with its former president, Mary Whitehouse, who was prominent in the 1970s.

Television's 'ordinariness' has always been seen as a central issue in trying to discuss its relationship with the audience. Controversial material, such as bad language, sex and violence, is seen to be more harmful when shown on television because it is arriving in our homes, possibly unannounced and uninvited by its audience. Organizations such as the **NVLA** have frequently called for stricter controls of television broadcasting, precisely because they believe that it is too easy for children or other 'innocent' viewers to gain access to inappropriate or shocking material.

This section, however, is concerned not with extremes of television material but with the shared experience of the most common forms of television viewing. The general concept of representation has already been discussed in Chapters 1 and 2. Here we are concerned with the ways in which representations of gender – **masculinity** and **femininity** – have been built into some of the genres on which television has built its popularity.

We will work from the assumption that the most common representations in our culture will be those which serve the **dominant** interests. Dominant groups will often promote themselves as 'normal', and marginalize those groups who are seen as different and therefore 'abnormal'. The position of dominant groups comes about through the complex forces of history, economics and social politics. Diagram 3.3 suggests how some key social groups are positioned in relation to the idea of dominant social interests.

These relationships are subject to change, as there is a constant struggle between the dominant groups' need to sustain their position and the subordinate groups' attempts to gain recognition and status. Nevertheless, the fact that dominant groups often control those environments where power

Diagram 3.3	The constituents of dominant and subordinate social groups.

Dominant	Subordinate
Male	Female
White	Other ethnic groups
Middle class	Working class
Middle aged	The young, the old
Heterosexual	Homosexual, bisexual
Able-bodied	Disabled

Dominant groups: those social groups who seem to have attained power or status within society, generally at the expense of other related groups. The dominance of particular groups is often achieved by the process of making their own viewpoints and values seem normal or 'common sense', whilst the values of others are marginalized, made to seem abnormal, unimportant or disruptive.

Subordinate: used to describe groups who find themselves in less powerful positions than dominant groups.

Naturalization: a form of realism in which the real world is presented as closely as possible to the ways in which we experience it on a daily basis.

Content analysis: a way of analysing media texts which involves drawing conclusions from looking at the text as a whole or looking at a large number of similar texts.

Textual analysis: a way of analysing media texts which involves drawing conclusions from a close examination of individual elements or small parts of a particular text.

can be contested and redistributed – the government, the law, the education system, the media – means that the struggle will always be a long, drawn-out affair and one that is not often visible to society in general.

Given the ways in which television production is organized, it would not be surprising to conclude that television tends to rely on the dominant views of gender roles and stereotypes of masculinity and femininity. Most broadcast and production companies are run by men or have institutional practices which have been consolidated by years of male input and decisions.

Through this kind of organization, dominant or accepted views of gender are continually reflected in the programmes that make it to our screens. In turn, the constant use of particular representations serves to **naturalize** them, therefore making them seem 'normal' and without alternative.

The study of gender roles on television has generally centred on two methods, content analysis and textual analysis. **Content analysis** relies upon gathering data about the amounts of various representations available from a large number of television programmes and draws conclusions from the relative proportions of these.

Content analysis has been able to show that the number of men on television outnumbers those of women by about three to one and that there are many more men in central, star roles. Women tend to be seen in a restricted number of positions and professions – for example, girlfriends, wives and mothers, or secretaries and nurses. Men enjoy a much wider range of roles and professions. From this we can see that television does not reflect the reality of our society (in which women slightly outnumber men), but that it might reflect the balance of power in men's favour.

Textual analysis concentrates on a relatively small number of programmes, or even just one, but attempts to look closely at these to show how the construction of gender representations is achieved. Through textual analysis it is possible to isolate and identify the strategies by which representations are built up and naturalized, and perhaps to identify how alternative versions might in turn be employed. The sections which follow, concentrating on sit-com and soap opera illustrate how this approach might be used.

Activity 3.7

- Videotape a selection of adverts from a variety of channels.
- Using this selection, perform a content analysis, focusing upon gender roles.
  - How many male and female participants are there?
- What kinds of roles do they play?
- What sorts of settings are they found in?
- What conclusions can be drawn from your findings?

SEX AND GENDER

Although these two terms are often used interchangeably (the male sex or the male gender), it is more useful for us to identify a fundamental difference in their meanings. The term **sex** will often be used by academics while defining those *biological* differences which separate men and women. These differences are determined by genetics and, by and large, there is little room for debate or change in our biological make-up.

Definitions of **gender**, however, are *cultural*. The qualities which are identified with masculinity and femininity are very much debatable and certainly subject to a great deal of change over time. As suggested in the previous section, these definitions tend to be controlled by those in dominant positions, that is men, generally. As such, definitions of masculinity tend to be loaded with more positive and powerful qualities, while femininity is defined in more negative or passive ways. It is also characteristic of this situation that definitions of masculinity tend to be wider and to allow more social roles than those of femininity.

Diagram 3.4, we can see how some of these stereotypical qualities are linked to our understanding of gender. Remember, these are not meant as descriptions of how men and women actually are, but rather they

Activity 3.8

- Continue the list in Diagram 3.4 by adding further qualities in each column.
- Choose a selection of female characters from popular television programmes.
- Which qualities do they seem to exemplify?
- Can you find examples which seem to contradict th table's assumptions?

Diagram 3.4	Stereotypical qualities of masculinity and femininity.
Masculinity	**Femininity**
Professional	Domesticated
Strong	Weak
Rational	Emotional
Competitive	Co-operative
Independent	Communal
Aggressive	Passive
Ruthless	Sensitive
Ambitious	Supportive

indicate the kinds of ideas out of which conventional representations tend to be built.

It is worth noting that female characters can certainly be constructed out of the qualities which tend to be associated with masculinity. However, more often than not, the character will be portrayed in a negative light and 'punished' through the narrative for her actions. For example, female characters who are ambitious and assertive, but lack emotional and sensitive qualities are often portrayed as a threat to a male protagonist and have to be overcome physically or emotionally.

TV situation comedy

ey terms

Series: a television programme whose episodes tend to be self-contained narratives, which can often be viewed in any order.
Serial: a television programme whose narrative or narratives continue from one episode to the next.

Situation comedy derives its humour by placing a small number of characters in a set of familiar locations or situations and allowing our knowledge of their traits, weaknesses or ambitions to generate laughter. The comedy may be verbal, physical or both.

The most obvious feature of traditional sit-coms is their lack of progression. They have a circular narrative structure in which characters return to their original state or situation at the end of each episode, ready to begin again in the next. Sit-coms, therefore, are generally in a **series** format, as opposed to the **serial** format adopted by soap opera, where narratives are continued from episode to episode.

Several recent sit-coms have combined elements of both the series and serial formats. *Friends* has some narrative strands which are carried through each episode, such as the relationships between Ross and Rachel and between Chandler and Monica. At the same time, there are usually one or two self-contained narratives within each episode. British sit-coms such as *Spaced* have also adopted this kind of structure to maintain a loyal audience.

Taflinger, in his examination of sit-com, divides the genre into three areas:

(1) The action comedy (or actcom) in which:

☐ narratives are action-orientated
☐ characters are not complex, but are consistent and predictable in actions and thought
☐ the settings are backgrounds to the action, with little sense of identity.

(2) The domestic comedy (or domcom) in which:

☐ narratives are character-orientated and based on domestic or personal crises
☐ characters are complex, with multiple and conflicting emotions
☐ the settings, generally either literally or symbolically domestic, reflect the personalities of the characters.

Picture 3.5   *Spaced* – a recent British sit-com aimed at a younger audience.

(3) The drama-comedy (or dramedy) in which:

☐ narratives are issue-orientated, often focusing on personal or social themes

☐ characters are generally complex and used to explore specific themes or ideas within a situation

☐ settings are used to establish an appropriate arena in which the relevant issues and themes can be raised or dealt with.

(Source: Sitcom: what it is, how it works – an examination of the situation comedy, Richard F. Taflinger, www.wsu.edu:8080/~taflinge/sitexam.html.)

In common with soap opera, many sit-coms share an emphasis on the family. The basic premise of many sit-coms involves a family or a group of individuals who function as a family. In addition, domestic locations are common; where the home isn't used, there is often a surrogate such as a café or a bar.

The changing nature of sit-com subject matter over the years often reflects real changes in society (e.g. the nuclear family sit-coms of the 1950s and 1960s replaced by various dysfunctional family arrangements

Activity 3.9

- Try to find some examples which illustrate Taflinger's three categories?
- Can you add any further features which the three types seem to have in common?
- Are there any sit-coms which cannot be placed into the categories?
- See if you can define further categories to take account of these.

Activity 3.10

- What kinds of issues do contemporary sit-coms deal with?

- Choose some specific examples to illustrate your argument.

in the 1970s, the introduction of Afro-Caribbean families in the 1980s in programmes such as *The Cosby Show* or *Desmonds*). However, rather than suggesting that the sit-com is a particularly progressive genre, we should see this as part of a predictable strategy whereby social unease can be handled and defused through the employment of humour.

SIT-COM AND ITS AUDIENCE

Although sit-coms may appear to lack the range and narrative complexity of soap opera, they are still very much concerned with social values and attitudes, and gender remains a key issue.

Often the humour of sit-com derives from a setting or situation which is in some way alien or abnormal; this implies a view of 'normality' that can be shared by the audience. However, as we saw earlier any definition of what is normal is likely to be generated by dominant groups – in other words, what is normal to white, middle-class, middle-aged programme makers. This is not to say that all sit-coms are based around dominant groups, but rather when other representations do appear, they tend to be 'explained' through dominant viewpoints.

Let us take an example from the sit-com, *Friends*. This series is based around the lives of six twenty-something New Yorkers, who share their apartments and leisure time with each other. The core characters form a symbolic family and the key themes of the show are lifted from a middle-class ideal of family life – loyalty, emotional dependency and, of course, friendship.

When outsiders are introduced, they are generally done so as a threat to the unity of this group and rarely achieve any sort of status within the show. One of the regular subsidiary characters, Carol, is Ross' ex-wife and the mother of his son. The marriage ended when she began an affair with Susan, with whom she now lives as a family.

In the opening episodes of *Friends*, humour was generated from the usually painful situation of a marriage break-up through the 'abnormal' nature of Carol's affair. Her homosexuality clearly contrasted with the 'natural' heterosexuality of the main characters, although the jokes tended to be directed at Ross' inability to maintain his relationship, rather than her behaviour.

Ultimately, however, Carol and her lover are accepted and retained in the world of *Friends* because they function as a normal family, *despite* their homosexuality. In this way, the potentially disruptive effect of a gay character in a mainstream sit-com is naturalized by the fact that Carol retains a middle-class view of familial relationships.

We, the external audience, are asked to share these viewpoints by becoming part of the community set up by the show. This process is aided by the presence of a laughter track, which both encourages a sense of the show's 'liveness' and spontaneity, but, more importantly, acts as our guide in determining reaction.

Through the use of audience laughter, we are invited to share the joke and the perspective from which the joke is told. In *Friends*, this is pushed further by including the audience's reaction to romantic and emotional scenes. (When Ross and Rachel kiss for the first time, the audience cheers and sighs happily.)

MEN IN SIT-COM

In comparison to soap opera, there seem to be many limitations to the ways in which complex characters can be created. Sit-coms tend to run in limited series with 30-minute episodes. More importantly, the need for familiarity and repetition in the narrative makes progression and development particularly difficult.

With this kind of formulaic approach, it is hardly surprising that sit-com should be so heavily reliant upon stereotypes to fill its environments. The images of men and women with which we are presented in sit-com have to be easy to recognize and relate to. They do, however, raise some key questions about the way in which we are positioned in relation to these types in order to generate laughter.

Earlier, we suggested that the humour of sit-com arises from the undermining of a shared set of ideas about what constitutes 'normal'. Unsurprisingly, then, the male protagonists of sit-com are often marked by some clear deviation from the dominant views of the qualities which make up masculinity.

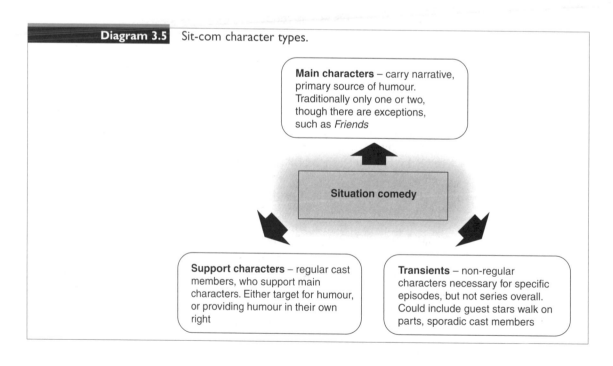

Diagram 3.5 Sit-com character types.

Main characters – carry narrative, primary source of humour. Traditionally only one or two, though there are exceptions, such as *Friends*

Situation comedy

Support characters – regular cast members, who support main characters. Either target for humour, or providing humour in their own right

Transients – non-regular characters necessary for specific episodes, but not series overall. Could include guest stars walk on parts, sporadic cast members

Activity 3.11

- List some other male characters from the sitcoms which you watch.
- What traits or characteristics make them funny?
- Do these deviate from our dominant views of masculinity?
- Is the opposite process at work in the female characters of the series?

Basil Fawlty in *Fawlty Towers*, for example, demonstrates masculine drive and ambition, but is constantly thwarted in his attempts to establish control by his overemphasis on the superficialities of class distinctions and social niceties.

Similarly, Del Boy in *Only Fools and Horses* suffers because he lacks the professional skills to realize his business plans and because he is handicapped by the brother and grandfather (or uncle in later series) whom he has to look after. In both cases, their comedy flaws derive from a misplaced feminine trait – in Fawlty's case, the desire for conformity and for acceptance into a class community and in Del Boy's case, the need to protect and nurture his family.

In the US sit-com, *Frasier*, there is a more sustained examination of male stereotypes, illustrating further how humour derives from our assumptions about normal masculinity. The Crane household exists as a kind of dysfunctional family unit.

Picture 3.6   *Frasier's* curious appeal means it has a very wide international audience.

Martin Crane is the father, his natural authority signified by his former profession as a police officer. His power and influence however have been curtailed by a gunshot injury, which has left him vulnerable and dependent on the care of others.

Martin's physical therapist, Daphne, lives in, superficially fulfilling the role of the mother by acting as housekeeper and cook. However, she is also constructed as childlike, through a naïve belief in her own psychic powers and by her British, northern, working-class origins which are seen as unsophisticated and primitive compared to the American West Coast, middle-class lifestyle which she has taken up.

Frasier exists as son, necessarily loyal to his father and Daphne; as mother-figure, responsible for the family's emotional well-being (he is a radio psychiatrist); and as father-figure, keeper and provider of the household. Two other characters make up the central roles. Niles, Frasier's brother and also a psychiatrist, and Roz, Frasier's radio producer.

Much of the comedy comes from the tensions between the various roles which the characters have to occupy. In addition, the humour derives from the inversion of typical assumptions about gender.

Both Frasier and Niles are *feminized* males. Their love of fine clothes, *haute cuisine* and the classical arts are matched by their dislike of classic male pursuits – football games, drinking in bars and eating in steak houses. The deviance of their characterization is emphasized by the contrast drawn to Martin Crane, who functions as a stereotype of masculinity and to Roz, who is a *masculinized* female, independent, successful and sexually assertive, preying on the single men around her.

The partnership between Frasier and Niles is coded as a kind of marriage. They dress in similar fashion, they share professions and lifestyles and find it difficult to maintain relationships with their partners. In fact, several episodes revolve around the jealously felt by one brother at the professional or romantic success of the other. However, the brotherly link is used to ensure that this kind of deviant relationship remains safely humorous and does not become too extreme or uncomfortable for the audience.

The structure would not work as successfully if Niles were a best friend instead of a member of the family. Buddy sit-coms, such as *Men Behaving Badly* or *Seinfeld* strive to avoid the kind of emotional closeness demonstrated in *Frasier*. In these series, male friendships are based around clearly heterosexual activities such as attending sports matches, going to pubs and bars or discussing women. Emotional bonds are rarely suggested or explored.

WOMEN IN SIT-COM

In the USA, there has been a long standing tradition of sit-com based around a female protagonist. *I Love Lucy* was one of the first examples of the genre in the 1950s. In the 1970s, *The Mary Tyler Moore Show* and

Rhoda were hugely successful and in the 1980s, *Roseanne* became a worldwide success. More recent examples such as *Ellen*, *Grace Under Fire* and *Suddenly Susan* confirm the potential for using female characters as the basis for comedy.

Predictably, most of the above have achieved success by **inverting** or **subverting** the accepted representations of their female stars and by providing a situation for them in which traditional models of femininity are shown to be inadequate. As before, by drawing attention to the subversion, the shows seek to demonstrate that we share a common understanding of what the normal would be.

Many of these sit-coms are based around the family, although often this is not of the nuclear variety. The independence and self-sufficiency of the protagonists is often suggested by their lack of steady partner, even though the lack is generally shown as a source of comic disappointment.

Despite not having a man, these women tend to play the role of mother to the disparate group of individuals with which they surround themselves. As such, the values of the nuclear family can be confirmed, even while the disappearance of such families in the real world is being acknowledged.

In the UK, there were relatively few sit-coms which focused predominantly on female characters. *Absolutely Fabulous*, hugely successful in the 1990s and still regularly repeated, provided an inverted family formation, in which the mother, Edina, is constructed as childlike, irresponsible and spoilt, while her daughter, Saffron, has to take a maternal role in looking after her.

Edina's lifestyle is encouraged and sanctioned by her best friend, Patsy. Both Edina and Patsy are approaching middle age, but are seen as independent and assertive figures, who ignore the conventions of female behaviour by adopting a masculine approach to life: hedonism, heavy drinking and sexual promiscuity.

Absolutely Fabulous asks us simultaneously to both condemn and to admire the actions of the protagonists. We can laugh at the way in which the rules of family life have been turned on their head, while comforting ourselves that we exist as part of a more 'normal' family situation. On the other hand, we note that by sticking to these rules, Edina and Patsy would lose the autonomy that characterizes their lifestyle and would be forced to conform. In this way, the sit-com is able both to celebrate the construction of a challenging female representation, while reminding us of the boundaries that have already been set as 'normal'.

The construction of gender representations within the sit-com generally serves to maintain our culture's dominant views about masculinity and femininity. This conservative approach is encouraged by the limited characterization and circular narratives which the genre demands. Above all, sit-coms tend to be a prime time genre, dependent on the widest audience possible for their continued success; as such it is a risky strategy to offer challenging or subversive material. However, it is possible to identify some element of struggle in the field of social relations if we look towards another hugely popular genre of television – the soap opera.

Activity 3.12

- Have a look at some more recent sit-coms, such as *Third Rock from the Sun* (US), *Malcolm in the Middle* (US) or *My Family* (UK).
- Compare them with some of the older sit-coms – what features of gender representation are common and which are new or different?
- What reasons might account for any changes and why might familiar elements remain?

TV soap opera

The term **soap opera** originated in the 1930s, when US radio serials were sponsored by major soap powder companies. Those serials, like their modern-day television relations, tended to concentrate on domestic and family dramas, using a large range of characters to populate a succession of interlocking narrative strands.

Television soap operas have adopted the **serial** format, in which narratives are carried over from one episode to the next and characters tend to develop over time, their actions informed by the detailed histories which they carry with them. This is in contrast to the **series** format, in which characters and situations are carried from episode to episode, but the narratives remain self-contained.

Mary Ellen Brown (1987) has identified eight characteristics, or generic conventions, shared by many soap operas which are listed in Diagram 3.6.

We will look at a number of these characteristics in order to examine the construction of gender.

SOAP OPERA AND ITS AUDIENCES

Both the content and the form of soap opera have led commentators over the years to claim that it is a 'female' genre, even when viewing figures have continually shown that male audiences are equally likely to watch and enjoy this type of programme. However, there is evidence to suggest

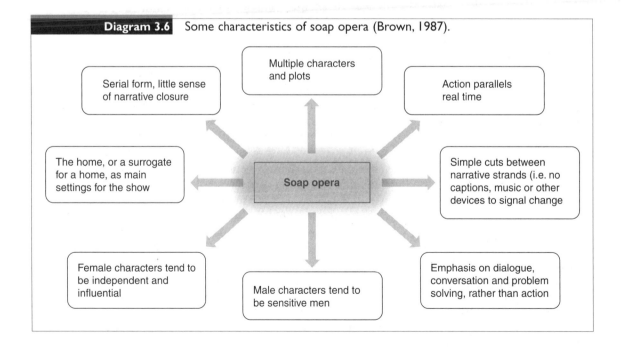

Diagram 3.6 Some characteristics of soap opera (Brown, 1987).

Multiple characters and plots

Serial form, little sense of narrative closure

Action parallels real time

The home, or a surrogate for a home, as main settings for the show

Soap opera

Simple cuts between narrative strands (i.e. no captions, music or other devices to signal change

Female characters tend to be independent and influential

Male characters tend to be sensitive men

Emphasis on dialogue, conversation and problem solving, rather than action

that soap opera does offer female audiences various pleasures which other genres cannot provide.

The focus on the home as a setting, identified by Brown, is complemented by an emphasis on families, either literally (the Mitchells and the Fowlers in *EastEnders*) or metaphorically (the motel employees in *Crossroads* or Tony and his lodgers in *Hollyoaks*). Culturally, the family has always been seen as the preserve of the female and, indeed, in soap opera, families are often led by powerful female figures or **matriarchs** (Peggy Mitchell and Pauline Fowler in *EastEnders*, for example).

However, in many other genres of television, the family is of secondary importance, used as a contrast to or an escape from the more important professional environments. Police and hospital dramas are often structured in this way: in *ER*, Dr Greene's professional life is regularly compromised by the 'pressures' of his domestic world. Over the course of several series, he has struggled through a divorce, been a single parent and, at the end of series seven, he effectively killed a patient who had threatened his new wife.

In soap opera, the family functions as the key social grouping and other elements, such as jobs and relationships, are always explained in terms of family forces. Thus, the running of the Queen Vic pub in *EastEnders* becomes merely another illustration of the shifting power within the Mitchell family and their allies or enemies. Similarly, the café in *Hollyoaks* functions more as an extension of the Morgan family home than a workplace.

In addition, the soap opera provides a space on television where the notion of the family can be explored and questioned by audiences in ways which do not seem to be available in other genres. While the idea of the nuclear or average family has diminished and changed drastically in the real world, many television genres, including advertisements, still cling desperately on to the idea that families must consist of two parents and the children.

In soap opera, the constant round of new and breaking relationships, legitimate and illegitimate births, secret and not-so secret affairs, adoption and fostering, false identities and mysterious pasts places almost every character into a complex and ambiguous family context. Through this the concept of the family and the idea that it should have clear 'boundaries'

Activity 3.13

- List as many British television soap operas as you can.
- How well do Brown's criteria seem to fit these soap operas?
- Are there any other conventions that you would add to this list?

Activity 3.14

- Choose one of the key families from a TV soap opera.
- From your own knowledge and research, draw out a family tree as accurately as possible.
- How easy or difficult is it to complete the tree?
- What conclusions about the structure of the genre can be drawn from this process?

Extend your knowledge

Television and its representations
Key text: *Television Culture*, John Fiske (Routledge, 1998)
- This is not always an easy book to understand, but Fiske has been instrumental in making the study of television a respectable pursuit for academics and media students.

- In this book, he looks at a number of television genres and demonstrates the ways in which audiences interact with the experiences of television.
- See if you can identify some of his main ideas and apply them to your study of media texts.

is stretched almost to breaking point. Family is central in its importance to soap opera, but there is no single definition of how a family *should* be. Love, loyalty and respect are qualities which are prized over simple blood links in the genre.

Linked to this questioning of the family are other challenges to 'normal' notions of female attitudes and behaviour. Soap operas often exhibit an ambivalent attitude to marriage, both as a ceremony and a way of life.

Soap opera weddings tend to be special events, although they are rarely presented as entirely happy affairs. Last-minute doubts, the arrival of old flames or the revelation of painful secrets are used to cast doubt on the wisdom of marriage. In *Coronation Street*, Mike Baldwin's marriage to his young bride went ahead, despite the fact that he had just discovered her affair with his son. In *EastEnders*, Ian Beale lost his bride, Melanie, after 2 hours when his lies about his daughter's leukaemia were revealed.

Weddings have traditionally been used as a positive moment of narrative closure in other forms of entertainment; soap opera however uses them as site of conflict and further narrative development.

Even if the wedding goes ahead, soap opera marriages are likely to be short-lived or unhappy times. This is partly attributable to the need for drama and conflict, something that happy marriages can rarely provide. On the other hand, it is often the female characters who are at the centre of narrative events, suggesting a power and an influence in relationships which is not often seen in other genres.

In *Television Culture* (1994) John Fiske argues that the lack of central characters or a single narrative viewpoint in soap opera provides a more **open** experience for the viewers. This allows a single narrative event to be interpreted in a number of different ways, allowing audiences to explore social or moral issues for themselves. In this sense, a married woman's affair could be understood as breaking the 'rules' of our culture and deserving of punishment; equally she could be celebrated for having the courage and independence to break out of a relationship which was difficult or oppressive.

Key terms

Open texts: media products whose form and content (though particularly the former) allow a large degree of interpretative freedom to the audience. This kind of text produces many different readings or meanings, none of which are seen to be more legitimate than the others, for example, art films, alternative forms of music or television, radical magazines
Closed texts: media products whose form and content are arranged so that only a limited number of interpretations or readings are possible by the audience.

Activity 3.15

- What recent soap opera narratives might be used as examples to illustrate the 'openness' of the text?
- What features do these narratives

seem to have in common?
- What readings are possible from the audience?

WOMEN IN SOAP OPERA

We have already identified the importance of **matriarchs** within the soap opera world and it would be true to say that soap opera provides a range of female roles which are rarely seen in other genres. The importance of

| Picture 3.7 | Jacqui Farnham takes over the bar in *Brookside* (Channel 4). |

female representations in this type of programme is not that they completely break with the cultural definitions and stereotypes identified elsewhere, but rather that they present a view of the world in which those qualities are privileged or respected more than elsewhere.

Gossip is a term which carries largely negative connotations and is most often used in connection with women (men are seen to *discuss* issues, while women *gossip*). However, this is a skill which is highly prized in soap opera. Brown's criteria indicate the importance of intimate conversation and problem solving as narrative features and the female characters are very often at the centre of this process. In this sense, it is often the characters most associated with the idea of gossip who play a pivotal role in both the community and many of the narrative strands (Dot in *EastEnders*, for example, or Vera and Audrey in *Coronation Street*).

What's more, the regular, real-time episodic structure of soap opera encourages gossip from the audience. Narratives unfold slowly, giving us plenty of time to predict and judge outcomes. The audience's privileged position in relation to the action means that we often 'know' more than the characters. This position of knowledge is further emphasized by subsidiary media, such as tabloid newspapers and magazines, 'giving away' the narratives before they occur. Far from spoiling our enjoyment, this information allows us to discuss and debate from an informed viewpoint and to join with a community of like-minded 'fans'.

By concentrating on dialogue and discussion, rather than physical action, soap operas allow strong, independent women to dominate their narratives. Many of the key settings of the genre are controlled and run by women. This obviously includes the home, but extends to important workspaces such as the Queen Vic pub (in recent years, run by Peggy Mitchell and then by Sharon Watts), The Woolpack in *Emmerdale* (owned by Bernice) and Bar Brookie in *Brookside*. While it could be argued that all of these spaces are merely an extension of the stereotypical representation of the women as *mothers* – nurturing, providing food and drink – their important position within the community as a whole gives the owners status and power.

As suggested earlier, soap opera women are also allowed power through their sexuality. The popularity of characters such as Kat Slater in *East-Enders* or Maxine in *Coronation Street* is based upon their ability to manipulate and control the male characters who are often attracted to them both sexually and emotionally. In other genres, this type of character would normally be evaluated negatively and punished for their actions, but in soap they are celebrated and ultimately rewarded for their independence.

Nor is it only *young* women whose sexuality is acknowledged. Soap is one of the very few genres prepared to deal with the sexual relations of its middle-aged characters. In *EastEnders*, a long running storyline involved Peggy's fight against breast cancer and frequently focused on her concerns about the effect of the disease on her relationship with her husband. More recently, she has been at the centre of a love triangle with Harry and Charlie Slater. In *Coronation Street*, Rita embarked on an affair with a married man whose wife was suffering from Alzheimer's disease.

Let us now take a look at how the male characters are positioned in relation to the female representations on offer.

MEN IN SOAP OPERA

Given that soap opera seems to privilege and promote certain qualities that we associate with femininity, it is not surprising that successful and long-lasting male characters might have to exhibit similar capabilities. Unusually on television, the range of male roles available seems not to be as varied as those for females. **Patriarchs** are far less common than **matriarchs**, with men usually fulfilling a secondary role in the family organization. This is most obviously seen in the 'henpecked' husband stereotype, usually played for humour (Jack Duckworth in *Coronation Street*, Barry Evans in *EastEnders*).

There are plenty of other examples where the family power structure is in evidence in more subtle ways. Pregnancy storylines, for instance, often centre on the tension between a strong and knowledgeable mother-to-be and an overanxious and ineffective father-to-be. Similarly, female

Picture 3.8   'Henpecked' husband Jack Duckworth in *Coronation Street* (ITV).

characters tend to police their communities, dictating the terms in those situations where the 'rules' of the family are broken. In *Coronation Street*, Gail Platt kicked Martin out of the family home following his extra-marital affair; *Brookside's* Emily Shadwick was responsible for a campaign of revenge against Susannah whose affair lead to the death of her father and brother.

This is not to say that there are no powerful male characters in soap opera. The figure of the businessman or entrepreneur is a common type (Ian Beale in *EastEnders*, Mike Baldwin in *Coronation Street*, Eric Pollard in *Emmerdale*). However, these characters are often excluded or demonized by their soap communities. They tend to be constructed from qualities which are typically masculine – assertiveness, strength, ruth-lessness – and which would identify the hero in many other genres. These elements, though, mark them as outsiders in the soap environment.

Interestingly, the only times that they become fully integrated into the community is when they exhibit feminine character traits, such as sensitivity, caring and the ability to demonstrate emotion. Examples of this might include Mike Baldwin's reaction to the death of his ex-wife Alma in *Coronation Street* or Ian Beale's financial ruin and subsequent relationship and marriage to his former nanny, Laura.

Activity 3.16

- Draw up a list of the male characters from your favourite soap opera.
- Divide these into 'good' characters and 'bad' characters. There may be some you cannot fit into either category.
- What kinds of qualities do the characters in each category have in common?
- Why are some characters difficult to fit in this way?

It is often the emphasis on emotion and sensitivity which separates the 'good' male characters (those we like, empathize with or want to survive) from the 'bad' characters (those we are encouraged to dislike or wish to see punished).

In *EastEnders*, Phil Mitchell and 'Nasty' Nick Cotton are alike in their willingness to manipulate others for their own benefit, their reliance on violence and their links to the criminal world. However, Phil is seen more positively because of his ability to sustain relationships (with Lisa or Sharon) and because he is seen as loyal to his mother and to his son. This is in marked contrast to Nick Cotton, who is often involved in schemes to exploit his mother, Dot (even trying to poison her at one point), and who accidentally killed his own son. Phil is allowed to remain in the community because he is a good son and father; the latter is regularly expelled because he cannot adapt to these roles.

The genre of soap opera is one of the areas in which issues of gender and representation are being contested on an almost daily basis. The fact that it is often dismissed as a 'valueless' form of television is one of the strategies used by dominant groups to undermine the kinds of positive female roles on offer. A close study of soap opera can bring to the surface many of the conflicts which underpin the construction of representations in our culture and its popularity reveals the relevance of these issues.

Examiners' tips

When you are writing about a complex form like soap opera, remember:
- Do not simply retell the narrative. Assume your examiner has a working knowledge of the text you are discussing.
- Try not to generalise too much about the audience, particularly in a negative way.
- Use specific examples to illustrate your ideas.
- Try to pay attention to the form of the programme as well as its content.

Case study 3: studying new media technologies

INTRODUCTION

You've just finished e-mailing your friends on your PC or WAP mobile in order to discuss the latest CDs and MP3s you've been listening to. You've got a DVD to watch later but now you're just about to sit down at your Playstation 2 for a session of game-playing. If this sounds like a familiar account of your leisure time, you might find it hard to imagine that 20 years ago these technologies did not exist.

Key terms

Hardware: the physical technology
which stores and displays information.
Software: the data or information to be stored by the hardware.
Digital: any electronic system which stores information in binary form. In this form, information is easily copied, transferred, compressed, combined with other sorts of information and rendered interactive.

Key terms

Technological determinism: the commonly held view that technology shapes, or determines, the kind of society in which we live.
Consumers: an alternative term for *audience*, often used when discussing the media as a business or institution to reinforce the role of profit and finance in the development of media forms and products.

The acceleration in the pace of technology over the past two decades has been astounding and arguably it is in the area of the media that these changes have had the greatest effect.

This section will look at the role of new media technologies within our society and try to examine how the development of technologies is related both to the *institutions*, who produce **hardware** and **software**, and to the *audiences* who consume them. We will look closely at the development of **digital** television and discuss how the medium has been altered by the introduction of new technologies, services and ideas.

ATTITUDES TOWARDS TECHNOLOGY

Let us go back in time for a moment. In the 1960s, a US magazine, *The Futurist*, was busy predicting what the world would be like in the year 2000. Science fiction writer Issac Asimov believed that all home appliances would be powered by batteries with nuclear isotopes. Meanwhile, certain scientists predicted that we would all be travelling in magnet-controlled flying saucer devices, similar to guided missiles for short journeys around the world.

Of course, little of what was expected has come true. In making this point, there is no criticism intended of the writers for their inability to see into the future. However, the examples illustrate a common tendency to view technology as a predictable series of developments, following a clear path of progress. Equally predictable seem to be the effects of these developments once they reach our society.

This way of thinking is sometimes called **technological determinism**. Like many systems of thought, it is so widespread that it appears to be common sense and unarguable.

However, to regard technology in this way is to ignore the complex role of institutions and audiences, or **consumers**, in determining the ways in which technology is developed and implemented in our society. For example, the technological determinist view would argue that, in any medium, new technology will automatically replace and outdate old technology. History, on the other hand, demonstrates that this is not always the case.

Cinema could be used as an example here. Over the course of the last century there have been many developments to the technology of cinema which film-makers and audiences have evaluated and accepted. Silent films became virtually extinct in Hollywood after the introduction of the first synchronized sound in *The Jazz Singer* (Crosland, 1927).

The processes of Technicolor and Eastmancolor, once they had become economically viable for studios, made black-and-white films practically redundant. However, there were other technological developments which were introduced only to be rejected by film audiences. The three-dimensional (3D) film was introduced in 1952 to boost cinema audiences as the new invention television was adversely affecting attendance. The first was a safari adventure film called *Bwana Devil* (Oboler, 1952) and 3D enjoyed a brief period of employment, before it became obvious that audiences

| Diagram 3.7 | In each case, the introduction of the new medium has been said to make the old medium redundant. However, the old media persist, though their role may be different. |

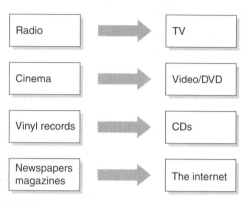

In each case, the introduction of the new medium has been said to make the old medium redundant. However, the old media persist, though their role may be different.

Radio → TV

Cinema → Video/DVD

Vinyl records → CDs

Newspapers magazines → The internet

would not accept wearing red- and green-lensed glasses during performances. Apart from a brief revival in the 1980s and the adoption of 3D technology for specialist film exhibitors such as IMAX, this spelt the end of the 3D movie as a mainstream format.

In his book, *The Soft Edge*, Paul Levinson (1998) employs a useful analogy to indicate how a society interacts with the introduction of a new technology. A caveman sits in his dark and gloomy cave, wondering what the weather is like in the outside world. He decides that the best way to have access to this information would be to create a hole in his wall so that he can see outside. However, the hole lets in the wind and the cold from which the caveman wishes to be protected. He therefore invents a basic piece of 'information technology': a window. The window allows an approximation of the outside world to become available to the caveman, without the negative effects such as the weather.

However, the window has some unforeseen effects for the caveman. Because he can see out of the cave, it follows that others are now able to see in; in inventing the window, the caveman has also invented the prehistoric voyeur. In addition, because, the widow is easily breakable, his cave is now more vulnerable to intruders than when it was solid wall.

The caveman has to evaluate the effects of his new technology, weighing up the foreseen with the unforeseen, the positive effects with the negative effects. In doing so, he finds that he can improve the ratio of positive to negative effects, by adapting his new technology – introducing curtains! Now he can look outside whenever he wishes, but he can also prevent people looking in. The window is still vulnerable to being broken, but this negative effect is compensated for by the improvements to his life.

This analogy indicates several important ideas about new technology. First, that new technology will often have unplanned effects on society. These effects can be positive or negative, depending upon which groups

ctivity 3.17

- Research the introduction of a new media technology (for example, Minidisc, DVD, MP3 or the X-Box).
- What are the benefits offered to the consumer?
- Are there likely to be any unexpected consequences or drawbacks?
- To what degree do you think that the product will be accepted, adapted or developed as a result of its consumer's needs?

Audiences are shown the first 3D film in 1952.

of society you belong to. (In the case above, the transparency of the window was not good for the shy and retiring cave dweller, but proved a positive thing to peeping Toms and cave-breakers!) Second, it demonstrates society's role in evaluating, adapting and implementing or rejecting new technology, undermining the myth that technology is always imposed on us.

The introduction of video technology into mobile phones puts us in a remarkably similar situation to that of our imaginary caveman. The ability to see or be seen by the people we are talking to could certainly be a powerful and positive effect in certain situations. But would this benefit be outweighed by the loss of privacy that the videophone would entail? Would we become more vulnerable to the intrusion of unwelcome and undesirable callers?

Before we look into the case study, we need to consider some of the terms and ideas which are central to this topic.

Some key terms and ideas

Almost every new digital medium has been sold to the consumer on the basis that it provides better quality of sound, visuals or experience than its analogue predecessor (for example, CD replacing vinyl, DVD replacing video or the digital mobile replacing the analogue mobile). However, this is not the only difference which new technology makes to our lives.

One of the commonly held beliefs of technological determinism is that new technology outdates and replaces its 'old' media equivalent, leaving the old technology redundant. However, there are many examples where old technology survives this process by fulfilling a specific social role for which it is uniquely suited.

Radio, for example, is one of the most durable of media, because it can be listened to in the car, in the workplace or anywhere while involved with other tasks. Vinyl records have been replaced by CDs as the main format for record sales, but they survive in the specialist markets of dance and club music, where DJ's find vinyl easier to mix and scratch.

Digitalization has allowed technology to deliver media products in faster and more compact ways. Information stored in a digital format can be **compressed**. This means that more information can be sent and received through the existing channels of communication in our lives: phonelines, mobile phone frequencies, television aerials, satellite dishes and so on.

The increasing amount of information on offer has led to the proliferation of technology: a massive expansion in the range of products from which a consumer can choose.

Technically, any channel of communication is limited by its **bandwidth**. By compressing information so that more of it can be sent and received, the bandwidth can be increased. In the future, it is likely that a combination of new compression technology and new bandwidth technology will allow the creation of **broadband**, whereby enormous amounts of information will pass almost instantaneously between institutions and audiences. Internet access will be quicker, for example, and internet content more advanced as analogue phone lines are replaced by digital lines and fibre-optic cables.

The nature of the digital signal and its mode of transmission also encourages multimedia presentation, combining visual, audio and print technology, and interactivity between the text and the audience, allowing them to participate more fully in its creation or transmission.

Key terms

Digitalization: the process through which analogue media are turned into their digital equivalents.

Compression: digital information can be 'squeezed' so that more of it can be stored in existing spaces. Compression can result in a loss of quality in the information. But it increases the possibilities for two-way communication, allowing more interactivity between institution and audience.

Picture 3.10   Vinyl records have found a niche market among DJs and clubbers.

Institutions are able to integrate technologies to increase profitability and efficiency. This process is known as convergence. Ultimately, the aim of many media institutions seems to be to merge all available media into a single signal, through a single piece of technology to the audience. We can already see this process in technologies such as PCs, which offer home entertainment options through DVD-ROM facilities or through televisions which offer in-built access to the internet.

We shall return to these key categories later when we look at a specific example of a new media technology:

☐ quality
☐ proliferation
☐ interactivity
☐ convergence.

Although we can predict some of the tendencies in the development of new media technologies, the results of these for audiences and societies can only be judged in retrospect. Those who have commented on the implications of digital technology for the future have tended to occupy a position somewhere between two extremes.

On one hand, the **technophile** believes in the positive benefits of technology and its potential to redistribute power within societies and

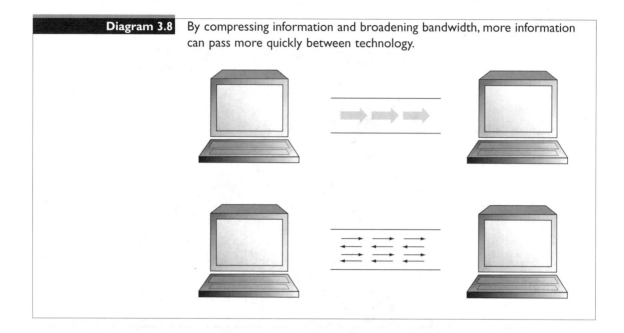

Diagram 3.8 By compressing information and broadening bandwidth, more information can pass more quickly between technology.

Activity 3.18

- Are you a technophile or a technophobe?
- List the advantages and disadvantages which you believe that technology is bringing to our lives.
- Which is the longer list? Argue your case with a partner who holds the opposite view.

across different cultures. The accessibility of information in a digital world should allow every individual to compete on an equal level with the institutions which surround them and should bring together communities joined by common interests, irrespective of geographical or social boundaries. This idyllic view sometimes goes by the name of the global village scenario.

On the other hand, the **technophobe** believes that new technologies can only serve to strengthen and support the power structures which already exist in the world, allowing those corporations who control our access to the technology an immense amount of influence on the economic and cultural development of the planet. In addition, there is a fear that it will create a two-tiered society, divided into the **information rich** and **information poor**, as not everyone might have the money or skills to participate in the digital communications revolution.

The technophobe is fearful of the potential of new technology to increase the power and influence of already dominant groups. In particular, the threat of **cultural imperialism** is increased, whereby the range of products and values which exist in a global culture is swamped by those products from the cultures which control the technology (usually the USA).

One example of this process might be seen in the medium of film, where the ready availability of Hollywood films in cinemas and on video or DVD has restricted the opportunities for film-makers from other backgrounds or cultures to find finance or large audiences.

Now, we are going to turn our attention to a specific example of a new technology in order to examine some of the key issues which surround the implementation and consumption of digital media.

Digital television

WHAT IS DIGITAL TELEVISION?

Digital television broadcasters make use of the established means of television reception (aerial, satellite dish and cable) to carry digital television signals. However, because digital information can be compressed, the broadcasters are able to make more efficient use of this bandwidth to provide many more channels, as well as additional services.

Digital television can be delivered to our homes in one of three ways:

☐ **Digital Terrestrial Television (DTT)**: currently offered by ITVDigital (at time of writing ITVDigital had gone into administration due to financial problems, so you can access updated knowledge when you study this topic). DTT signals can be picked up through a conventional television aerial and decoded by the digital set-top box supplied.

☐ **Digital Satellite Television (DST)**: currently offered by SkyDigital, DST signals are received by a small external satellite dish and decoded by the set-top box supplied.

☐ **Digital Cable Television (DCT)**: currently supplied by companies such as Telewest and NTL, DCT signals are carried along underground fibre optic cabling which is connected to subscriber television sets.

The digital television landscape contains some familiar landmarks. Terrestrial television channels (BBC1, BBC2, ITV1, C4 and C5) are free-to-air on all digital television services, along with a number of other digital-only channels created by these institutions such as BBC Four, BBC Knowledge, CBeebies, BBC News 24, BBC Parliament, ITV2 and E4.

However there is now far more competition for these established networks in the form of specialist channels, **narrowcasting** to audiences based around specific interests or genres of television.

In addition to the channels offered, most of the digital television providers are also promoting other services which can be accessed through our sets such as e-mail facilities, shopping, banking and subscription events such as **pay-per-view** and **near video on demand.**

In order to benefit fully from the interactive services on offer, it is necessary in most cases to connect a set-top box to a phone line, creating a **return path** which allows two-way communication to take place.

At the moment, analogue and digital television channels run side by side, allowing consumers a choice of format. However, it is envisaged that in the near future, analogue systems will be turned off permanently. BSkyB ceased analogue satellite transmissions in 2001. Terrestrial channels are obliged by law to maintain an analogue service until the government believe that sufficient digital coverage is available for all viewers.

The initial timetable for digital television's takeover suggested that the switch off of analogue signals would occur between 2006 and 2010, although it would not be surprising if this was later extended. After analogue television transmissions have finished, the government plans to sell the analogue frequencies to telecommunications companies, earning the country somewhere in the region of £8 billion. Technology is constantly changing and by the time you read this section, innovations will have been made to this area of television technology.

DIGITAL TELEVISION AND THE AUDIENCE

Key terms

Digital decoder: the hardware required to transform a digital signal into its analogue equivalent so that the signal can be viewed by a conventional television set. Normally, this is a box through which the aerial or satellite dish connects to the television. Also known as a digibox.

Let us look at some of the benefits which digital technology promises to bring to audiences and their consumption of television. Again, it might be useful to think about these in the four categories which we identified earlier: **quality**, **proliferation**, **interactivity** and **convergence**.

Quality

The robust nature of the digital signal compared to that of analogue television has allowed suppliers of digital television to promote its product on the basis that digital television offers the audience an unprecedented level of sharpness and definition in the picture quality, along with a reduction in the amount of interference present, compared to analogue terrestrial and satellite signals. Digital television is also promoted on its ability to provide digital quality sound.

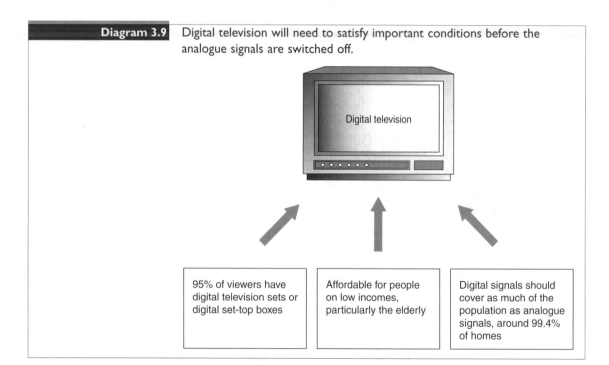

Diagram 3.9 Digital television will need to satisfy important conditions before the analogue signals are switched off.

Digital television

95% of viewers have digital television sets or digital set-top boxes

Affordable for people on low incomes, particularly the elderly

Digital signals should cover as much of the population as analogue signals, around 99.4% of homes

Picture 3.11 One day all homes will receive digital television, either via set-top boxes or minidishes or via built-in television sets.

Multiplexing: is the process of simultaneously broadcasting a number of different signals through a single path of transmission (in this case a digital satellite frequency).

However, these claims are complicated somewhat by the fact that most of us are still watching analogue television sets. The need for **digital decoders** to transform the signal into an analogue format reduces the quality of the signal, so that it is only slightly better than the best analogue pictures received through an aerial or a satellite dish.

The consumer magazine *Which?* published a report in June 1999 which was highly critical of claims from the digital television industry. In addition to questioning the superiority of the picture quality over analogue, their researchers pointed out that the compression of digital images which is necessary to **multiplex** the existing bandwidths might also affect the quality of the image, particularly where there is a lot of information to be compressed (an example of this might include a pan across the crowd at a football match).

In addition, while it is true that digital signals are less liable to suffer from interference from buildings, weather and other such forces than their analogue equivalents, certain conditions can cause the total break up of the digital television picture (the build up of static before an electrical storm, for instance). The latter criticism only applies to DTT and DST; digital cable is, of course, free from most sorts of external interference.

Finally, *Which?* compared the sound quality of digital television with that of the best NICAM stereo analogue service and declared that any improvement was imperceptible to human hearing.

Proliferation

Undoubtedly, the development of digital television has allowed the audience more choice in terms of what they watch than ever before (but there is an argument that we now just have more choice of the same kinds of programmes, but no truly new programmes).

In the space of a few years, we have moved from a choice of five channels broadcasting a variety of different programming for all sections of the audience to a multi-channel environment, in which the broadcast channels are supplemented by a huge variety of specialist, narrowcast channels, providing specific types of programming for specific niche groups within the overall audience.

Examples of narrowcast channels include:

- ☐ **UK Style**: dedicated to programmes on the home, garden and cookery.
- ☐ **Extreme**: coverage of extreme sports and pastimes.
- ☐ **MTV**: music video and music/youth programming.
- ☐ **Discovery**: documentaries.
- ☐ **Nickleodeon**: children's programmes.

Scheduling: the process of placing shows on the appropriate channel and at the appropriate time to gain the largest or most suitable audience.

One of the most obvious effects of this increase is to change the way in which we watch television. In a limited channel environment, competition for large audiences at particular times of the day (for example, mornings or *prime time* 7.00pm to 9.00pm) emphasized the importance of channel competition and **scheduling** to ensure that the largest percentage of available audience would be watching at any one time.

The schedulers employed a variety of techniques to create a sense of **channel loyalty** in the audience, using popular and established shows to generate large audiences, many of whom they hoped would be **inherited** by the new sit-com or quiz show which followed. **Hammocking** new programmes between shows with guaranteed audiences is another popular prime time strategy.

Of course, audiences are not so easily influenced as this might suggest. From your own television viewing experience, you will recognize that you adopt a number of tactics to undermine the schedulers' intentions. Video recorders allow audiences to **timeshift**, moving programmes from their carefully positioned slots to times that are more convenient for their own, independent viewing habits.

Asynchronous: a term adapted from computer jargon, which indicates that behaviour is no longer restricted by traditional notions of time and order.

On a more basic level, you probably watch television with a remote control in your hand, channel 'zapping' or 'hopping' at your convenience, destroying the notion of channel loyalty by constant movement between programmes, perhaps even watching two or three simultaneously.

The proliferation of channels will eventually remove the idea that audiences can be loyal to two or three broadcasters. Audiences will be able to decide for themselves what kind of programmes they wish to watch and at what times they wish to watch them, in effect becoming their own schedulers. It is a common feature of many new technologies that they empower audiences in this way, allowing them to adopt an **asynchronous** approach to their media consumption.

Activity 3.19

- Draw up a 'fantasy schedule' for an evening's viewing, including all of your favourite types of programme.
- Now have a look at a detailed listing guide for digital channels. How close can you get to your ideal evening's viewing by channel hopping?

We will still need some sort of guidance however. With a choice of over 700 channels, we might find that proliferation is daunting or just plain confusing. Perhaps we are missing out on the programmes that we want to watch because we have too much material through which to sift.

In this scenario, the importance of the **electronic programme guide (EPG)** becomes obvious. This onscreen guide displays information about the content and timings of programmes that are showing now or later on every available channel, as well as the one which you are watching. It can be called up in picture or as a separate service. The more dependent we are on the EPG to guide our choices, the more powerful this tool becomes for the institution which controls it.

For example, the groupings of different types of channel together on the EPG may well determine our perception (and, therefore, use) of those channels. On SkyDigital's DST, it is clearly in the institution's interest to group its flagship channel, Sky One, alongside the established, previously terrestrial, channels, BBC1, BBC2, Channel 4 and Channel 5. Similarly, by placing the Sky News channel at the head of a group which includes CNN, BBC News 24 and ITN, the EPG is implicitly privileging the Sky channel.

Picture 3.12   The electronic programme guide is used to navigate around a multi-channel environment.

The EPG is also helping to establish a number of predetermined categories into which existing and new channels will have to fit, potentially undermining the notions of choice upon which much of the digital environment prides itself.

In this scenario, it is possible to identify 'ghettos' in the EPG where audiences are never encouraged to stray. How many SkyDigital viewers, for example, sample the delights of Asian popular music and film on the B4 channels? Or where do you position a channel such as Rapture TV which offers its youth audience a mixture of extreme sports coverage, along with dance music and programmes on the UK club scene? Is this sports or music? (These complications were undoubtedly a contributing factor when the channel ceased broadcasting in 2002.)

These kinds of decisions reveal the importance of the EPG as an institutional tool, which is attempting to govern the audiences' use of digital television in ways which are much more subtle than the scheduling strategies of the past. We have much more choice to determine our individual viewing, but perhaps that choice is not as infinite as first seems.

Interactivity

Digital technology promises to bring the same kind of interactivity to television which has been brought to other media, such as music or games. In doing so, it may fundamentally alter the ways in which we consume and understand the medium. On one level, there is already evidence of this in the sports broadcasts offered by SkyDigital's interactive coverage.

In these broadcasts, most often of major sporting events such as football or rugby union matches, viewers are given a number of options to transform their viewing experience. Different camera positions may be chosen, highlights and replays accessed, statistics and trivia revealed or alternative commentaries from fans to replace the views of the professional commentators. The audience's choices allow them to customise the viewing experience, reflecting individual interests and priorities.

However, we may feel some disappointment that our interactivity is limited by the needs and demands of the broadcaster. The cameras cannot respond to our individual requests and we remain focussed on events chosen by the director in his gallery. The audience might want to see whether Martin Keown has managed to recover from the foul just committed, but the director will be more interested in the action at the other end of the pitch. Highlights and replays will be limited to those chosen by the broadcasting team, again not necessarily what the audience wants to see. Nevertheless, this technology represents an interesting development in the television viewing experience and has already begun to appear in broadcasts other than sports, such as music concerts.

We could say that the proliferation of channels provides a kind of interactivity that audiences will not have experienced in a limited channel envi-

ctivity 3.20

- Look at a list of the channels available on SkyDigital.
- What categories can they be divided into?
- What conclusions can be drawn from their positions on the EPG?

ctivity 3.21

- Draw up a list of other sorts of programme that would be suitable for interactive presentation
- What makes a particular style of programme appropriate?
- What kinds of programme would not work as interactive experiences?

ronment, since we are much more active in making our choices and more independent in deciding what kind of material we want to watch and when we want to watch it. Many of the digital television providers also have the facilities to allow audiences to choose specific types of programming to watch irrespective of timing or scheduling.

At the moment, this process tends to be focused on films through services such as Sky Box Office or U Movies Direct. These are NVOD channels (near video on demand) through which individual films run every 15 or 30 minutes during the day, allowing subscribers to choose when they want to watch a particular movie – for an extra cost.

In the future, it is likely that NVOD will be replaced by VOD, in which we can order our films to begin at any time, not just every quarter of an hour. After this development, it is easy to see how the service could be spread to cover every sort of programming: sports, soap operas, documentaries and so on. The potential of this kind of interactivity is that it allows audiences truly to be in control of their own schedules, tailoring the massive selection of programmes on offer to individual tastes in ways that have never been possible before.

By fragmenting the audience this way, however, there is a risk that we will lose some of the benefits which television can bring as a collective experience. The image of the family gathered together around the television set in the evenings is now a nostalgic memory, thanks to the cheapness and convenience of portable television which mean that many viewers probably watch television in their bedrooms or other personal spaces.

Nevertheless, television does play an important role in creating a sense of community, based on our shared experience of the medium. How many of the conversations you have with your friends during the day revolve around what you watched last night, whether that was your favourite soap opera, a music performance or a football match? If we are all watching our own schedule, then the social groupings which depend on the collective experience of popular culture might begin to drift apart, hastening a fragmentation and a move towards individualism which has been identified elsewhere in the digital future.

Convergence

Like many other media, television has been the focus of the integration of previously separate technologies and activities into a single digital experience. All of the major digital television providers offer services alongside their programming which were initially in the realm of separate media, such as the internet. E-mail, shopping, games and competitions have become part of the television experience through services such as SkyDigital. Nowadays, the common feature of most of our entertainment and information is a screen of some kind, so perhaps Media Studies will change its name before too long as there will be only one medium, the screen, and become renamed **Screen Studies**?

For audiences, this kind of convergence offers convenience and speed in their already rushed and pressured lives. No need to leave the house to purchase the latest CD from your favourite artist, since you can do this from your living room. Ordering pizza to accompany a showing of your favourite movie is also achieved at the touch of a few buttons and, if you want to discuss the result of Monday night's football with a friend, it is easy to use the television's built-in email service to do so.

Potentially, this kind of convergence can be used to enrich and expand the televisual experience. Already, television advertisements can be linked to an interactive service so that if we are interested in a particular product we simply press a button to order it. In future, the programmes themselves could be linked this way, allowing us to buy music from the artist currently performing on *Top of The Pops* or tickets to a concert following a profile of a particular artist.

However, as was pointed out in the introduction to this section, the availability of a particular technology does not guarantee its acceptance by an audience. In April 2001, SkyDigital had somewhere in the region of 5 million subscribers. Despite this user base, only 600,000 transactions had been carried out on its interactive Open service and in October 2001, Open was replaced by SkyActive, as a means of encouraging greater use of the features available. Why is it that audiences have not embraced this particular form of convergence?

In a speech to the Royal Television Society in 1998, Elisabeth Murdoch, then of Sky Television, expressed her doubts that audiences would accept the convergence of lean forward and lean back technologies.

> *For years now, the word convergence has gone side-by-side with digital, a convenient way of explaining how TVs and PCs will get married and live happily ever after. Well I'm sorry to be the bearer of bad tidings, but there's been a divorce ... It's increasingly clear that people's use of the TV and the PC are hugely different experiences ... I really find it hard to believe that people will switch from their web page to EastEnders without leaving their desk. Even now, each industry will learn and borrow from one another. TV will continue to be the dominant medium for lean-back leisure rather than lean-forward interaction. Yet both pieces of technology will happily sit together in the home of the future, fulfilling different needs for their owners, which makes the PC and the Internet a very serious competitor. We're all competing with other media now more than ever.*
> (Source: BBC News)

Murdoch believed that audiences who have made a conscious decision to undertake the relaxation of television watching, would not be prepared to interact to any great degree with the material they are consuming. This may be true even though the same audience in another context (for example, using the internet) are more than willing to explore the potential of this kind of interactivity.

Examiners' tips

There are no right or wrong answers when debating a topic such as this. You will get marks for:

- using the correct terms for technology and the key terms associated with studying it
- reference to specific examples from media industries and new technologies
- reference to facts and statistics as evidence to back up what you are saying
- the ability to manage a debate by looking at it from all angles or as directed by the exam questions.

From these examples, we can begin to appreciate the complexity of the issues surrounding audiences and their consumption of different forms of technology. Simple predictions about the impact and effects of new technologies are always likely to be inaccurate because they ignore the range of ways in which audiences use the media and the different kinds of pleasure that they receive from them.

The situation is further complicated by the institutional contexts which surround these technologies. New technology is rarely introduced simply to make life better and more convenient. Profit, control and brand image are important factors tied up with the introduction and promotion of digital media; let us now turn our attention to the companies who provide digital television in its various formats in order to examine their role in the process.

DIGITAL TELEVISION AND ITS INSTITUTIONS

Although it would be pleasing to believe that new technologies are always introduced in order to make the lives of their audiences better, or more convenient, or more varied, this is very rarely the case.

New media can offer all of these things, but it is equally important to recognize what they can also offer to the companies and institutions responsible for introducing the technologies. In simple terms, this means profit. However, profit has to be secured through several different means and digital technologies generally offer the institutions more control over the ways in which the product itself is used. This provides more control over the **brand image** of the product and more knowledge of the audiences consuming the product.

In the arena of digital television, we can see more clearly how the technology has aided the institution. Let us focus upon SkyDigital's **DST** service as our example. BSkyB's analogue service offered the consumer a multi-channel platform: the same as the digital equivalent. However, the nature of the analogue satellite signal meant that consumers were able to receive channels beyond those licensed to the Sky service.

For example, foreign language channels from Europe, particularly Western Europe, were a regular, if not often watched feature, of the Sky customer's schedule. Viewing cards could be purchased which enabled access to encrypted channels (normally 'adult' viewing). Satellite enthusiasts commonly swapped information across bulletin boards and websites about channels that could be received at certain frequencies or by moving the dish to point at a certain set of coordinates.

While this kind of activity did little harm to Sky's revenue, it does present a problem in terms of their public image. No broadcasting company wishes their name to be raised consistently in connection with illegal viewing of suspect material. In the long run, that kind of publicity can affect the potential profitability of an institution.

The switch to a digital television service allowed Sky to regain control of the channels available through their technology. In fact, the Sky viewer

Watermark: an encryption technique which ensures that broadcast material can be viewed live by subscribers, but cannot be recorded or copied for later viewing. The name derives from the *watermarking* of paper currency as a measure to prevent counterfeiting.

Activity 3.22

- Look at some of the channels on offer to digital customers and discuss who you think the target audiences might be.
- What kind of products do you think would be advertised on these channels?
- If you can video your chosen channels, compare your predictions with the actual advertising content.

Key terms

T-Commerce: the activities of buying and selling through your television set.

now has many more channels available to them, but, significantly, these are all licensed or approved by the television provider. No 'extra' channels can be received, irrespective of how the **digibox** is used or the satellite dish moved.

More control is also offered over how the viewers use the channels provided. The ability to **watermark** a digital signal can prevent unencrypted material from being copied and transmitted elsewhere. Currently, only the Sky Box Office channels are affected, meaning that a viewer can watch the broadcast but not tape it for later use. Potentially, however, every channel could be treated this way. Whether the audience would accept a television service which was uncopiable, and could not be archived or time-shifted is another matter.

We saw in the previous section how the proliferation of channels offered the viewer more choice and more freedom to create their own schedule. In this context, it is obvious that the institution will benefit from the increased subscriptions paid by an ever-expanding customer base. However, proliferation does throw up a challenge for television institutions.

With more channels, the potential audience is spread thinly across the available material and the mass audience once guaranteed for the terrestrial stations can be replaced by small, niche audiences. Yet many television companies depend on the revenue raised through advertising for their survival. If the audience is small, why would an advertiser pay money to have access to it?

The answer is that, although the audience is small, the institution knows much more about it. Narrowcasting creates niche audiences, small groups of viewers who share interests, values or lifestyles.

This kind of audience is valuable to advertisers since they can tailor their products and advertising, very precisely targeting only those groups who are likely to buy and consume their product. Sports channels, for example, tend to attract young, male audiences, with a relatively large amount of disposable income and free leisure time. This kind of audience buys and consumes in predictable ways, and are often targeted by companies selling fashion, especially sports-based fashion such as trainers, alcohol, electronics and other gadgets.

In addition, the technology also provides the potential to build an even more detailed picture of the audience which can then be sold to advertisers. The digibox and viewing card have the ability to store records of the families viewing habits, including when the television is watched, what channels are viewed, how often they are switched over and so on. Using this kind of information, a very accurate account of a family's lifestyle can be constructed, particularly when this is combined with the personal information which is gathered in the initial contract and through subsequent individualised market research.

Potentially this information can be personalized further, by offering individual start up screens for different members of the family, so that the profiles can be made even more specific. If and when **t-commerce** becomes a part of our daily lives, then records of products and our purchase patterns can also be added to this profile.

New media technologies are opening up new and exciting opportunities for consumers and their relationship with the media. However, these technologies are not being introduced simply to improve our lives. Technology allows institutions a great deal of control over their products and this, in turn, can lead to increased profits and domination of the marketplace.

Case study 4: studying media ownership and institutions

INTRODUCTION

ctivity 3.23

- List the last media product you saw, read or listened to in the following categories:
  – television programme
  – advertisement
  – pop song
  – magazine
  – website.
- Where did each of these products come from? Who owns them? How are they making money from them?

Think about all of the media images and sounds which you have probably seen and heard in the past 24 hours. How many of these do you know the origin of? Who owns the pictures and sounds that you have been consuming? And why is it important anyway?

Most of the time, we are being asked to think about the meanings of media products as texts, rather than about where they come from. However, in order to understand these meanings fully, it is equally important to understand who has produced the products, for whom they have been produced and why they have been produced. This section will concentrate on the area of media ownership and examine the importance of institutions in determining how, and why, we consume the media.

Institutions are the companies and organizations which are responsible for the funding, production, distribution and promotion of media products. Every media product, irrespective of its medium or format emerges from one kind of institution or another, although its origins might not always be clear cut or apparent. Sometimes this is because institutions choose to keep their role in the production of an artefact relatively inconspicuous; sometimes it is because we, as audiences, prefer to think of our favourite products as individual, rather than institutional, efforts.

Our frequent lack of awareness about institutions comes as a result of a strong tradition of art and culture in our society. Two of the most important beliefs about art which we hold are that it is the result of an individual skill or talent and that it comes about from the artist's irresistible urge to express him or herself. Media products, on the other hand, are almost always the result of collaborative efforts and are almost always produced to make money. Nevertheless, these features of the product are sometimes played down in order to guarantee some kind of quality or value for that product.

Of course, this is true in different media to different extents. The institutional context of an advert is fairly obvious to an audience (at least it should be if it is doing its job correctly). However, the context may be less clear for us when we are watching a film or listening to music.

Nor is this simply a matter of being well-informed. The institution from which a product is produced can have an active effect on its meaning or an audience's expectations of it. Take the example of *Pulp Fiction* (1994,

| Picture 3.13 | *Pulp Fiction*: a Disney movie? |

Activity 3.24

- Choose one of the major Hollywood film studios and research into the subsidiary companies which it owns.
- What kinds of films are produced by the studio through the different companies?
- Are there any surprising relationships?

Key terms

Conglomerate: a large corporation or company whose continued growth is achieved by buying or merging with other companies, who can support one another's business interests.

US, dir. Quentin Tarantino). This film was funded by a small production company called Miramax, a company well-known for becoming involved in low budget, hip, violent, thrillers.

However, the film was distributed and marketed by a different company, Touchstone. Touchstone is a subsidiary of Disney Enterprises, so it is not too far off the mark to call *Pulp Fiction* a Disney film. Do you think the film would have achieved the cult status it has today if it had been sold to audiences as a Disney movie? Equally, what would have been the effect on the animated features sold to a family audience by the same people who brought us *Pulp Fiction*?

The same kind of issues can be seen in the music industry, where major labels often buy or form subsidiary companies in order to cater for particular genres of music or niche audiences. Often this process can be used to give an artist or band some kind of credibility for an audience which is likely to reject the products of one of the majors as being too mainstream or too commercialised

A knowledge of media ownership can be used as another tool of analysis for the Media student, since it enables us to make connections between many different kinds of products and media in order to discover how and why we consume the media in the way we do.

In this section, we will look at some of the ways in which the relationships between institutions and audiences have been explained by media theorists. Then we will look in detail at a large media **conglomerate**, AOL Time Warner, to see how knowledge of this institution can help to increase our understanding of its media products.

INSTITUTIONAL MODELS

Let us look at some of the different 'models' that have been suggested as a way of trying to illustrate the relationship between institutions and audience. A model is a theoretical set of ideas which attempts to explain or make clear events that we perceive in the real world. We can apply each of these sets of ideas to an example of a media product, *The Sun* newspaper, in order to see them in action

One of the most common models used is the **manipulative model**. Essentially, this set of ideas sees audiences as somewhat passive, and whose ways of thinking are easily changed by the media products which they consume. Media products are constructed by powerful groups within our society, generally defined by gender (male), class (middle class) and age (middle aged). These groups use the products to ensure that their own ideas and values remain widely believed or accepted. Importantly, this is seen as a conscious process, in which institutions are deliberately manipulating their audiences.

Tabloid newspapers such as *The Sun*, owned by Rupert Murdoch's News International Corporation, are frequently criticized for their obvious bias in coverage of political events and for the stereotypical ways in which certain groups are presented in the paper, especially women and certain national or ethnic groups.

The manipulative model suggests that when this kind of material is presented as 'news', the audience are led to believe that the representations are truthful or accurate and accept them as 'real'. The success of the tabloids is achieved by the skill with which they are able to pass their viewpoints as facts. In this way, those groups who have tended to control the media are able to ensure that their interests and viewpoints are the

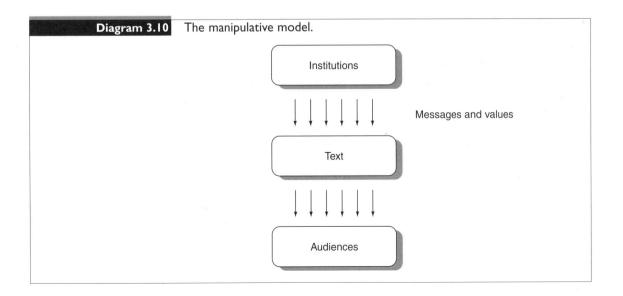

Diagram 3.10 The manipulative model.

most widely circulated and, therefore, most likely to be accepted. In this way, the dominant groups can maintain their privileged positions and social stability can be achieved (see page 77 for definitions of dominant groups).

Opponents of this way of thinking have argued that it does not take into account the choices which audiences have in their media consumption. The manipulative model seems to rest upon the idea that almost all media products are concerned with articulating a very similar set of ideas, whereas experience tells us that there are in fact many different views on offer in many different products. If *The Sun* is a successful newspaper (of course, it is currently the most successful in the UK with a circulation of approximately 3.6 million copies), it might be because it has adapted itself to reflect the views of a substantial proportion of the population.

This way of thinking about the media is sometimes called the **pluralist model** or the **market model**. Pluralists believe that different groups and interests within society are constantly competing for audiences and that the most successful of these interests are those that manage to appeal to the biggest audiences. This model suggests that audiences are very active in the ways in which they choose and consume their media.

Pluralists will point to *The Sun*'s change of political allegiance during the 1997 election campaign as an example of the model in action. Although the paper had been a fervent supporter of the Conservative Party for over 20 years, it came out in support of Tony Blair's New Labour during the campaign and continued to do so during the 2001 election. In both campaigns, initial polls demonstrated a massive amount of popular support for the Labour Party.

Pluralists point out that this support was not generated by the paper (since the paper had been promoting Conservative values), but that the

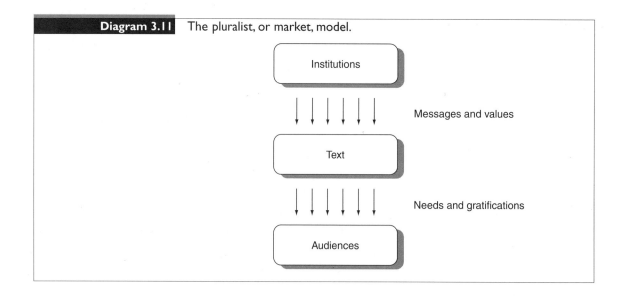

Diagram 3.11   The pluralist, or market, model.

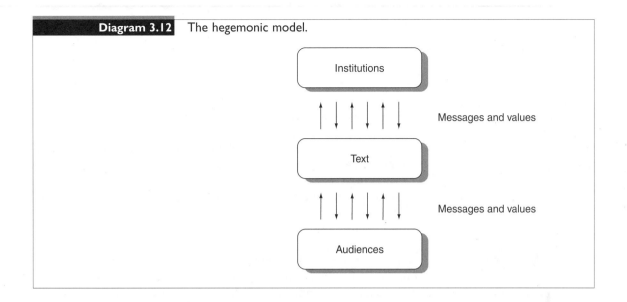

Diagram 3.12 The hegemonic model.

The Sun had to change in response to its readers' changing allegiances, or risk losing a large proportion of its audience.

A third model, the **hegemonic model**, offers a way of thinking about institutions and audiences which rests somewhere between the two views suggested above. The hegemonic model acknowledges that much of the media is controlled by a relatively small group of people (who are generally male, middle class and white) and that the viewpoints associated with these groups inevitably become embedded in the products themselves, though the promotion of these views is rarely conscious. Instead, dominant views are seen as 'normal' or 'common-sense' and are given greater emphasis in order to build up a consensus or agreement among the audience.

However, some parts of the audience will try to **resist** this process, making choices about their purchase and consumption of products challenge the idea of consensus. Resistance can take the form of fairly ordinary, individual, responses – writing a letter of protest or complaint, deciding not to buy a product. Occasionally, as in the example below, resistance is expressed in a more obvious, collective form.

THE SUN AND THE HILLSBOROUGH DISASTER

On 15 April 1989, Sheffield Wednesday's stadium, Hillsborough, played host to an FA Cup semi-final between Liverpool and Nottingham Forest. Overcrowding at the ground led to a massive crowd surge crushing hundreds of spectators against the fences which had been erected to stop crowds invading the pitch. Ninety-six fans died as a result of the crush, the majority of whom were Liverpool supporters.

ctivity 3.25

Using examples from other media, see if you can illustrate these three models, explaining the relationship between the institution, the products and the audience.

ey terms

Mainstream: a term used to describe those areas of the media which tend to be highly commercialized. Mainstream media products reach large audiences and tend to make big profits for their institutions.
Alternative: in a media context, this is used to classify a text whose form or content differs from the mainstream equivalent.

The following Monday, *The Sun* ran a front page story under the headline of *The Truth*. In the story, they accused Liverpool fans of picking the pockets of victims, urinating on dead bodies and fighting with policemen who were trying to give first aid to the casualties. These allegations were unfounded and deeply upsetting to a community still in shock from the previous days.

As a result, there was an immediate boycott of the paper on Merseyside, causing the paper's circulation to drop by over 200,000. Despite later retractions and apologies for the article, the paper is still treated with disgust by many in Liverpool, including a large number of shopkeepers who refuse to stock it.

Successful products from successful institutions tend to be able to acknowledge resistance and to **incorporate** alternative ideas so that those consumers who initially resisted the values of the product can be drawn back into its audience.

If we turn our attention away from the tabloid press, we can see the hegemonic model at work in other media. The popular music industry seems to be based on a consistent cycle in which **mainstream** music (with all of its associated commercial values) is resisted by groups of performers and audiences who introduce **alternative** or more challenging genres.

In the 1970s and 1980s, the punk movement provided a working-class reaction against the packaged, commercial rock music which was dominating the charts. With songs that rejected any notion of melody and harmony, anger, frustration and energy were more important than musical skill or song writing techniques. More recently, the garage scene has grown out of a similar disillusionment with the commercial compromises of jungle and hip-hop. It promotes deep sub-bass lines and super-fast beats per minute ragga-influenced dance music as part of an underground culture linked to pirate radio and illegal estate clubs or parties.

However, even these genres inevitably became (or are likely to become) incorporated into the mainstream and commercialised, drawing their initial audiences with them or leaving the audiences to seek out other new and challenging genres, which will subsequently become incorporated once again.

THE MUSIC INDUSTRY AND NAPSTER

The introduction of new technology often has the effect of renegotiating relationships between institutions and audiences. In the last few years, the music industry has found itself in a conflict with Napster, a company set up to share music across the internet. The events of this contest provide a good illustration of the hegemonic model in action

Napster was founded in 1996 by Shawn Fanning, an 18-year-old college dropout from Iowa, USA. He had created an application which allowed individual PCs to share files with one another by using a central server as a portal or gateway. This method of joining PCs together is known as

ctivity 3.26

- What do you think are the likely developments in the future of the music industry?
- Look at some examples from other media and try to work out whether there are any predictable patterns
- What other media are most likely to provide parallels?

peer-to-peer networking. Fanning and his friends were big music fans and his software was set up to allow them to swap music files, stored in a format known as MP3, among one another. As a result, in 1999, US CD sales dropped by 39%. Individual artists, with the backing of their record companies, began to take legal action against Napster for infringing their copyright and non-payment of royalties.

In 2000 and 2001, the music companies began to fight back, suing Napster and winning the right to force Napster to filter out the songs which breached copyright agreements. Napster users began to undermine this effort by deliberately misspelling the names of artists and songs, but more importantly, in the meantime many other file-sharing sites and software was springing up for use by the audience. Some of this software, such as Gnutella and FreeNet, dispensed with the need for a central server and offered PC users the ability to create a true peer-to-peer network by **daisy-chaining** together a string of machines. The lack of a centralized system or company makes it almost impossible to track or control the usage, so once again music files become freely available.

The music companies were soon to realize that, on its own, legal action was either ineffective, or at worst, actually increased the problems with which the internet was providing them. In the summer of 2001, a different approach was adopted. This saw the music companies recognizing the benefits which MP3 files and peer-to-peer networking offered to audiences and setting up their own services. Universal Music and Sony set up a service called Duet, while the other three majors, BMG, Warner and EMI went into a joint venture called MusicNet.

With the establishment of these two services, we can see how these institutions have **incorporated** the technology which was being used to resist their dominance and attempted to re-establish their control of the music market in the process.

Whether the audience will accept this approach remains to be seen. Many commentators have suggested that the audience has become too accustomed to having music freely available and too sophisticated to accept technology which they can no longer control. If this is the case, it is likely that audiences will continue to offer further, different forms of resistance to the music corporations and that further negotiation will be necessary.

Examiners' tips

- The examples in this chapter can be used as models for studying other texts, topic areas and media products.
- Use the key terms and theoretical models referred to in this chapter and apply them to other objects of study.
- The annual *Guardian Media Guide* and www.mediaguardian.co.uk are both excellent sources of up to date information about media institutions and new technologies.

AOL Time Warner

Let us now have a look at a specific example of a media institution and examine how its ownership has effects on the company, the audiences and the products themselves. When AOL and Time Warner merged to form a giant media corporation in 2000, it sent a shockwave through its competitors. The importance of the merger and the lessons that it can teach us about the future of media ownership are enormous. We will begin by looking at a brief history of the two parent companies.

AMERICA ONLINE

Internet service providers: companies which provide access to the internet. Normally these companies provide the user with a software package and a password. You can then browse the World Wide Web and send and receive e-mail.

In 1991 America Online was formed and began to combine its previous experience in online technology with a clear business plan and some aggressive marketing and immediately became one of America's major **Internet Service Providers (ISPs)**. The initial success of AOL surprised many analysts. The company offered flat-rate internet access and was swamped by customers to the extent that the service almost crashed completely.

In the early 1990s, AOL was the target of several big information technology companies, including Microsoft. The chief executive, Steve Case, refused to become a subsidiary of a bigger company and continued to build AOL throughout the USA and then into Europe and the UK. By 1994, the strength of the company was such that Case could begin his own round of shopping, acquiring and merging with companies that would strengthen and support the business. Rival ISP, CompuServe was bought out in 1995 and later the browser company Netscape also became an AOL **subsidiary**. Software development companies became targets as AOL looked to create an **instant messaging** service which would allow online users to 'talk' to one another while surfing.

Various strategic alliances with big corporations from Dell Computers, through Nokia and Ericsson to automobile company General Motors have placed AOL in an unchallenged position within the industry. They currently provide internet services for around 35 million subscribers, 10 million of whom are in Europe and the UK.

Subsidiary: a company wholly owned by a larger and more powerful parent company.
Instant messaging: a communications service allowing you to 'talk' privately with another individual online. Usually, the system will alert the user when somebody from their private list is also online. There are several different systems available and no agreed standard between systems.

Key terms

Browser: a web browser
is a piece of software
used to locate and display
web pages. The two most
popular browsers are
Microsoft's *Internet
Explorer* and Netscape's
Netscape Navigator.
Walled garden: this
refers to a browsing
environment that
controls the information
and websites that the
user is able to navigate.
Typically this approach is
used to direct users to
favoured content or to
protect users from
unsuitable material.

Key terms

Mogul: a term used to
describe various powerful
individuals who run or
finance media companies.

AOL provides a different kind of service to those of other ISPs. AOL users have their own **browser** (not the familiar Internet Explorer or Netscape interface) and a large collection of exclusive and favoured sites to which customers are directed and encouraged to use. This kind of **walled garden** approach demands a constant stream of content to keep the customer satisfied and coming back for more. AOL's merger with Time Warner in 2000 was seen by many as the ideal combination of technology (AOL) with content (Time Warner).

TIME WARNER

The history of Time Warner stretches much further back into this century than that of AOL. Warner Brothers was one of the five major film studios which dominated Hollywood during its golden age of the 1930s and 1940s. As the system began to collapse, Warners expanded into the realms of music and television to create a corporation known as Warner Communications. Warner Communications was a pioneer in US broadcasting, controlling a considerable fibre-optic cable network throughout the USA and launching a number of new networks, including the highly successful HBO channel (Home Box Office, best known in this country for producing shows such as *Sex and the City* and *The Sopranos*).

In 1989, Warner Communications merged with Time Incorporated, a giant publishing media and publishing company, known in the USA for producing *Time* and *People* magazines. In 1996, Time Warner underwent a second merger with Turner Broadcasting, the media company run by **mogul** Ted Turner, which owned several successful television networks such as CNN (24-hour international news service) and TCM (classic film channel).

Warner has often been at the forefront of technological change in the entertainment industries, though with varying degrees of success. Its synchronized sound system, introduced in 1927's *The Jazz Singer*, led Hollywood films into the sound era. In 1975, it was a pioneer of satellite broadcasting in the USA, establishing several new satellite channels which successfully competed with the traditional networks. However, these were relatively short-lived ventures and closed down, despite huge investment.

Given the rapid take-up of the internet, it was an obvious area into which Time Warner would head. But, despite a massive amount of investment into the technology and its promotion, Time Warner were unable to build up sufficient usage for its internet service to make a profit.

Despite the fame, quality and sheer amount of its products, Time Warner seemed to lack the expertise and understanding of the new media world which would be required to exploit the opportunities presented. By merging with AOL, Time Warner might finally achieve the kind of symbiosis (mutual dependency) which would enable its products to be sold and consumed by the next generation of media audiences.

Let us now look in detail at the opportunities which the merger of these two companies will bring to the institution and the ways in which the audience of their products might be affected.

AOL TIME WARNER AND THE INSTITUTION

In basic terms, each company has something that the other wants. AOL has the experience, technology and strategies to make a success of any online venture. Even more importantly, they have a massive share of the online market with around 31 million subscribers using the AOL service.

Time Warner has two important assets. First, content. The availability of material ranging from news (CNN) to music (Warner Music), film (Warner Bros) to print (*Time* magazine) will enable the company to offer very attractive packages of products to customers, in a market where many ISPs are struggling to find enough content to sustain their service or to give it a unique identity.

Second, Time Warner has an extensive cable network throughout the US which will allow AOL to develop broadband services with the knowledge that there is a ready-made market for these. Time Warner's initial ventures into this market have not been successful. In the 1980s, the company attempted to set up a video-on-demand service through the cable network

| Picture 3.14 | *Cats and Dogs* – an AOL Time Warner product. |

Activity 3.27

- What are the differences between marketing/advertising using 'old' media (print or television) and 'new' media (websites)?
- In what situation would one form be preferable to the other?
- What differences are there in the audiences that they can target?

Key terms

Data transfer: the movement of information (text, sound or video) electronically from one source to another. Conventional modems, connected to analogue telephone lines, allow this transfer to happen at a relative low rate of 56,000 (56k) bits per second (bps). New broadband technologies will increase the transfer rate tremendously.

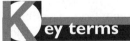

Key terms

Transnational: a corporation whose various elements are no longer based in a single country but spread around the world in order to create a global operation.

in Florida, with very little success. Their 1999 venture, the Pathfinder web portal was equally misconceived and struggled to attract revenue, despite the company investing $500 million in the enterprise. With AOL's expertise and customer base, a successful strategy should be possible.

Both sides of the partnership have important **gateways**. The AOL browser represents a trusted and familiar online entry point; the Time Warner cable network reaches into millions of home in the USA.

Traditional media companies have struggled to understand the dynamics of the web. Conventional marketing and conventional patterns of consumption have little bearing in the online world. Many companies have wrongly assumed that they can simply throw up a site, then sit back and wait for people to visit.

Time Warner's broadband potential is the key to success. The range of potential content to be offered means very little if customers are struggling to download material at the 56 **kbps** that their modem offers. **Data transfer** at this speed makes downloads of video, and even audio material, frustratingly slow and unreliable. By linking up with the Time Warner cable network, which is the second biggest in the USA and a potential reach of 20% of all America's household, the new company has the ability to push its content quickly and conveniently to a huge market of subscribers.

However, the merger will not only have an impact on the US market. Time Warner is a **transnational** corporation, whose brand name and products are recognized and trusted in territories all over the world. AOL is a relatively new company, keen to widen its subscriber base by establishing itself in other countries and areas. This process becomes easier through its alliance with Warner and because the technology of the internet is in itself transnational, and no longer controlled by individual states.

The process whereby national borders are broken down and differences between societies and their cultures are erased is known as **globalization**. Globalization is the aim of many big corporations, since it provides the biggest possible opportunity for selling their products. Opponents of globalization point out that the process often involves individual cultures being swamped by the products and the values of other more powerful cultures (normally American or Western values).

AOL TIME WARNER AND THE AUDIENCE

During the press conference arranged to announce the merger of AOL and Time Warner in January 2000, many of the executives of the new company were keen to promote the deal's 'positive impact on society'. Ted Turner, the former chief executive of CNN, declared that it would create the 'most exciting and most socially conscious company the world has ever seen'. While there have been a number of initiatives to offer help to deprived social groups, these still seem to be extreme claims. They do however indicate how important it is for AOL Time Warner to be seen as working for the benefit of the consumer.

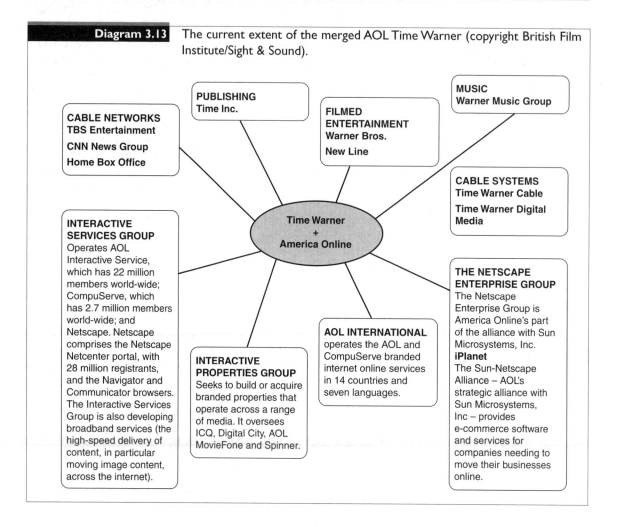

Diagram 3.13 The current extent of the merged AOL Time Warner (copyright British Film Institute/Sight & Sound).

AOL subscribers (around 30 million people) are likely to feel the impact in the short term. They will have noticed a lot more material being presented to them from the Time Warner stable, material to which they might never have had access before such as music or film and television clips. In the long term, these subscribers should benefit from broadband access to the internet, provided by Time Warner's cable network, which will increase speeds and lower connection costs.

AOL Time Warner claim that the marriage of their skills, technologies and content will speed up the development of the services provided on the internet, as well as the process of convergence. AOL's links with telecommunications companies such as Nokia and Eriksson suggest that it will not only be the PC which is their focus, but television, mobile phones and PDAs will all be targeted as interactive devices.

Steve Case, the chairman of the combined group, set out his agenda for the company. 'Our brands, services and technologies already touch hundreds of millions of people. We will embed the AOL Time Warner experience more deeply into their everyday lives.' Other observers, however, are more sceptical about the potential effect of the merger. AOL Time Warner might offer a huge amount of services and content to their customers, but these will all be from two companies. As more and more competitors are shut out, customers might be deprived of wider choices and this could ultimately drive up prices.

When the two companies initially announced the merger, the US Federal Communications Commission placed a number of conditions on the deal to address these concerns:

☐ Customers using the AOL Time Warner cable network should have a free choice of ISP and not be forced to use AOL.
☐ AOL's instant messaging service should be made available for competing ISPs to use.
☐ The US phone company AT&T were forced to sell their 25% stake in Time Warner's cable systems in order to ensure that competition for broadband services remained healthy.

Vertical integration: the extension of a firm's activities into earlier (backward integration) or later (forward integration) stages of production of its goods or services.

These conditions should provide AOL customers and other internet users with some reassurance of choice and competition in the short term. However, the effect of this deal on the audience is likely to be a long-term one. If other media conglomerates are to compete with the size, power and potential of AOL Time Warner, a great deal of consolidation will need to take place, as internet and media companies merge or acquire each other.

In a few years, the media landscape will probably be dominated by a small number of huge, **vertically integrated**, **transnational** companies. Whether or not, these companies will be able to provide a sufficiently wide range of content to ensure that their customers are satisfied remains to be seen.

CHAPTER 4

Being creative: production skills

Approaches to practical production and evaluation

The chapter is organized as follows:

- [ ] Part 1: how to write an evaluation.
- [ ] Part 2: general advice and production principles.
- [ ] Part 3: video production.
- [ ] Part 4: print production.
- [ ] Part 5: audio production.
- [ ] Part 6: ICT-based production.

The emphasis in this chapter is on:

- [ ] careful planning and record-keeping in the **pre-production** stage
- [ ] demonstrating technical skills in the **production** and **post-production** stages
- [ ] **reflecting** on and **evaluating** your work.

Sometimes students put in months of work on their production only to find that when they show it to their target audiences their intentions are not understood. This can be disappointing and frustrating. Bearing in mind that this can happen to professionals, following the advice in this chapter will help you to avoid some basic mistakes.

Remember that Chapter 2 is an essential aid to your practical work as it contains all of the key production terms you will need to know and use when producing, and writing about, your own media production, so be sure to refer back to it.

Examiners' tips

- Choose your brief or subject matter wisely.
- Aim high – but not too high.
- Research and plan very carefully.
- Show that you know the conventions of your chosen genre or format.
- Be flexible and make the best of difficulties or necessary changes.
- Persevere when dealing with problems: they can always be solved if you are determined.
- Be prepared for your work to take you much longer than you ever expected.

COMPUTER SOFTWARE: AN IMPORTANT NOTE

It is important to state here that we cannot hope to give you precise instructions for using the various software programs that you might encounter, especially given they will be updated more frequently than this book, and

Picture 4.1   Students Matthew Rains and Ryan Carmon working on an animated short *film noir Deceit.*

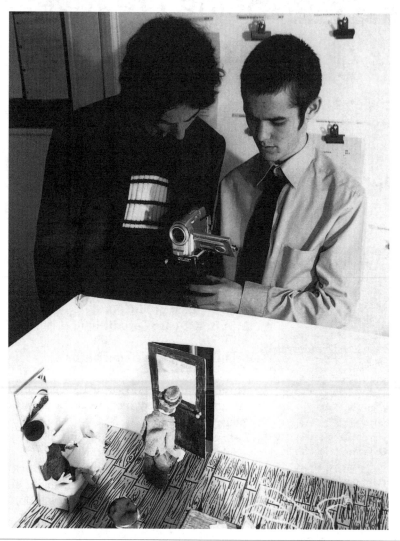

we do not have sufficient space. Also, schools/colleges may use different formats, most using PCs, but an increasing number using the media professionals choice, Macs.

For detailed instructions on using digital video-editing software, image manipulation software or web design packages, refer to the manuals or online support available. There are also office and classroom (or 'idiots' or 'dummies') guides available from bookshops (online bookshops are a good place to start looking), so try to encourage your tutor to purchase some for the Media Studies department or library.

Part 1: how to write an evaluation

To gain the most marks for practical coursework you will have to show that you have a better understanding of the media through experiencing the processes of production for yourself – hands on.

This is why you need to write an **evaluation, production log or commentary,** which **reflects on**, **analyses** and **evaluates** your own work. It is vital therefore that you see this as an important part of your work from the beginning, rather than as an unconnected activity you do in a hurry at the end. This is why we have begun this chapter with advice on the written work that will support your practical production.

KEEPING RECORDS

The first step to writing a good evaluation is to **keep a record of all stages of your work from the start**, including notes on discussions that take place, with your tutor or your group, during the planning process.

GROUP WORK

Although you might be working in a group, you will be required to produce written evidence individually, so be sure to keep your own records and evidence of planning and development. Even if you are a member of a group, you will each be graded individually (and will not necessarily all get equal marks), so you need to retain evidence of what skills you have developed and which aspects of the production that you personally had responsibility for. You will also have to produce your own individual commentary/production log/evaluation.

You also need to keep a note of your **individual contribution**, such as researching sound effects, music, or costumes and make-up. These notes, which can be kept in a diary or log, are essential when you write your evaluation. You may be asked to include the original notes in an appendix, so keep them in a folder. The more organized you are from the beginning, the easier this work will be.

Keep first drafts of scripts, storyboards and mock-ups for print work or websites, as these too may be required for the appendix of your coursework, as evidence of your ability to plan. Keep copies of original photographs and any **'found' images** that you have used.

Found images: Images found from existing sources, such as the internet or magazines.

EVALUATING YOUR OWN WORK

Students at any level can find it difficult to stand back from their own work and reflect on it objectively. Yet this is what you will get marks for here.

| Picture 4.2 | Keep a note of your progress and individual contribution during the whole process. Matthew Scrivener writes up his progress on his radio documentary. |

It is particularly difficult if there is very little time between you finishing the production and writing your evaluation, as is often the case with tight deadlines. Therefore you need to find methods which will help you to be objective about your own work.

SHOW YOUR WORK

One of the most important aspects of any evaluation is an examination of the strengths and weaknesses of your production. To help you identify these, show your finished production to representative members of your target audience and other audiences if possible.

You need to invite constructive comments to help you write your evaluation and therefore it is helpful to devise a questionnaire which will give you some written comments that you can take away with you.

KEEP TO THE WORD LIMIT

Make sure you know exactly how many words are required and stick to the word limit. Writing more than you need to will waste your time and will not attract more marks, as a word limit is part of the assessment. The advice below on the written material that should company your production is split into four separate sections to make it clearer, but you can easily adapt it to the specific requirements of your awarding body, which you should follow precisely.

WRITING 1: THE BRIEF AND YOUR RESEARCH

- ☐ Outline the **brief** you were given, or that you have chosen, showing how it will link to your study of topic areas or genres.
- ☐ Outline the **aims** of your project.
- ☐ Detail all class, group and individual **research** that you undertook on your chosen genre or topic, including points on sub-genres and conventions. Give details of other media texts that you looked at and how useful they were.
- ☐ What **inspired** you and what ideas did you reject?
- ☐ Show how the form and content of your production will match your **target audience**. Be as specific as possible. Include points on the age, class, gender, education and interests of your target audience. What other media products (mention actual texts here) might they enjoy?
- ☐ What kind of **institution** might have constructed your production?
- ☐ If you have to relate your production to a specific **topic area**, such as documentary or advertising, explain clearly which aspect or topic area you are exploring and how you intend to do this.

ctivity 4.1

Evaluation questionnaire for your target audience

Use the following questions as a guide to developing your own questionnaire, which relate directly to your own production, and use them with an audience:

• Place the production in a particular category (such as a docusoap) and explain why it fits into that category.
• Pick out several aspects that you particularly enjoyed or thought were successful and explain why.
• Pick out any parts of the production that you thought were less successful and explain why.

• What kind of audience do you think this production is aimed at? Be as specific as possible, suggesting other media products (films, television programmes, music, newspapers) they might enjoy. Mention age, gender, income and interests.
• Where and when might this production be seen/heard/sold?
• What kind of institution do you think might have produced it?
• Identify which messages and values are being conveyed by the production.
• How effectively do you think they are communicated?

WRITING 2: PLANNING THE PRODUCTION

Give an account of the decisions made during the planning stages in your group or by yourself:

☐ How were the individual **roles** allocated? Give details of all specific responsibilities.
☐ Include details on **recces** (reconnaissance) into locations, sets or studios.
☐ How did you **cast** any actors, presenters, interviewees, participators? Mention any letters you wrote arranging auditions or interviews and include them in your appendix.
☐ How did you plan to use the **technology** that was available to you? Give details of the equipment and its possibilities and limitations.
☐ How did you decide on and obtain any necessary props, sound FX, costumes and make-up?
☐ How did you **organize** the production itself? Include details such as shooting scripts, call sheets, and booking time in the computer rooms or recording studios.
☐ Give details of any **test** shots, test recordings or drafts that you made as part of your planning.

WRITING 3: CONSTRUCTING THE PRODUCTION

- ☐ Explain your technical decisions and revisions during production and post-production.
- ☐ Detail any **changes** to intended shots/dialogue/locations/original plans and explain why you made them.
- ☐ Mention any **problems** you encountered with the equipment, your crew, your actors, or the weather and give details on how you overcame them.
- ☐ With specific reference to your finished production, did you follow **conventions** or try to challenge them?
- ☐ Give a brief account of the **editing** process, explaining how the technology available affected your finished production.
- ☐ Explain why you chose certain stylistic elements, such as **sound** FX, colours, typefaces or music.

WRITING 4: EVALUATION

- ☐ Identify the specific aspects of the production for which you were **individually responsible**.
- ☐ Explain what you **intended to communicate** to your target audience through your production. Include points on the appropriate key concepts, such as representation, narrative and ideology.
- ☐ If required, link your production to the topic area you have studied, explaining exactly how you have explored the key issues.
- ☐ Relate your production to **the genre** you have studied and show how you have followed or challenged its **conventions**.
- ☐ Compare your own product to **actual media texts**.
- ☐ How have **actual audiences responded** to your product? Use some quotations from their responses to your questionnaire (see above).

Examiners' tips

- Be sure that you understand the codes and conventions of the genre or format that you are using.
- You might decide to play with them, by subverting them, but you need to understand what they are to begin with
- and what effects they have on an audience.
- Have a look at Chapter 2 for information on genre, codes and conventions.

☐ Offer some **close textual analysis** of one or two sequences or pages that you think were most successful and show how you achieved this. Comment on shots, acting styles, codes of dress, location, *mise-en-scène*, lighting, rhythm of editing, layout, design, mode of address, language of the written text, etc.

☐ How far do you think you have achieved what you set out to do? Comment on the **limitations or weaknesses** of your production

☐ On reflection, what is your **overall impression** of your finished production and **what have you learned?**

Part 2: general advice and production principles

PRE-PRODUCTION PLANNING

Whatever your chosen medium, planning is essential. It will result in a higher standard of finished product and evaluation and will save you time. Planning is the most important part of your practical work; in media industries, no-one gets any money to make a product until they have produced satisfactory evidence of detailed planning.

If you are making a video, for example, the pre-production processes of a detailed storyboard, script, shooting script and call sheet (see the section on **video production** below) will save time and make for a more professional production. You will be marked on your planning and organization, as well as on your production and evaluation (see separate section above).

CHOICE OF BRIEF

You are likely to be given a certain amount of choice in your production work. Think carefully about what is most appropriate for you. You may prefer to work individually, in which case **print production** or **ICT-based production** probably offer the best options. If you prefer to work in a team then **video** or **audio production** might suit you best.

If your practical work is linked to a particular topic area, such as Film and Broadcast Fiction, you are most likely to work in video. Work on documentary could be undertaken in video, radio or photo-journalism. As you will be spending a substantial amount of time on the production, make sure that you choose a topic and subject that will engage and interest you.

Aim high, but don't be over-ambitious. If you are required to make a finished production, rather than a pre-production exercise, you want to achieve a high degree of finish, but you do not have the time, money or resources to make a film such as *Terminator 3*. Use the following exercises to help you think about what you can achieve.

Write down your answers to all the questions in Activity 4.2. Show them to your Media Studies tutor and to other members of your group

Diagram 4.1 A brief section from a student commentary on their own production.

Production Log Section 1

The brief that we were given was to construct the opening sequence to a thriller. To do this we had to do research into similar media texts. We looked at 'Scream' (1996, US, dir. Wes Craven), which contains elements of horror and elements of thriller; therefore we were able to see how the filming of a thriller was constructed. 'Scream' helped to show that thrillers follow certain rules so that they are classified as thrillers. It showed that to build tension, the camera should move from the different points of view of the characters, particularly the threat and the victim. 'Scream' showed that there had to be a vulnerable victim or vulnerable victims, there also has to be some kind of threat such as the killer. A thriller usually addresses fears that are present in society.

We also observed the narrative of 'Seven' (1996, US, dir. David Fincher), which uses other elements of thriller genre, such as dark places and small areas so that it looks claustrophobic. It makes particular use of film noir conventions, especially in its chiaroscuro lighting. In 'Seven' it is usually raining which adds to the feeling of entrapment and claustrophobia, increasing the tension present in the movie. In 'Seven' there are enigmas in the narrative, which are not resolved immediately to the viewers causing suspense. In thrillers the threat is usually extinguished and the restoration of normal moral values is shown at the end.

ctivity 4.2

Choosing the brief
Ask yourself the following questions:
- How much **time** do you have?
- What do you want to **communicate**?
- Who is your target **audience**?
- What **equipment** is available?
- Can you make your **ideas clear**?
- Are you clear about the **conventions** of your chosen **genre**?
- Will you be **following** or **challenging the conventions** of your genre?

- What **institution** might have produced your production? Where might it be seen or heard?
- Is your chosen **medium appropriate** for the **subject matter** or **topic area**? An arts or music programme may be far more effective as a radio programme than a television programme, for example.
- Can you be prepared to **change and develop your ideas**? It is quite likely that you will have to reject some ideas if they prove impractical.

or class. This will help you to clarify your aims and to see how realistic and achievable your ideas are.

Brainstorm your ideas until you are clear about your aims. What are you trying to achieve?

Diagram 4.2 A student's first brainstorm for a new film website.

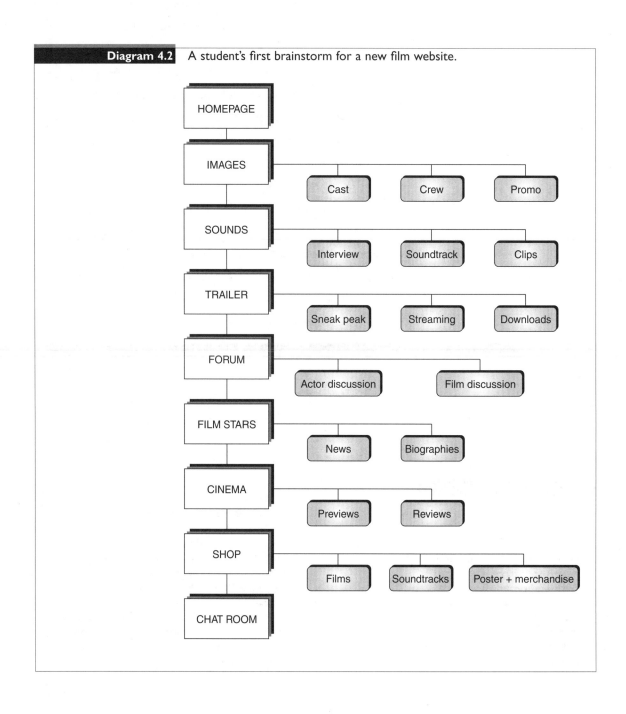

RESEARCH

Research real media products. Spend time looking at as many products as possible that are similar to, or contain elements of, the product you want to produce. Think about what gives you pleasure as a spectator, viewer or reader and this will help you to identify which elements you want to employ in your own production.

Research audiences. If you are creating a new radio programme or a new magazine, do some basic research to check that your target audience will be interested in your product. If you have time, conduct interviews with a representative range. If you are working in a group of four and you each interview about 10–15 people, you will have a good basis on which to work once you have analysed their responses.

EQUIPMENT

The quality of your ideas and planning is more important than having the latest or most expensive equipment. Some excellent productions have been constructed using very low-tech equipment, but there have been very many high-budget productions that are dismal failures. Find out exactly what equipment you have access to and think about working within your limitations. Specific details on production equipment are in the production sections of the different media forms below.

TECHNICAL SUPPORT

Even if you have a Media Studies technician, they may not be experts in your chosen medium. Try to find alternative sources of technical support, such as older media students (especially before they leave school/college), tutors or computer experts. Talk to them about your plans before you start production. Look at and listen to previous students' work and find out how they constructed magazines, radio programmes or websites.

This part of your planning will help you to see what is possible using the equipment available to you. It should also avoid disappointment and frustration and will mean you have someone else to turn to when you encounter technical problems.

PRODUCTION PROCESSES AND THE CONTINGENCY FACTOR

If you have worked hard on the planning stage, you will reap the benefits later. However, you need to be prepared for things going wrong. Even on professional productions, bad weather or illness can hold up a film shoot and lose the production company a great deal of money.

Try to build a contingency factor into your plans, just as the professionals do. Give yourself an extra day or two, to catch up in case of delays. When you book equipment, always over-estimate the amount of time you need to allow for unforeseen difficulties.

Although some problems can seem insurmountable, a combination of determination and flexibility will see you through.

Part 3: video production

Producing a video can be very rewarding but it is a complex process which is very time consuming. You need to be prepared to give up lots of free time in order to produce a successful video.

You will be expected to demonstrate the following skills:

☐ the ability to research and plan for your production
☐ control over the technology used
☐ using a variety of shot distances and frame shots
☐ selecting *mise-en-scène* and lighting
☐ editing so that meaning is clear to your target audience
☐ using sound with images and editing appropriately
☐ analysing and evaluating your production.

You may be using **analogue** video, **digital** video or **film**. Not many schools or colleges offer their students the opportunity to work in film, and therefore we have concentrated on video production in this section of the book, as you can use video to produce a film or television product.

EQUIPMENT

You will need the following equipment:

☐ An analogue or digital video camera with video cassette.
☐ A tripod.
☐ External microphones.
☐ An analogue or digital editing suite.
☐ Actors/presenters.
☐ Costumes/appropriate clothes.
☐ Make-up.
☐ Props.

Optional requirements:

☐ a lighting kit
☐ a stills camera.

Film is usually shot at 24 frames per second, giving the impression of continuous movement, while video operates at 25 frames per second. Increasing numbers of you will have the chance to work in digital video, and some argue that the quality of digital video will soon rival film. However, even if you only have access to analogue video, you can still produce impressive videos. More advanced technology does not automatically result in higher quality work. But whether you are working in film, analogue video or digital video, the general principles of production are the same.

3.1 VIDEO PRE-PRODUCTION

Brief

Choose and consider the brief carefully, taking into account your own skills, the skills of your group members, your interests, time schedule and the available equipment. Remember to keep within your limitations.

Research

Your work needs to be **consistent**, **convincing** and **confident**. The best way to achieve this is to research carefully throughout the planning stages. You may find that it helps to continue your research into the production stage. Film directors often watch other directors' work, not only while they are planning their film, but also during the shooting of the film.

- ☐ Make sure that you are familiar with the conventions of the genre you have chosen.
- ☐ Study videos, television programmes or films in your genre and use textual analysis skills (refer back to Chapter 2) to analyse them, noting what you like about them and would like to emulate in your own work. This should include points on lighting, editing, music, dialogue and even specific shots which you would like to experiment with.
- ☐ Don't forget to research your target audience as well (see the section on general advice above).
- ☐ If you are making a documentary, watch a whole range of documentaries so that you are clear on the particular style that you are adopting. Mixing styles can work, but this should not look like an accident. You will need to explain exactly why you chose to do this in your evaluation.
- ☐ Keep a record of your research as you go, as it is often difficult to remember exactly which products you studied. One way of recording your research into existing media products is shown in Activity 4.4.

ctivity 4.4

Research into similar media texts

Record your research in separate columns of a table (this example is based on research into opening sequences of thrillers, but you could substitute any genre/format)

Text	Camerawork	Enigma codes	Music	Lighting	Editing
The 39 Steps (Hitchcock, 1935, GB)	High angle slanted shot of box office bars, symbolizing entrapment. Man's shadow moves into frame, suggesting menace. Slant of shot connotes a world where something is wrong.	What are the 39 steps of the title? Who is the man? What does he look like?	Mr Memory's signature tune played by the music hall band. Apparently light in tone, but low slow undertone of cellos contrasts with this and suggests the sinister.	Word 'Music hall' suddenly lights up against black background. The blackness symbolizes evil and the mystery of the 39 steps, while the sudden light suggests that the mystery will be solved and evil conquered.	Three quick cuts only reveal lower half of hero, adding to the enigma code. We don't see Hannay's face clearly until shot 22. This gives him a sense of mystery.
Witness (Weir, 1985, US)					
The Big Sleep (Hawks, 1946, US)					

Institution

Examiners' tips

Make sure that you are clear about the kind of institution that will produce your product. For example, if you are producing the first five minutes of a television documentary on heavy metal music, you need to think about whether it could fit into a BBC series such as *Panorama* or whether it is more likely to be produced by an independent company such as Ginger Productions for Channel 4 and be able to explain why in your evaluation.

- Acting is not part of your assessment, so choose people who are likely to be best for the part and not necessarily members of the group. This will give you more time to concentrate on the skills that are being assessed.

Actors

- If you need adults or children, or police or teachers, try to use real ones rather than get someone to pretend, as this often looks amateurish.

You will need actors, presenters or voice-overs for your production. Devote some time to finding people who can act convincingly and rehearse them carefully. Voice-over actors are also important; for example, if you are producing a serious documentary on terrorism, a voice-over in the style of a comedy actor would obviously not be appropriate.

| Diagram 4.3 | Arrange your interview dates well in advance by letter. |

Dear Mr Hopper,

I am producing a short television documentary on local clubs for my A-Level Media Studies assignment.

I would be very grateful if you could spare the time for a brief interview to explain the particular appeal of your club.

I could offer the following dates and times ...

Interviews

If your production requires interviews, make sure that you arrange these by letter, e-mail or telephone, giving precise details of times and locations. Even in your own institution, you cannot expect to interview a teacher, lecturer or fellow student successfully without explaining your aims to them and arranging the interview in advance.

Production team roles

Key terms

Synopsis: a brief outline of about 200 words, give a brief outline of the plot or subject matter of a film, television programme, novel or radio play.
Script: the written text of a film, play or broadcast

Find out from your tutor exactly which skills are being tested and decide as a group how you can each get an equal opportunity to develop a range of specific skills, but not necessarily all of them. It is important that specific responsibility for each aspect of the production is allocated to individual members of the group, even if you rotate this. As you are most likely to be working in groups of four, some of the tasks will need to be shared.

Synopsis

Write a **synopsis** of the film or programme. Indicate the genre, comparing your intended production to similar media texts. Indicate the setting and introduce the main characters or sequences.

| Diagram 4.4 | Video production roles. |

Crew

The following roles need to be allocated to members of your group:

Director	– in overall control of the production, rehearses and directs actors
Producer	– controls schedule, makes arrangements for actors and locations
Camera Operator	– shoots the video as director wants, looks after camera
Sound Recordist	– checks sound levels, uses earphones and mic for dialogue
Lighting	– organizes lighting set-ups or checks position of camera in relation to sun/other 'natural' lighting
Continuity	– logs the shots and checks costume, hair and *mise-en-scène*
Costume	– researches, provides and cares for costumes
Make-up	– provides and deals with characters/presenters' make-up
Set Designer	– plans and provides the props and dresses the set

Optional

Assistant Camera	– pulls focus, provides tracks, looks after camera
Choreographer	– arranges dance or fight movements

Scripting

Write a **script** for the actors, interviewers or presenters. It is easiest to allocate this job to one or two group members.

Test the script out on your group, friends, tutors and family. Think about how much of your dialogue can be conveyed through expressions, camerawork and music. Then cut as many words as possible. Redraft again to improve it further. Every word should *fight* to deserve a place on your page. A useful guideline is that one page of dialogue is equivalent to 1 minute of screentime.

Hold a read-through with your actors, interviewers or presenters. If the script still does not seem convincing, then redraft it until it does.

Storyboarding

Film directors like Steven Spielberg use storyboard artists to produce detailed storyboards which they follow meticulously, especially for action sequences. Storyboards are often reproduced in books on the making of a film or in the special features on some films on DVD.

Diagram 4.5	The opening of the synopsis of *Chicken Run*.
	It is night and all seems quiet on Tweedy's Farm. But someone – or something – stirs in the shadows. It is Ginger, a chicken with a mission. She and her fellow flock are determined to escape the chicken farm where any chicken who doesn't make her egg quota can meet a fowl fate.

Diagram 4.6	How to set out a script – a scene from *Chicken Run*.

```
Scene 6400
EXT. DIFFERENT PART OF THE COMPOUND - MORNING

Bunty lies on her belly on a modified bunk which sits in
suspenders like a rock in a slingshot.
STRETCH - Chickens pull it back.
Nick and Fletcher sit in their `bleachers' - watching.

                    NICK

          Hurry! You're keeping me in suspenders!

                    ROCKY

          Release

They let go. Bunty rockets forward. There's a length of rope
attached to it. It uncoils then - THOING! - goes taut. The
bunk stops. Bunty shoots forward.

                    GINGER

      FLAP!

She flaps across the frame on the cart, past the rats.

                    NICK

          Poultry in motion!

She flaps furiously then - BLOOP! - slams into the chain link
fence.

The rats howl.

Then Bunty bounces off the fence and flies back into the
rats' bleachers, sending them tumbling.
```

After the storyboards have been drawn, the directors discuss the details, such as the camera positions, lighting set-ups and the scene composition with the director of photography (DOP). The storyboards then are issued to crew members and form the outline from which the crew works. In post-production, they are a useful visual reminder for the editor.

Storyboards will help you to focus on the visual elements of your production. From the way that professional media producers use storyboards you can see how important it is to spend time working on your storyboard.

Key terms

Storyboard: this is a series of drawn camera shots in a camera sequence.

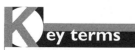

Storyboarding advice

- ☐ Every shot needs to be drawn in a separate box. If you try to cover three shots in one you will encounter difficulties during shooting. Include details on choice of shot, shot length, angle, framing, lighting, dialogue, sound FX, music and any other helpful information.
- ☐ Draw a first draft in pencil as it is very likely that you will want to change or add some more shots. You may want to make changes after discussing the storyboard in your group, trying some test shots or **reconnoitring** (see below) the location.
- ☐ Keep your original storyboards with your log so that you can account for the changes you made in your commentary.

Picture 4.3 Frames from the storyboard for *Men in Black*.

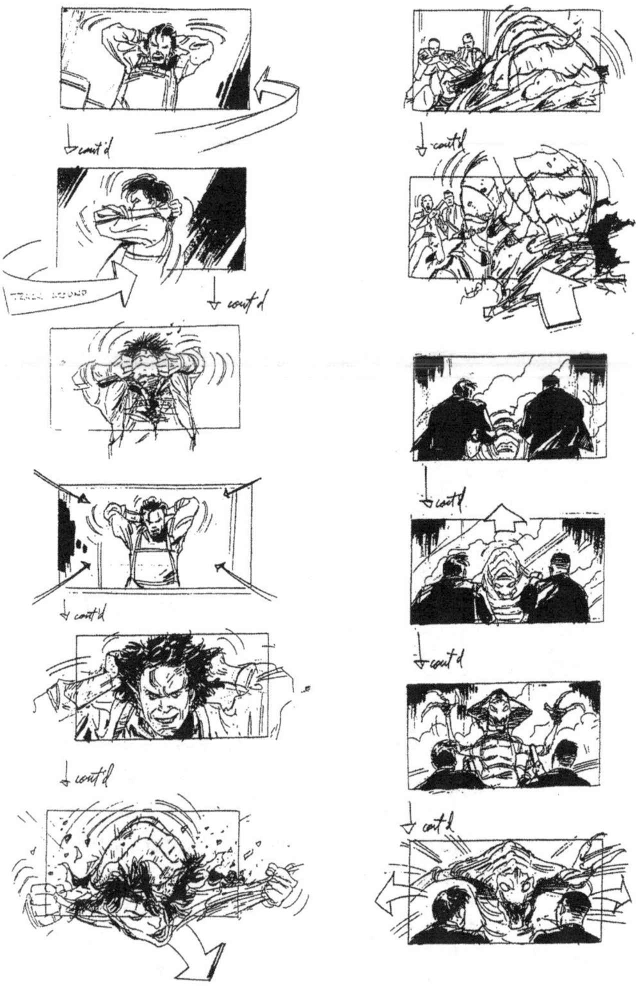

Diagram 4.7 How to draw a storyboard – a student example.

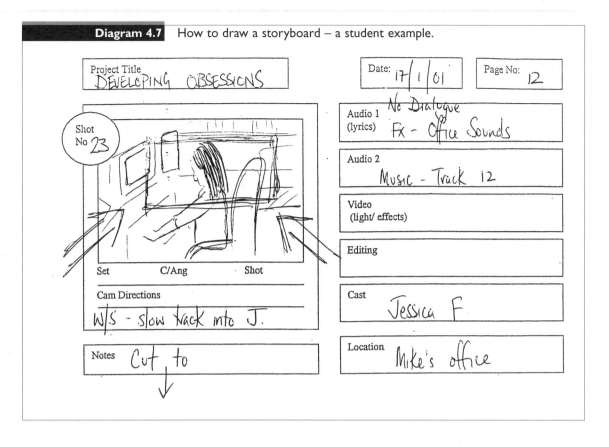

Recce (reconnaissance)

- ☐ Go to your planned locations to check that they are suitable **before** you start production.
- ☐ If you are planning to shoot in a public place, you must inform the police and the local council or company that owns the shopping centre. It is particularly important that you advise the police if you are going to stage fights or use props such as guns. The public will (understandably) inform the police if they see anything suspicious and there are many cases of shame-faced students having to explain their actions to the police.
- ☐ Many film directors take stills of their locations to check they match their vision of the film. If you have time, this is good practice and could save you time in production.
- ☐ Try some test video shots in advance (at the location if possible), especially for any complex sequences.
- ☐ Check whether other people will be walking through your location and think about what you will do if their presence interferes with your shoot. It is a good idea to prepare notices informing the public in advance.

Shooting schedule

This will save time when you start production, as you can group all the shots from one **set-up** together. For example, it will be better for lighting if all exterior shots at one location can be taken in one afternoon, while all interior shots at another location can be taken together. This means that you are less likely to have to alter the lighting and your shoot will proceed more quickly.

Call sheet

Produce a call sheet for every day of the shoot. Make sure that everyone gets a copy. This will help you to be organized and to take swift action if anyone does not turn up.

Equipment

☐ Discuss the capabilities of the camera and the editing suite with your tutor or technician early on. Then you won't find yourself in a situation where you have made a sophisticated tracking shot the focal point of your video only to find that you have no tracks or dolly.

☐ Make sure that you turn up on time to collect your equipment. This will show your Media Studies tutor that you are organized.

Diagram 4.8	A shooting schedule for a student production *Deceit*.	
Shot no	Set	Characters
3	A	DM + Doc
4	A	Doc
5	A	DM
6	A	Cop
7	A	DM + Doc
8	B	Dupré + DM
9	A	DM
10	B	Dupré
11	A	DM
12	A	Cop + DM
13	A	Cop
14	B	DM
15	A	Cop
16	B	Dupré + DM
17	B	Dupré + Doc + Cop
2	C	Killer + (Cop)
1	D	Killer

- [ ] It will also give you time to make checks that you have everything you need, including batteries, battery charger, tripod, mains lead, and so on.
- [ ] Check that you have access to a mains socket in order to recharge batteries if necessary.
- [ ] Look after the equipment very carefully. Handle it with respect. If you do damage equipment it is likely that you will be liable for any damage or loss and you will be inconveniencing other students.
- [ ] Return the equipment on the date and time you have agreed. Otherwise you could jeopardize your relationship with the Media Studies department and fellow students.
- [ ] If you have damaged anything, be honest about it so that it can be repaired as quickly as possible.

Camera care

These rules apply to all cameras: still, analogue and digital.

- [ ] Do not let the camera get wet or expose it to extreme temperatures.
- [ ] Do not drop the camera or leave it on the back seat of a car where it might fall.
- [ ] Keep the camera free from dust and dirt.
- [ ] Always keep the camera in its case when not in use.
- [ ] Make sure that the camera is firmly attached to the tripod.
- [ ] Take the camera off the tripod to move it.
- [ ] Care of the camera must be the responsibility of the camera operator or the camera assistant.

3.2 VIDEO PRODUCTION

Sound

- [ ] Remember that sound: music, dialogue and sound FX are all just as important as the visual elements. Student video work is often seriously let down by the lack of attention to sound.
- [ ] Think of the sound perspective as the 'ears' of the camera.
- [ ] Always use earphones as this will let you listen directly to what is being recorded.
- [ ] If you are including dialogue in your video, make sure that you use an external gun or rifle microphone on a boom pole (see Picture 4.5) for the best results. Then get the mic as close as you can to whoever is speaking without it being seen in the frame.
- [ ] An alternative to the gun mic is the radio mic which can be hidden under clothes. If you are lucky enough to have access to these, they can be very efficient. (See the section on Audio Production for more information on microphones.)
- [ ] Be aware of any background noise, such as traffic, a ticking clock, or aeroplanes overhead, which will affect the quality of your sound. If your

Picture 4.4   Try to use a boom mic for best results.

ey terms

Boom mic: an external microphone on a long pole which can be held above or below the line of shooting to record sound at source.
Gun mic: an external mic on a short stick which can be held by a recordist or

mounted on the top of the camera.
Radio mic: a cordless external mic.
Rifle mic: like a gun mic.
Atmos: short for 'atmosphere', ambient sound that derives from the location itself.

sound recordist says there was a problem with the take, re-shoot the take even if the visual elements and the acting were perfect.

☐ If you do have to use the mic on the camera, then remember that it is close to the camera operator, so he or she must be careful not to make a sound.

☐ Always record two minutes of atmos (ambient sound) for editing purposes. Keep everyone on the set and make sure this is recorded at the same level as the rest of the takes using that set-up.

Shooting procedure

Your shoot will proceed efficiently if you establish a clear and consistent procedure for every take. The procedure in Diagram 4.9 covers everything for video shooting.

Diagram 4.9	Procedure for video shooting.
Director:	*Quiet on the set.* *Everyone ready?*
Camera operator: Sound recordist:	Indicate that they are ready or inform the director that there is a problem
Director:	*Roll camera!*
Camera operator:	*Camera rolling.*
Assistant camera operator/continuity	*Shot 1, Take 1*
Director:	*Action!*
The shot proceeds here	
Director (allowing 3 seconds at the end of the take):	*Cut!*

☐ Camera and sound switch off.
☐ Camera operator, sound recordist and continuity state their opinions on the quality of the take.
☐ Director decides if take is NG – no good or G – good.
☐ If NG, the cycle is repeated for a second take.
☐ If G, the crew proceeds to the next shot.

LOGGING

All shots should be logged throughout the shoot. This will speed up the editing process. The continuity person or the assistant camera operator can take responsibility for this. A note should be made if there was a problem with the sound, camera or continuity, even if the director decided against another take.

Continuity

If in doubt about a continuity problem, check by replaying the material and then go for another take if necessary. Continuity's job is to keep a check on all details of the set, actors' costumes, hair, make-up, movement and dialogue.

Mise-en-scène

Always check the *mise-en-scène* by looking through the viewfinder to see what is in the frame. If the background, props, costume and make-up are not appropriate, these details could spoil your video.

Diagram 4.10	A detailed log sheet will speed up your editing.

00:50 - 00:54	Shot 3	Take 1 & 2
00:54 - 01:16	Shot 3	Take 3
00:00 - 00:06	Shot 4	Take 1
00:00 - 00:08	Shot 5	Take 1
00:00 - 00:04	Shot 6	Take 1
00:00 - 00:01	Shot 6	Take 2
00:00 - 00:04	Shot 6	Take 3
00:00 - 00:02	Shot 11	Take 1
00:00 - 00:08	Shot 11	Take 2
00:00 - 13:00	Shot 7	Take 1
00:00 - 00:01	?	
00:00 - 00:05	Shot 12	Take 1
00:00 - 00:05	Shot 13	Take 1
00:00 - 00:07	Shot 14	Take 1 & 2
00:00 - 00:08	Shot 15	Take 1
00:00 - 00:05	Shot 9?	
00:00 - 00:12	Shot 8	Take 1
00:22 - 00:28	Shot 8	Take 2
00:00 - 00:16	Shot 8A	Take 1
00:00 - 00:07	Shot 10	Take 1
00:08 - 00:09	Shot 16	Take 1
00:00 - 00:03	Shot 16	Take 2

NB: Log of all shots on tape.

Direction

☐ Restraint is very important when directing actors for film or television. A slight movement of the eyes can be very expressive if shot in close up.

☐ Pace is important, as are pauses. If you are asking your actors to act one line for a close-up always go back a few lines so that they have something to react to.

☐ Remember that moments when nothing seems to happen can be very powerful in film and television.

Camerawork

☐ Practise some test shots first, especially if you are planning a tracking shot or a pull focus.

☐ Always use a tripod unless you have a very good reason for employing a *ciné-vérité* style.

☐ If you are stuck without a tripod for some reason, you can place the camera on a table, but this situation is best avoided if possible.

☐ Make sure that any eye-lines are matched between people.

☐ Take care when looking through the viewfinder. Notice any details of the *mise-en-scène* which do not look quite right for your video and either change the position of the subject or change the position of the camera.

Picture 4.5	Placing characters at opposite sides of the frame, gives them off-screen space and suggest a spatial relationship. Source: *What Women Want* (Eileen Lewis, MA film, Canterbury Christ Church University College).

☐ Make sure that your subject is placed exactly where you want them within the frame. If you are planning to edit a sequence of two people having a telephone conversation, you need to place one of them to the right of the frame facing inwards and the other to the left of the frame facing inwards. This is a convention which needs to be followed as it gives imagined off-screen space to the unseen character.

☐ There are six zones of off-screen space: above, below, left, right, behind the scene and behind the camera. Think about using them creatively.

☐ Make sure that you have got exactly the amount of sky or background that you want in the frame.

☐ Don't be afraid to shoot some big close-ups which can be particularly effective.

☐ Be careful to zoom gently, unless your production style demands a sudden zoom. Pans and tilts should also be used sparingly and operated slowly.

☐ Make sure that you rehearse each shot or sequence before you start recording. This will help you anticipate any problems that might occur during shooting.

☐ Check your lens is clean and only use special cloths to clean it.

☐ With the lens cap on, record 15 seconds of black before your first shot. This is especially important if you are going to use analogue editing.

Analogue cameras pre-roll

Always count at least 6 seconds at the end of each piece before stopping the recording. Whenever you stop the recording, the tape will roll backwards (known as pre-roll). In order to avoid erasing part of your previous take, you must allow at least 6 seconds at the end of each take.

Lighting

Spend time looking at paintings and other films in order to think about the kind of lighting you want for your film/television programme. Never underestimate the importance of lighting. It is one of the most important techniques to create mood and establish character.

Examine the low-key chiaroscuro lighting of *noir* films like *The Maltese Falcon* (Huston, 1941), with its strong contrasts between light and darkness and its shadows which make the characters 'shady' and ambiguous.

Look at the blue lighting used by Ridley Scott in the neo-*noir* *Blade Runner* (1982). This helps to construct the harsh coldness of the dystopian world of the film.

Lighting set-ups

You may be lucky enough to have access to a set of '**redheads**' (so termed because of their red casing, giving out 800 W of light) or **blondes** (yellow casing, giving out 2 kW of light). The lights can be adjusted by turning a knob and by altering the position of the flaps called **barn doors**. As artificial light sources have a different colour temperature to daylight, you need to place **gels** (coloured filters over the light) to achieve the right colour balance. A blue gel will convert artificial lamps to look like daylight, while you need an orange gel to convert daylight to artificial light.

Picture 4.6	The 'shady' character of 'Sam Spade' (Humphrey Bogart) is emphasized through the chiaroscuro lighting.

Unless you are aiming for a **low-key** effect (see below), use the standard three point set-up. This involves the **key light** (the main light source normally placed near the camera), **back light** (behind the subject to emphasize its depth and shape) and **fill light** (usually placed on the other side from the key light, but lower down to fill in shadows).

Think about whether you want to create a **high-key** or **low-key** effect. A high-key effect will eliminate most of the shadows, while a low-key effect may mean working without a fill or back light. If your video requires a *film noir* effect, you will choose low-key lighting, possibly by using just one light in order to create shadows and harsh lighting. You can choose to soften the lighting with **scrim** (a fine gauze placed over the lights), or by bouncing the light off the ceiling with a reflector or a white board. This will avoid harsh contrasts.

Using natural light

☐ If you are shooting outside, make sure that you choose the time of day that gives you the light quality appropriate to your video. Think about sources of light and where the shadows are.

☐ If you have **a white balance** (adjusts the internal filters on your camera), set this on every shoot or you will have problems with colours. Zoom in on a white object using the same lighting conditions as those you will use when recording, making sure that it fills the frame, and then push the white balance button until the viewfinder display reads 'White Balance OK'.

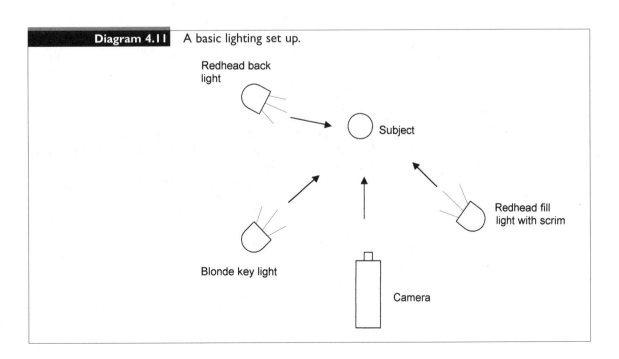

| Diagram 4.11 | A basic lighting set up. |

- [ ] Many digital cameras will do this for you automatically, but you need to adjust brightness controls for different conditions.
- [ ] If you are shooting a subject that is strongly back-lit, the **iris** needs to be opened up to give correct exposure to the subject rather than the background. Some cameras do this automatically, but check in case you want to operate it manually, in order to have more control.
- [ ] If you choose to use natural light, check where the main light source is coming from. Then move your position with the camera and your subjects (if possible) until you get the exact light quality that you want. Usually this will be one where the light falls on your actors or subject, with the sun or light behind the camera.
- [ ] Do not shoot into the sun or place your subject in front of a window unless you particularly want a silhouette effect.

3.3 VIDEO POST-PRODUCTION

Editing requires patience and persistence. It is also extremely time consuming. It may also be the case that you are booked into editing suites for specific amounts of time because of difficulties with resources and this can make the editing process quite stressful. However, remember that it is also a very creative process and should give you a finished product that you can be proud of.

Digital video editing

- [ ] If you are lucky enough to have access to digital video editing, you will end up with a much better quality product than you would from analogue editing as there is no degradation of the image.
- [ ] Another advantage over analogue editing is that you can alter a shot at any stage in the editing process, without spoiling the rest of your edit.
- [ ] You will build up an **EDL**, or editing decision list as you work, and your work will be stored as a project.
- [ ] You also have a huge range of effects and transitions available to you such as slow motion, split-screen and dissolve edits. However, remember that there has to be a reason for every decision you make in editing, so do not use these effects gratuitously.
- [ ] Try some practice editing using found footage first. This will help you to familiarize yourself with the basics of digital editing.
- [ ] It is likely that your editing system publishes guidelines on use on its website. The website will give you up to date information and may help with trouble-shooting if your tutor or technician are not available.

Analogue editing

The edit controller synchronizes your two video machines to the same running speed. You then select the 'in' points and the 'out' points for each edit. You can still produce some excellent work on analogue video editing equipment, provided you follow a few simple rules:

| Picture 4.7 | Digital video editing – your editing decision list is displayed onscreen and you can play it through at any time. Laurie Ritter works on his music video. |

☐ Always use brand-new videotapes, rather than recording over pre-recorded ones.

☐ Do check that you are happy with each edit as you build your video as it is quite difficult to go back and change an inappropriate edit once you have finished. In **assemble** editing the audio and video tracks are transferred to the recorder together and each edit is built up, one after the other.

☐ **Insert** editing will allow you to transfer sound and video tracks separately. If you are producing a music video your sound track needs to be laid down first in order to match the rhythm of your visual edits to the rhythm of your audio track.

Basic principles of editing

These principles are the conventions, or unwritten rules, that you need to follow if you are aiming to produce a film, video or television programme in a particular genre. Here are a few of the most basic principles, common to analogue and digital editing:

☐ The **edit** is the transition between two shots. The cut is the direct transition from one shot to the next and is the most common form of edit.

☐ The **mix** is the overlapping of two shots which gives a more gradual transition from one shot to the next. This may be in the form of a dissolve, where as one shot fades out of view, the other shot gradually becomes more visible. This edit may be used to indicate a change of time or setting or when you want to make a strong link between the fading shot and the new one. This should last between one and three seconds for it to be effective.

☐ Another form of mix is the **wipe**, but bear in mind that these often look dated. Only use this edit if you have a good reason for doing so and remember that you will have to justify it in your commentaries.

☐ The last form of edit is the **fade**, or gradual transition from a shot to black, occasionally white (**fade out**), or from black to a shot (**fade in**). You can use this at the beginning or end of a scene in your production or for a change in time or setting. Again, only use this edit if you have a good reason and match your sound to the edit. Whilst it is the convention to fade up from black at the beginning of a programme, you may want a straight cut from black for dramatic effect.

☐ **Cutaways** are shots of related objects or details that you can use to improve the quality of your editing or to avoid a **jump cut** (a cut where there has been no change of camera angle but a slight change of movement by the subject, so that the audience feel that something is missing).

☐ Avoid **cutting on movement**. Your work will look amateurish if you cut on a pan, tilt or zoom. Wait until the pan has stopped before you make your edit. Allow a moving car to move out of the frame or to come to a stop before cutting to a shot of it parked.

☐ **Action match** is important: if a character or vehicle leaves the frame on the left, they should enter the next shot on the right. This will maintain continuity.

☐ Professional editors often **underlay** the beginning of the sound track of the next shot to a second or less of the visual image of the previous shot. This technique provides continuity and helps to prepare the audience for a change of focus, scene or time.

☐ Avoid **crossing the line**. Sometimes called the 180° rule, this means that all shots that are edited together need to be taken from one side of a line. If you are filming two people talking, an imaginary line should be drawn between their eyes (**eyeline match**) and this line should not be crossed. Otherwise the result could be very confusing for the audience.

xtend your knowledge

Key text: *Grammar of the edit* by Roy Thompson (Focal Press, 1993).
• This has many useful tips and more advanced points on editing.

Diagram 4.12 The 180° rule – editing between camera 1 and 3 will confuse the audience and make it look as though the two people are facing the same way. You need to edit between camera 1 and camera 2 to avoid crossing the line.

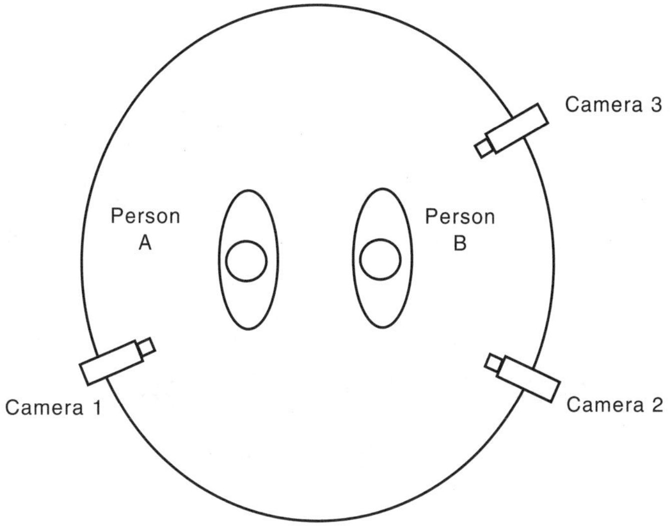

Part 4: print production

This area of production includes newspapers, magazines, comics and advertisements.

You will be expected to demonstrate the following skills:

☐ the ability to research and plan for your production
☐ using the technology appropriately for the task
☐ control over the technology
☐ showing an understanding of the conventions of layout, graphics, colour and page design
☐ using an appropriate mode of address
☐ integrating illustration and written text
☐ manipulating found images
☐ analysing and evaluating your own production.

One advantage of this area of production is that you may have access to this equipment at home and therefore will not need to rely on your college's or school's equipment. Another is that you can be equally successful working as an individual or in a group on a print production.

EQUIPMENT

You will need:

- [ ] a computer
- [ ] a desktop publishing program
- [ ] a scanner
- [ ] a colour printer
- [ ] a stills camera (digital if possible).

For simplicity, the advice given below assumes that you are producing the front cover and some inside pages of a magazine, but it can be adapted for any print production, including newspapers, advertisements, CD covers, flyers, etc.

4.1 PRINT PRE-PRODUCTION PLANNING

Research the conventions

Look carefully at a whole range of magazines, including ones that are not aimed at your target audience. (See Chapter 2 for more detail.)

Front covers

Compare the front covers of a range of magazines. How does each try to attract its target audience? Using a magazine that is aimed at a similar target audience to your own, make a list of the conventions that it uses in order to attract it.

Masthead

Decide on a title that is appropriate to your target audience and design the masthead. This is a key part of brand identity and you need to spend some time on getting it right.

House style: the style of layout and language of a particular publication or the style of a particular institution.

Visual style

Start to think about the visual style that you want to construct. Consider colour, layout, images and the overall visual impact that you want. You need to create consistency throughout the pages of the magazine that you construct to ensure brand identification: a **house style**.

Picture 4.8	Some successful student magazines – *Reel* by Alex Diggens, *Oxygen* by Russell Hope, *The Rim* by Gavin Fraser and Graham Tong, and *AMP* by Sam Blake.

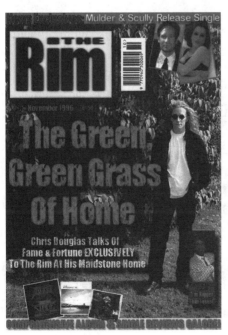

Typography

Decide on the typography. You have hundreds of choices of fonts and sizes. Serif or sans-serif font? Shadow or outlining on your front cover? Experiment on the computer until you find the one you want. Always think about your target audience and what will appeal to them.

Layout

Will your text be justified (lined up on the right and/or left of the page) or not? If you are appealing to a youth audience, you may want to vary the justification, to give the impression of rebellion or lack of conformity. Do you want your cover lines to be placed in text boxes? If you are using a model or an image, will you overlay the image so that it partially obscures the masthead? Do you want your cover to look cluttered or stylish?

Mode of address

Decide how you will address the reader. Will you act as a friend, big sister, or authoritative voice? What kind of language will you use for your cover lines?

Diagram 4.13   Different fonts and text effects can produce very different moods.

Front cover	2	3	4	5
MASTHEAD IMAGE	Advert aimed at target audience	CONTENTS PAGE	Advert aimed at target audience	EDITORIAL THE TEAM
• Cover line • Cover line • Cover line				Advert

Diagram 4.14 A mock-up will give you a good idea of the final look of your magazine.

Research

Ask a representative group of your target audience some questions about their interests, about what they would like to see in your magazine, and about how much they would be willing to pay for it.

Produce a mock-up

At quite an early stage, produce a hand-drawn mock-up of your finished magazine so that you get a clear idea of the overall look. The best way to do this is to fold some blank sheets of A3 paper in half and place the pages together so that you have the right number of pages for your magazine. Number the pages and draw your layout for each page roughly in pencil.

Discuss your mock-up with the other members of the group and with members of your target audience. If necessary, adjust your plans and redesign the pages. Then produce a more detailed mock-up in colour.

4.2 PRINT PRODUCTION

Images

The images are just as important, if not more important, than the written articles. Decide which images you can produce yourself and which you need to find. You will want a variety of images, including photographs and **graphics** (cartoons, sketches or designs) to enhance the visual style of your magazine.

Found images

Found images are those which you have found from existing sources such as the internet or other magazines. You are likely to include some of these if you are producing a celebrity or film magazine. However, in order to demonstrate your own creativity, you should try to manipulate these images for your own purpose. You may crop them (cut parts from the image) so that the original meaning is altered or you may juxtapose (place them next to) the image with other images to form a collage. To manipulate found images digitally, you will need a program like Adobe Photoshop.

Original images

Your brief may demand that you provide a certain number of original images in your print production. In any case, you will be rewarded for any original photography which is then included in the finished product. You can use any kind of camera to take the photographs for your production, but the advantage of digital still cameras is that you can link them straight into the computer and then import the images into your work without loss of quality.

Remember to plan your photographs well in advance so that if something goes wrong you have time to retake them. Just as with video shooting, think about lighting, framing, composition and the position of the subject and the camera.

One way of avoiding the use of found images is to find a look-alike of a famous film star or model and photograph them yourself. With careful use of lighting, costume, make-up, pose and background this can prove a very creative and effective exercise.

When you have scanned your photographs into your magazine pages you can decide whether you want them to be printed in a box or within a coloured frame to give it emphasis. You may then want to place your captions inside the photograph in a different coloured box. Smaller photographs or drawings can be placed within the article so that the text **wraps** itself around the image. Your software program should offer you a 'text wrap' box to help you with this technique.

Keep evidence of all photographs you have taken yourselves and a record of the sources of any found images, together with the found images themselves, before you manipulate them. They need to accompany your commentary as evidence of your work.

Writing the articles and the contents page

Start to write the articles, contents page and editorial (known as **copy** until the magazine is published). It is best to word-process at this stage as this will give you a better idea of the amount of space your writing will take up on the page. You will need to keep redrafting until your pieces are the right length and consistent in their mode of address.

Make sure that your cover lines correspond to the titles of some of the articles and work hard at them until they are appropriate for your target audience. One way of checking this before you print your work off finally is to show some of your copy to members of your target audience and your lecturer/teacher for feedback. This will help you with your redrafts and to cut your pieces down.

Layout

Your method here will depend on the resources at your school or college. You will probably work on the layout using a **DTP** program (a desktop publishing program which allows you to create a layout involving text and images or graphics). Using the DTP method means that you can try out different column widths, headline sizes and fonts. You can also design your own graphics and wrap text around your photographs.

You may also use the **cut and paste** method (cutting out word-processed text, images and graphics, assembling them on the page, then gluing them down). The first may be easier because you can try out a whole range of layouts, fonts and colours immediately, but some DTP programs can be restrictive. Provided you word-process your written text and colour photocopy the final result onto photographic paper, it is possible to achieve an excellent product using the cut and paste method.

For the cut and paste method, you can prepare each page by drawing guidelines on the paper with a blue non-reproducing pencil, to show exactly where images, graphics and written text will go on the page. Then cut the copy to the exact size and stick it where you want it.

4.3 PRINT POST-PRODUCTION

Printing

Print off some test copies of your finished product and make sure that you have not made any factual or spelling errors by showing your work to your tutor. When you are confident that all your pages are accurate, print them off on good quality photographic paper to do your work justice. Try to present them life-size and in realistic contexts, for example, put a newspaper article or advert *in situ* on a page.

Part 5: audio production

You will be expected to demonstrate the following skills:

- ☐ the ability to research and plan for your production
- ☐ recording appropriate material
- ☐ using a microphone to ensure sound is appropriate
- ☐ editing so that the meaning is communicated to the target audience

☐ using generic conventions effectively
☐ analysing and evaluating your production in a wider context.

You may be using an audio cassette recorder, MiniDisc, **DAT** (digital audio tape) recorder or ¼-inch reel-to-reel tape recorder. You must use an external microphone, so if your department does not have one, try to borrow one from another department. If this is not possible, this is not a good option for you, as using a microphone is likely to be one of the technical skills which is being tested.

EQUIPMENT

You will need:

☐ an audio recorder, either cassette, MiniDisc or DAT
☐ a microphone
☐ an audio mixer, digital editing suite or ¼-inch reel-to-reel cassette with splicer and chinagraph pencil
☐ actors/presenters
☐ interviewees
☐ a studio/soundproof room.

Try to choose the microphone which is most appropriate for your production. Microphones have different pick-up ranges and are therefore suitable for different purposes.

MICROPHONES

☐ **Omnidirectional**: picks up sound from all directions, often used with portable recorders and emphasizes the natural acoustics of a room. Good for interviews and location recording.
☐ **Cardioid (uni-directional)**: heart shaped, records from one direction only, useful for music balance or speech from a single person.
☐ **Hypercardioid**: similar to the cardioid, but with a small response area at the back of the mic as well.
☐ **Bidirectional**: a figure of eight shape, this mic picks up from two sides and is good for radio drama or studio interviews where two people sit opposite each other.
☐ **Gun or rifle mic**: directional with a small pick-up area, often used for news gathering. This often comes with a cover (often called a 'Hairy Harry' or 'Dougal' – after the *Magic Roundabout* dog!) to reduce wind noise.

Think about the endless possibilities of the medium of radio. This will help you to use the medium to its best advantage. You can present events and places which would be impossible if you were working in video. This is partly why historical drama or science fiction are so successful on radio.

Radio is a very intimate medium, allowing you as a producer to get very close to your subject. You can use it in the same way that a film-maker might use an ECU (extra close-up). This means that it might be the most appropriate medium for a serious documentary that includes eyewitness accounts or for an intimate audio diary. Your task is to create visual images for your audience.

5.1 AUDIO PRE-PRODUCTION PLANNING

Research the conventions

Listen to as many examples as possible of the genre that you are working in. There is no point in trying to produce 5 minutes of a radio play if you have never listened to one. Become as familiar as possible with the conventions of the genre, and also the conventions of the different radio stations.

If you are working in a group, it is a good idea to record some of the best examples individually and then to listen to them in a group and note which elements you find successful and which ones you want to reject for your own programme.

Target audience and mode of address

Establish a profile, or clear picture of your target audience. This is best done through interviews with a representative group to find out their interests, what other media texts they enjoy and what their generic expectations are likely to be. You can then develop a clear notion of your mode of address.

For example, if your main target audience is 15–25-year-old male Nu-Metal fans, your mode of address will be relaxed, with colloquial words attached to that genre of music. If your audience is middle class and middle aged, this language would not be appropriate. The clearer you are about your target audience, the more convincing your mode of address will be.

Structure

Think carefully about the structure of your piece. It will almost inevitably be part of a longer programme, but your sequence will not be impressive if it comes to an abrupt halt, unless it is a dramatic cliff-hanger. Whether you are making a radio news bulletin, a radio advert, a radio drama extract, a music programme extract or a documentary you need an introduction, a development and some sort of conclusion.

Research the subject matter

Even though you may be planning a radio show on a subject that you feel you are knowledgeable about, you must research it thoroughly. For example, students could easily spend 4 weeks researching a 5-minute sequence from a documentary on a music artist and selecting music tracks before they get to the recording studio. The research will make your programme more convincing and successful. Make sure that you keep the evidence of this research for your commentary.

Scripting improvised programmes with interviews

Even if you are aiming to produce an 'improvised' sounding show, you must have a script. Students' productions which are scrambled together at the last minute or at the moment of the recording are generally abysmal. Your script will show the shape and structure of your programme, and the presenter's, interviewer's or actor's words. It is just as important to script an 'improvised' sounding piece as to script a drama. Lack of preparation and rehearsal is a recipe for disaster in improvised pieces and will lose you marks.

If you are using interviews you obviously can only script your questions in advance but you need to know how long you want each interview to take. This example of a script from presenter Paul Lewis for BBC Radio 4's *Moneybox* programme on 16 September 2001 shows you how professional broadcasters write scripts with interwoven interviews.

Presenter: Paul Lewis

ATTACK   **Duration: 1'09'**

Hello and welcome to a rather different programme. The awful human cost of the terrorist attacks on New York and Washington becomes clearer by the day, and the more news we get the more we know of the horrors of those thousands of individual human tragedies.

We'll be talking to economists, market experts and investment specialists. But first with me is Peter Day senior BBC Business Correspondent, who has been broadcasting for more than 20 years and is presenter of *In Business* on Radio 4.

Peter – you have done many of your interviews in the iconic building that is now a pile of rubble – what does its loss mean?

You have travelled the world looking at the global view of business and the economy – was this a world-changing event?

Will it affect video conferencing? Change the way we work in large groups in vulnerable sites?

Peter Day BBC Business correspondent thank you.

(Source: *Moneybox*, 16 September 2001, BBC Radio 4)

 **ctivity** 4.5

Building a character
- Base a character on someone you know a little.
- Write down the following details: age, gender, education, background, occupation, parents' occupations, hobbies, tastes in music, cars, reading, sport, food, drink, holidays.
- Think of a catch phrase for that character.
- Write a monologue for your character beginning 'As the alarm went off ....' Include your character's catch phrase.
- Now pair up with someone else in your group. Read your monologue to them. Devise a situation where the two characters meet and script that scene together.

Scripting radio drama

There are many exercises that you can use to help you develop characters for radio drama. One example is given below, but you will find more useful advice in Robert McLeish's *Radio Production* (Focal Press, 1997) and in Peter Lewis's *Radio Drama* (Longman, 1981).

Be prepared to change your script, including new ideas and rejecting others. Have a read-through with presenters and actors and change anything that does not sound convincing.

Try to vary the pace and rhythm of your script, but remember that a **beat** refers to a brief pause of $\frac{1}{2}$ second, a **pause** is a maximum of 5 seconds and a **silence** (very rare) a maximum of 10 seconds. Practise your script, varying the beats and pauses.

Sample of a script for a radio drama:

BEANS MEANS FINES

INT. SMALL, QUIET SUPERMARKET IN THE 1970s. LATE AFTERNOON.

FX: MUZAK PLAYING. RUSTLE OF PAPER AND CLICK OF TILL

1. JACK: (SIGHING) 10 more minutes to go, Stan.
2. STAN: (APP) You going out somewhere tonight?
3. JACK: No such luck.
4. STAN: Have a look in the paper, see what's on the box.

FX: (RUSTLE OF NEWSPAPER)

5. JACK: Huh, not much. (READS) Hey, fantastic! The Sweeney! 'Supermarket Strike. Detective Inspector John Regan and Detective Sergeant George Carter find themselves in a supermarket dealing with an absent-minded shoplifter. (BEAT) Cor, I wish Carter would find himself in here, I'd soon smooth his ruffled brow and stop that Regan shouting at him.
6. STAN: Nothing like that ever happens here, love. Come to think of it, nothing ever happens.

FX: SUDDEN CRASH AS PYRAMID OF TINS COLLAPSES IN NEXT AISLE (MID DISTANCE)

7. STAN: What was that?

(Source: *Beans Means Fines*, Canterbury Christ Church University College, Kent)

Variety

Your radio programme will be much more successful if it includes a variety of voices, music, background sound, sound FX and different segment lengths. The variety of voices will provide the illusion of depth. Remember also that if people don't speak on radio they cease to exist for the audience who have to *hear* that they are there.

Presenters and actors

There are no marks available for your ability to present a programme well or for your acting, but these skills are essential for a successful radio programme. Therefore you should cast actors and presenters with a good variety of voices and who will take the production seriously.

5.2 AUDIO PRODUCTION

Test all your equipment carefully before you begin. Check sound levels using your **VU** (volume unit) meter or **LED** (light emitting diode) meter. If you are using a sound mixer the level of the output may be measured by a **PPM** (peak programme meter). Do not let the sound levels move into the red band or your sound will be distorted. Try also to ensure that you do not have sudden dips and peaks in sound levels.

If you do not have a recording studio, make sure that the acoustics of the room you are going to use are as good as possible. Avoid rooms where there is an echo, or traffic noise, and times when bells may go off, or other students may be making a noise during a recording.

Listen to your recording before finishing the session to check whether you need to re-record any sections.

Sound FX

Creating sound FX is great fun, but don't overdo them (unless you are deliberately doing so to parody the conventions and add humour to your programme). The FX act as aural clues for the audience. Don't make the mistake of thinking that your audience needs guidance on everything that takes place in your programme. It is better to make a situation clear in the dialogue so that the audience believes it is happening. For example, crunching cornflakes in a biscuit tin doesn't sound exactly like someone walking up a gravel path, but this technique will convince the audience if you back it up with the dialogue.

If you are working in radio drama, you will also need some ambient sound, such as traffic or birdsong. All of these are available on BBC sound FX tapes, but it is even better if you create your own (if you have time). You may record your FX at the time of the recording – these are called spot FX, or add them later in post-production.

Music radio show

If you choose this option, think about how many presenters you want, and whether you want interaction from other members in the studio (like most popular breakfast shows). Do you want to include interviews? If so, always chat to the interviewee to warm up. If you want to include phone-in competitions make sure that you have the equipment to record the phone-in voice convincingly.

Radio drama

The position of the mic in relation to the actors is crucial. The audience's understanding of the characters, the scene and their point of view is established by the distance of the actors from the mic. The actors make it clear through dialogue and through moving that they are moving position, leaving or entering the scene. The actors need to move slowly, walking back to give the illusion of distance and speaking more loudly as they move away. If they can move closer to the mic, speaking more quietly, they will create an impression of intimacy for the audience.

Picture 4.9 Students editing a radio drama. Students Rob Feasey and Sarah Stevenson edit their radio drama, *Wall to Wall*.

Music

If you are using music for any radio programme, think of it as a framing device, like the frame of a picture. It is important that the frame should match the picture inside – the verbal content and mode of address of your programme; otherwise it will sound unconvincing and inappropriate. The music will also be very important in establishing the mood and the pace of your programme.

5.3 AUDIO POST-PRODUCTION

Reel-to-reel editing

This is a great way to learn about sound editing. Make sure that you practise on some material you are not planning to include before you start on your own production.

First you will transfer all your material onto a ¼-inch reel-to-reel tape recorder. Wind your tape slowly backwards and forwards until you find the precise section that you want to cut out and mark it with a chinagraph (yellow or white) pencil.

Then cut the tape by placing it on a block and splicing it with a scalpel or razor blade. You stick the remaining sections of the tape back together with ¼-inch splicing tape. About 7½ inches of tape will carry two or three words, so you can be quite precise with this method and cut out any mistakes, stutters or awkward pauses which you want to eliminate. Finally, you transfer your edited tape onto a master tape.

The sound mixer

The sound mixer will allow you to balance a number of different inputs, such as a microphone, a CD player or a DAT player. You can then mix these different inputs together, adjusting the levels to your satisfaction and record the final result onto an audio cassette tape, MiniDisc or DAT.

Digital audio editing on computer

It is important to practise using some material you have recorded for this purpose first. Familiarize yourself with the editing programme, which works in a similar way to digital video editing. You will be able to input your recording onto a number of different tracks (for dialogue, FX, music) and then mix them together as you want, adjusting levels.

In the same way as digital video editing, you will be asked to name your clips and you will create an **EDL** (edit display list). You will also see your clips represented as sound waves, which will help you to control sound levels and the rhythm of your editing.

You will be able to fade up and down where you want and mix in music at any point. If you do make a mistake you can easily change what you have done and re-edit. When you are happy with your edit, you will output it to an audio cassette, MiniDisc or DAT.

Part 6: ICT-based production

This area includes computer games and websites.

You will be expected to demonstrate the following skills:

☐ the ability to research and plan for your production
☐ combining images, text, sound and video appropriately
☐ using ICT effectively for the combination of such material
☐ producing material so that it communicates clearly to its target audience
☐ analysing and evaluating your own production.

A typical task set by the awarding bodies is to construct a homepage and a number of supplementary pages from a new entertainment webzine. For simplicity, we have concentrated on that task in our advice to you, but the advice can easily be applied to other ICT-based tasks.

EQUIPMENT

You will need:

☐ a computer
☐ access to the Internet
☐ a colour printer
☐ digital stills camera or scanner and 35 mm stills camera
☐ portable storage medium, such as floppy disk or CD for sending to moderator
☐ software for designing a website (optional).

6.1 ICT PRE-PRODUCTION PLANNING

Research the conventions

This brief is probably best tackled working as an individual or with one other student.

☐ Research as many other entertainment websites as you can, noting the conventions they use.
☐ Notice how easy or difficult the interfaces are to navigate.

Target audience

Your target audience is likely to be computer literate and often spend periods of time on the internet.

Devise a questionnaire for members of your target audience, asking them which sites they visit on a regular basis and whether they are most attracted by the content, layout or visual style of those sites. This will help you to identify how you will appeal to your specific target audience.

Think also about how you can draw attention to your website through other sites' hyperlinks, advertisements and search engines.

Subject matter

Research your subject matter thoroughly. If you are writing reviews of films, for example, use other film magazines such as *Empire* (www.empireonline.co.uk) and the *Internet Movie Database* (www.imdb.com) for background information which will make your reviews more professional and polished.

Hyperlinks

Hyperlinks are an integral part of your website as they are a fundamental aspect of the **interconnectivity** (the way that one piece of information on one site can lead you to many other pieces of information on other sites) of the internet. Use the information from your research into your target audience to decide which other sites will interest them and will be useful as hyperlinks.

Mode of address

Think about the language that you will use for your written text, the overall visual style of your pages and any audio material that you will use. All of these combine to construct your mode of address. (The section on print production will also be helpful to you.)

Colour

One of the ways of establishing a brand identity for your website is to choose a colour scheme which will give consistency. The pages will then be immediately recognizable to your target audience as belonging to the same site, just as a magazine maintains its consistency of style throughout. Think about the connotations of your colour scheme: red combined with black may look quite forceful and aggressive, while light blue and white seem more subdued and formal.

Produce a mock-up

Try producing some mock-ups of your pages on blank sheets of paper so that you get a clear idea of the overall look.

Either discuss your mock-up with the other members of the group or with members of your target audience. If necessary, adjust your plans and redesign the pages. Then produce a more detailed mock-up in colour. Make your decisions on fonts and colours at this stage.

Picture 4.10   A student works on research for the homepage of his website.

6.2 ICT-BASED PRODUCTION

There are various programs that will help you to produce your website. However, if you are experienced in computer techniques all that is necessary to produce a simple website is a text editor program, such as Notepad in Windows. You will need a basic knowledge of HTML (hypertext markup language the simple computer language in which most websites are written).

You may find it easier to use a webpage editor that allows you to see immediately what the output will be. This gives you immediate feedback and requires less technical knowledge.

Constructing the pages

- ☐ Write the articles and the written text for the other pages. Keep redrafting the written text and reorganizing the layout. Look at other similar websites until your pieces are the right length and consistent in their mode of address.
- ☐ Decide whether you will place your navigation bar down the left hand side of the page (the usual convention) and whether you will use accompanying images to illustrate the links.
- ☐ Make sure that your homepage is appropriate for your target audience as this is usually the first page they will see.
- ☐ Show your website to members of your target audience and your teacher for feedback before you finish. This will help you to produce a website of which you are proud.

Images

One of the possible pitfalls of using this brief is the overuse of found images (images which you have found from existing sources such as the internet). The best way of avoiding this is to take your own original photographs. As with the print production work, you could use actors to represent famous actors or stars.

Either scan photographs into the computer or upload photographs from a digital camera. JPEGs (compressed graphics files which can contain up to 16 million colours and are therefore suitable for photographic images) are probably the best format for photographic images.

If you are using found images, you must make sure that you manipulate them by cropping them or using them in the form of a collage (a collection of images which have been reassembled to construct a different meaning from the original one). Make sure that you have access to one of the image manipulation programs such as Adobe Photoshop. Otherwise it is best to use your own images as far as possible.

6.3 ICT-BASED POST-PRODUCTION

Publishing your website

The first step in publishing your website is to gain access to some web-space (the hard disk space on a computer that is always connected to the internet). This will allow 24-hour access to your site, so that you do not have to be connected for your target audience to visit your site.

There are several ways of gaining access to some webspace. Your ISP (internet service provider, such as Demon or Freeserve) may offer you some webspace as a part of your contract or you may have to purchase it from a separate service operator. Many big companies and all universities have their own servers which are always connected.

You then upload all your files that are part of your website, including graphics, audio, images and the essential HTML source code, to that web-

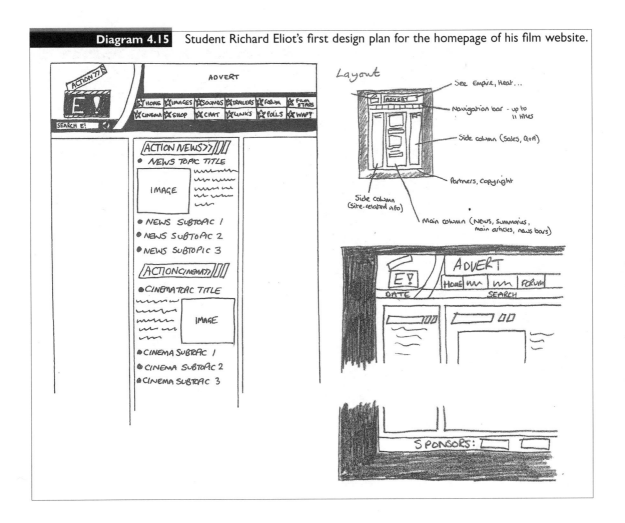

Diagram 4.15 Student Richard Eliot's first design plan for the homepage of his film website.

space. Depending on where your webspace is located, your website will be assigned a URL (universal resource locator – the address which can indicate the position of a file on a webserver anywhere in the world).

For instance, if you chose to name your site Fred Flintstone and Demon were hosting your site, your URL might be: http://www.fredflintstone.demon.co.uk/

You have already thought about the genre or category of your website as part of your Media Studies work. If you would like your website to appear in the databases of a **search directory** (a search facility which will give your potential audience brief information about your site), you need to identify the most relevant category for your website and apply to have yours included.

Other ways of publicizing your website include banner advertisements on other sites, offering to display hyperlinks to others' pages if they display hyperlinks to yours and, finally, word of mouth.

Examiners' tips

Final reminders
- In all practical production work, your success will depend on the preparation in the pre-production stage.
- Throughout the process, keep looking at actual media texts so that you can compare your work against them and check that you are showing an awareness of the conventions.
- Keep a record of all stages of the working process.

- See the links between your practical production work and the media concepts and theories that you have come across in the rest of the course. This will help you to reflect on and evaluate your work with insight and intelligence in your commentary.
- If you take this advice, and have a clear knowledge of your awarding body's requirements, you should get you the marks you are hoping for.

CHAPTER 5

Improving your study skills

Introduction

FADE IN:
INT. EXAM ROOM – DAY

CU on blank page. Camera tracks backward to reveal STUDENT, with head in hands, sobbing quietly.

    CUT TO:

Wide shot of exam room. Everyone is writing furiously, except STUDENT.

    CUT TO:

Mid shot of TEACHER, holding a stopwatch

TEACHER: Put your pens down everybody; that's the end of your exam.
FADE OUT

If that sounds like a familiar scenario, this chapter is designed to help you to increase your confidence in your approach to preparing for assessment. Although Media Studies is one of the most innovative subjects in the curriculum, if you want to be successful, it does demand some more traditional study skills.

This chapter will look at some of the key study skills that you will need:

- ☐ note-making
- ☐ research
- ☐ essay writing
- ☐ revision.

Media Studies has particular demands and skills, which are different to other disciplines, for example, many exams now ask you to analyse a print or moving image text that is unseen. Nevertheless, you will also find that the general study skills will help you with all of your studies.

Note-making

Media Studies is a dynamic subject and to ensure that students remain interested and engaged in the work, tutors constantly change and update the materials and texts upon which you will focus. Textbooks, like this one, are an essential part of learning the skills and concepts which are important to the subject; however, no textbook can provide a complete range of up-to-date examples for students to use year after year.

Therefore much of your learning will be dependent on the work you do in class, with your tutor, with fellow students and on your own, from a wide variety of sources from the internet to books and journals. To get the most out of this kind of work, it is important that you develop effective note-making skills as soon as possible.

Remember that the notes that you make will form the basis of your preparation and revision for examination. In some cases, there may be a gap of 1 or 2 years between the time that you make the notes and the time that you sit the exam. So it is vital that your approach to note-making is one that will enable you to remember why you took the notes in the first place.

IN GENERAL

Let us look at some of the general points about note-making before moving on to specific methods.

When you are making notes for any activity:

- [ ] do **not** write in full sentences
- [ ] pick out **key words** and **phrases** wherever possible
- [ ] use **abbreviations** and a **shorthand form** which you will understand later
- [ ] use **clear headings** and **subheadings**
- [ ] use **numbers** and **letters** to list ideas in order or for priority
- [ ] use **bullet points** to list ideas of equal importance
- [ ] **highlight** or **underline** key points
- [ ] use **colour** to pick out important ideas or to link together related or similar information
- [ ] **date** and **number pages** to make it easy to understand them later.

Make sure that you understand why you are making notes at any particular time, since this will affect how you take them. Of course, sometimes you will be making notes for more than one purpose ('I need these notes to write an essay for class, but I will also need these to revise from later'), so be aware that they will have to satisfy more than a single task.

One key function of your notes is that they should be easily recalled or remembered. Clarity and organization are central to achieving this.

Picture 5.1   Making effective class notes is crucial.

Your notes will obviously contain lots and lots of information. In order to ensure that this information is given a context and will be useful later on, you should try to give your notes a clear structure. Ideas and arguments should be built into your notes as much as possible so that the information you have makes sense in terms of the topic you are covering and the reason you are covering it. Having structured notes will also help when it comes to planning your essays and revising.

LINEAR NOTES

The most common form of note-making, although not the only (and not necessarily the best for you), is linear note-making. Linear notes are generally hand-written on lined paper.

The aim of linear notes is not to fill up as much of the page as possible. You are not writing an essay yet. Don't write on the full length of the line and don't write on every line. Aim to leave a lot of white space on the page.

You should get into the habit of leaving a margin on the right, in case you want to add extra points later. You should also get into the habit of writing on every other line; again, this will allow you to make later additions or alterations. Write important ideas on the left-hand side of the page and the details on the right.

Make sure that the headings you use help you to remember the information. Highlight or underline them so that their importance is clear. Use sub-headings and sub-points to give more detail to the main topics. Number or letter these if they need to be prioritized. This will help you when you come to revise. If possible, use non-written signals to clarify your notes – colour, arrows, diagrams – but do not overcrowd or complicate the page.

Diagram 5.1   Linear notes are useful to record key points or facts.

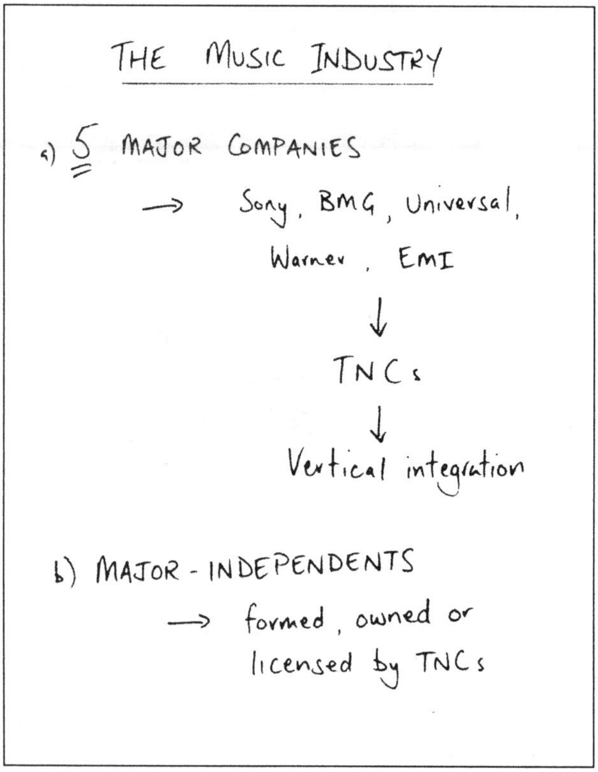

OTHER WAYS OF NOTE-MAKING: MIND MAPS

Activity 5.1

- Look at the section on pp. 113–114 about the Hillsborough documentary and *The Sun*.
- Try to summarize the main ideas and important points in both linear notes and mind maps.
- Which is the easiest method for you to use?
- Which set of notes will be the easiest for you to remember?
- Could you combine elements of both methods.

If you find it difficult to take notes in a linear style or, more importantly, if you find it difficult to understand or remember these notes when you go back to them at a later date, you need to consider other ways of note-making. Another very effective form of note-making is the **mind map**.

In mind mapping, we ignore the lines on the page and put down information as a diagram, in which the important parts are linked to one another graphically, through arrows or colours. Main topics and headings tend to be placed in the middle of the page, and the detail, subheads and sub-points spiral outwards from the central ideas.

The beauty of mind maps is their individuality. There is no set format – you should choose a method and a pattern that works for you. Make full use of visual signals in order to link related ideas and to create some sort of structure for the information you have gathered.

Try to develop your own methods of ensuring that the context of a topic remains obvious:

☐ use colours to indicate argument and counter-argument
☐ use the left side for dominant viewpoints and right side for challenges
☐ use different size arrows to demonstrate the progression of a set of ideas
☐ use diagrams to set out major and minor areas of interest
☐ write out key quotes, facts or statistics and their source (writer, title, publisher, date) at the time of finding them, as it might be difficult to remember where you found them later.

Diagram 5.2   The main forms of media communication.

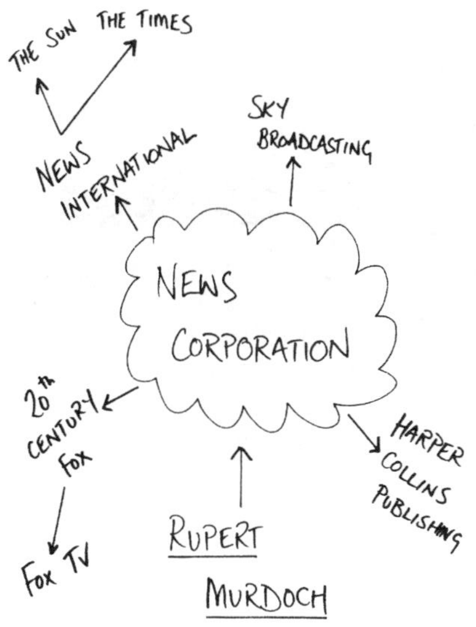

Making notes from moving image media texts

The key to making good notes is, as always, to be aware of **why** you are taking them. There are many different reasons for the use of film or television material in class, including unseen examinations, and you need to be clear what is expected of you:

- ☐ the sequence may contain relevant information about a particular topic, e.g. a documentary or a discussion programme
- ☐ you may be asked to examine the style and form of a particular sequence, e.g. to illustrate a discussion on genre
- ☐ you may be asked to concentrate on a particular element of construction, e.g. lighting or montage, in order to prepare for your own production work
- ☐ the sequence may be used to illustrate some aspect of representation.

If it is possible, watch the video a number of times. Before you start, examine the question you are going to answer and identify any key words which point to the elements that you need to focus on.

Do not write anything on the first viewing. Watch and listen to the sequence **in detail** and prepare yourself for the note-making.

On each successive viewing, try to concentrate on different elements at a time. Remember what it is you are looking for. Do not write in full sentences. Use key points and key words. Use abbreviations and short-hand wherever possible (e.g. CU = close up, LS = long shot).

When you watch the video for a final time, tick off the key points you have already made and add any relevant detail. Take some time after the screening to check your notes and make additions or alterations while the sequence is still fresh in your mind.

Note-making from video is not an easy task. The more practice you get, the better you will become at it.

Examiners' tips

- Divide your note-making pages into subheadings for each aspect you are focusing on (as required by the examination or essay question), then it is easier not to miss anything out.
- There's no excuse for not practising these skills at home; record a television programme or use a film on video/DVD for practice.

Activity 5.2

- Look at the opening sequence of any film or television programme on video/DVD.
- Using categories such as *mise-en-scène*, editing, soundtrack, narrative and character, try to analyse how the sequence has been constructed for its audience.
- What kind of shorthand or abbreviation can you use to make this process easier?

Essay writing

ANALYSE THE QUESTION

To produce a good essay you need to be aware of your audience and their expectations. In most cases, the essays you write will be read by your tutor, who knows you, or an examiner, who doesn't. In either case, you need to make sure that you know exactly what they want from the question.

Look carefully at the essay title you have been set and immediately underline the **key words**. Take these titles as examples:

Q: ***Discuss*** *the view that **mediocre films** were all that were produced by the **Hollywood Studio System** during its so-called Golden Period.*

Q: ***Evaluate*** *the effectiveness of the **laws and codes of practice** which have been set up to control **the press** in this country.*

Q: ***How important*** *is the process of **convergence** for **new media industries?***

Activity 5.3

- Ask your tutor for some past papers and identify the relevant questions from the areas you have studied.
- Analyse the questions by highlighting the key words and terms.
- Are there any patterns in the way in which the questions are asked?
- What can you learn to help you with your revision?

(1) In each case, the question begins with a **directing** term, which should indicate the approach that needs to be taken in each question. **'Discuss'** indicates that both sides of an argument need to be considered in the essay. **'Evaluate'** suggests that a view has to be discussed and judged as right or wrong, good or bad. **'How important'** questions demand that you develop an argument which judges the extent of a situation. You may come to a conclusion which suggests 'very important' or 'not very important'

(2) The last key word of each of these questions gives you the topic area in which you need to focus – the Studio System, the British Press and New Media Technology. However, you are not expected simply to write everything that you know about each of these topics.

(3) The third key term helps you to focus on a particular area, debate or feature of the whole topic. In the first case, this is the quality of films emerging from Hollywood during this time. In the second, it is the codes of practice of the press which have to be considered. In the final example, you are expected to focus upon convergence as a key element of new technologies.

The questions you are set might not always be as clear cut as the above examples, nor will the key terms always be ordered as above. Nevertheless, you should be able to gather sufficient information from the question to ensure that you know exactly what to write.

PLANNING THE ESSAY

Activity 5.4

- Choose a media-related topic for discussion or debate, for example the effect of violent films on their audiences, the intrusion of privacy by tabloid journalists.
- Using this structure, outline the main points you might make if you were asked to write an essay on the topic.
- Compare your plan to that of a partner.
- What differences and similarities are there in your approaches?
- Which do you think would make the better essay and why?

The most important work to be done for any essay occurs **before** you start writing. This is true whether or not you are working under timed conditions. Once you have effectively analysed the question, you must begin to **plan** your response.

Planning involves deciding:

☐ What points you are going to make
☐ What order you are going to make them in.

Use your notes or revision materials to decide what information is going to be relevant for the essay. Do not be afraid to leave out information which is not relevant, even if you have spent a long time collating it. *Remember to look for the key words in the question.* Throughout the planning process, make sure that you refer back to the question to see that you are answering it relevantly.

Read back over your plan to make sure that:

☐ your points answer the question
☐ your argument moves logically from one stage to the next
☐ you have included examples to illustrate general ideas.

Diagram 5.3 shows an example of a generalized essay plan. It is not the only way to structure your answer, but it may give you some idea of how to start planning.

Diagram 5.4 shows a suggested strategy for preparing answers to exam questions, either from past papers or ones you have written yourself.

Diagram 5.3 One example of a general essay plan.

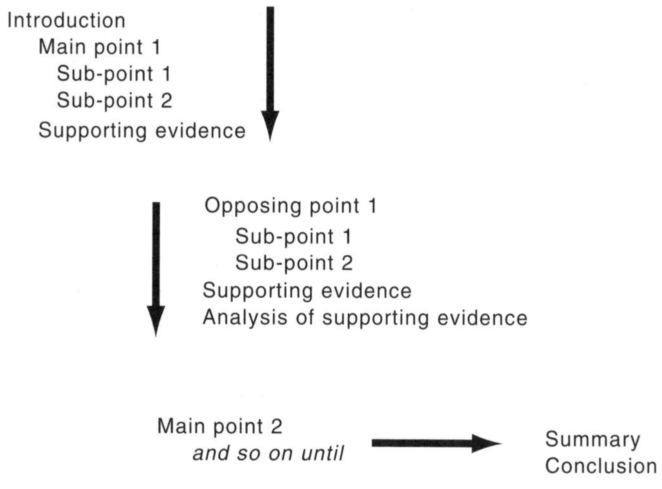

Introduction
Main point 1
Sub-point 1
Sub-point 2
Supporting evidence

Opposing point 1
Sub-point 1
Sub-point 2
Supporting evidence
Analysis of supporting evidence

Main point 2
and so on until ⟶ Summary
Conclusion

Diagram 5.4   One useful strategy for preparing to answer exam questions.

Exam Answer Strategy – REVISION AID GRID

Fill in the exam question title you are revising and complete your revision notes under each section below – you will probably need to use one sheet of A4 per question, but copy the grid format. Use this grid to practice your exam answer strategy

How exams are marked
- By the degree to which you answer the question set and the level of knowledge, understanding and analysis you demonstrate
- By the official exam board mark scheme criteria
- By quality of language (spelling, grammar, punctuation and presentation)
- By reference to detailed examples.

EXAM QUESTION –	SHORTCUT ANSWER –	TEXTS –	POINTS –	EXAMPLES/EVIDENCE –
• Identify the key words and phrases that show you what is required; re-phrase it, to show you understand the question. • Address the question at the start of your answer – no 'waffly' introduction' – and keep addressing it through answer; this shows the examiner you are on task. • Never set your own agenda or offer a pre-prepared answer to a past question.	• What is the essential answer to the question or central debate which will form the basis of your answers? The 'shortcut' answer, in other words. • This shows you how to target your answer and the purpose of your argument.	• Which media texts/products have you studied in depth for your answers? • These are where your examples will come from. • Watch/read them AGAIN! • Know them in detail – key personnel names, key ideas, key facts/dates, etc.	• What are the main points (and sub-points) which make up your answer? • Each point should form the basis of a stage of your argument, either supporting, contradicting or debating the question. • Each point/sub-point should be in a separate paragraph.	• You must have an example as evidence to back up each point you make, such as a reference to a industry, products/process, programme/program, news story, article, scene/sequence from a film or TV programme, or aspect of a text, such as its theme, narrative etc. • Use them liberally throughout the answer – it will get you marks for each relevant one!
Your answers here	*Your answers here*	*Your answers here*	*Your answers here*	*Your answers here*

Research and reading

Activity 5.5

With a partner, draw up a list of research tasks which might be undertaken for any research project.
See if you can decide which would constitute **primary** and which would constitute **secondary** research.
What are the advantages and disadvantages of each type of research? Which would you prefer to use and why?

At some point during your course it is going to be necessary to carry out some sort of research independently. This may be to help with a presentation or to carry out a more formal activity such as an extended essay, a production log, evaluation or for a research-based exam.

Generally, the research you can carry out falls into two categories: **primary** and **secondary** research.

Primary research involves direct contact with the text or topic that you are studying. This might mean viewing or listening to the text and other related products, or interviewing those involved in the construction and selling of media artefacts. Primary research might also include talking to members of the audience about their consumption of media texts.

Secondary research involves looking at research and writing which has already been carried out by others to see how it can support and extend your own arguments. Generally, this involves reading and researching from academic and industry books, papers and the internet.

The best research tasks tend to offer a mixture of both primary and secondary research, although secondary research is obviously easier to locate and carry out.

Picture 5.2   Thorough research will boost your knowledge and self-confidence.

PRIMARY RESEARCH

Once again, the most important element of primary research is to understand why you are doing it, because this should guide the sort of information which you are gathering.

Research from other media texts

Primary research using other media texts must be carried out in a systematic fashion. Have your research topic written down in front of you. This is most usefully phrased in the form of a question. Keep this topic in your thoughts throughout the task.

Always write down the **source** of your research (in the case of a film, title, date, director, country of origin) and the names of the relevant creative personnel and date your notes.

Research from interviews

When you are interviewing people on a one-to-one basis, it is essential that you have prepared effectively to encourage the interviewee to talk about the relevant topics and to record what is said:

☐ prepare questions in advance, based on the task you have been set
☐ order questions, so that the interview proceeds logically from one point to another
☐ begin with general questions, then move on to specific enquiries.

Allow your interviewee to speak as freely as he or she wishes and listen to the answers that they give. They may raise an issue which you have not yet considered, but which you would like to pursue, and you should be flexible enough to introduce new questions into your plans.

Audience research

Audience research can be **quantitative** or **qualitative**.

Quantitative research involves collecting data on the statistical behaviour of audiences; looking at issues such as how many people consume particular media, how long they spend consuming it, how much of a share of the whole market a product has and so on.

This kind of research is very difficult for the individual to carry out and has very little meaning when the numbers of people questioned are small. In any case, quantitative research from professional organizations (such as BARB and ABC) is readily available in print and on the internet.

Activity 5.6

- Choose your favourite television programme or magazine and use BARB or ABC to find out as much as possible about its audience and those of its competitors.
- What kinds of conclusions can be drawn from this information?
- How do you think institutions use quantitative research?

Activity 5.7

- Choose an area of debate or discussion which interests you and draw up five questions from which you can get responses from the rest of your class or group.
- Which questions are the most successful in generating useful information and why?
- Why did other questions not work so well?

Qualitative research looks at the reasons why audiences consume particular media and the kinds of meanings and pleasures which they take from the media. It is more easily carried out, particularly where you are focussing upon particular types of audience, defined by social categories (gender, age, ethnicity, etc.) or by specific interests (music fans, football players, role play enthusiasts, etc).

Good research will again be generated by good preparation. Questionnaires are a common source of data in this scenario, but they are only useful if they have been well-designed with the needs of the research project in mind. When you are drawing up a questionnaire, try to keep the following guidelines in mind:

☐ Always think about the research task while you are drawing your questions up.

☐ Keep the design of the questionnaire simple to follow, but vary the kinds of questions which are asked.

☐ Questions which demand Yes/No responses are used to define tendencies in group behaviour and to make general points about an audience's media usage.

☐ Questions which demand a free response (i.e. the interviewee can write a few sentences) are used to elicit personal responses, which can act as examples or illustrations of general points.

If you can, carry out a trial of your questionnaire with a small group, to see if there are any potential problems either with interviewees understanding the requirements or with the kind of information which is being returned.

SECONDARY RESEARCH

Undertaking secondary research will probably involve you in making a large number of notes, so it is vital that you remain well organized and focused on why you are undertaking this research.

It is a good idea to keep a research file, separate from your class or lecture notes. Initially, all of the information which you gather can go into the file, though you should regularly 'spring clean' your research. This involves organising material into relevant categories, removing material which is duplicated or no longer needed and ensuring that you have covered all of the areas of research which are necessary.

Remember that the information you gather needs to be treated with a degree of scepticism:

☐ do not assume it is a fact, simply because it is in print

☐ be aware of alternative points of views and arguments from other sources

☐ note who has written the information. Do they have an agenda or vested interest? Are they trying to persuade you?

☐ note when the information was written. Is it out of date? Has newer information become available?

Examiners' tips

If you are using primary or secondary research in your answers, bear in mind the following advice:

- Research findings are rarely sufficient in their own right. They should be used to support an argument that you are building or to provide an alternative argument that you wish to consider.
- Don't waste time in exams listing lots of data from your research, much of which will probably be irrelevant. Try to identify the most important elements from your research and use this to illustrate general tendencies.
- Try to be analytical about your research. Demonstrate its strong points and be prepared to acknowledge weaknesses. The ability to analyse these areas is often more important than the findings of the research.
- Always give the sources secondary research and don't try to pass off somebody else's work as your own. It is likely that an examiner will be able to spot someone else's 'voice' in your answer.

You may well have to provide **references** and a **bibliography** while writing up your research. **References** are used to indicate the sources of information in your writing and are normally presented as footnotes, at the bottom of the page, or at the end of a section or chapter. A **bibliography** is a list of the sources used in research, whether directly quoted from or not, and it is usually found at the end of an essay. The information on the back of your cards can be used to provide both of these elements.

Revision

Unfortunately, the time is going to come when the pleasure of studying the media gives way to the necessary task of taking your exams. The pressure and anxiety which this transition can cause, however, can be greatly relieved by some effective preparation and revision.

Revision is most successful when it is carries out in an active way. Very few people are able to learn productively simply by reading and rereading notes and books. More often than, this process becomes automated so that you go end up going through the motions of reading without really taking any information in.

Most experts believe that the memory works best when it is stimulated by more than one sense. In fact the more senses that can be devoted to the act of remembering, the more you are likely to be able to revise. The following techniques are suggestions for revision which attempt to create active processes. You do not have to use them all, but choose two or three which you think will help you. A varied approach to revision is a good thing.

BE PREPARED

The last thing that you want when you take your first look at an exam paper is to be surprised. Gather as much information as you can about the exam, the type of questions, what the examiner wants from you and the best way to deliver this well in advance of the exam session.

Your tutor will help you out with this as much as they can. You can also help yourself by getting hold of relevant materials such as past papers, mark schemes for those papers or examiners' reports on the past exams. If your teacher is not able to supply you with copies of these, you might try contacting your exam board or going to their website, from where this kind of material can often be downloaded.

Using this information, work out your strategy for each paper you sit.

- [ ] How long is the paper?
- [ ] How many marks are awarded for each question?
- [ ] Are there predictable patterns in the kinds of questions which are asked?
- [ ] Which areas tend to be focused upon?
- [ ] Are there any topics that you will not need to revise?

Picture 5.3　Don't be clueless – revise well in advance to prevent last minute nerves.

STUDENT AS EXAMINER

Use the mark schemes to put yourself into the position of the examiner. Using these you will be able to see precisely what each question is demanding and the ways in which candidates are expected to approach the tasks. Use the mark scheme to remark some of your old essays. What mark would you give yourself based on what you have written? How could you improve the essays to gain higher marks?

Examiners' reports are written by the examiners of each paper you sit and are sent to schools and colleges by the awarding bodies. They are useful for picking up general hints and advice about approaching the exam and hopefully your tutor will share some of the advice in them with you, as they are at liberty to use them with students.

The reports tend to emphasize the importance of good technique – answering the question directly, using specific examples to illustrate your answers, allocating your time sensibly, writing legibly in the exam and so on – and you should be able to pick up good practice through these.

ORGANIZE

When you are sure you know what material will be required for your exam, sort through your notes. Discard the notes you are certain you won't use and sort the rest so that they are organized for each exam. Where necessary rewrite your notes and where you think there may be gaps in your information, try to fill these through research from textbooks or friends' notes.

Try to learn information as part of a wider argument, as this will give you a structure and a way of preparing for essays quickly under timed conditions. Draw up practice essay plans and learn the different combinations that a question might demand.

After you have organized and re-written your notes on the key topics you are studying, it might help to reduce these longer notes to prompt revision cards (using index cards or similar). These can then be flicked through in the final days before the exam or for short bursts of revision.

VISUALIZE

Although Media Studies involves much less 'parrot-fashion' learning than many other subjects, there are still occasions when you will need to learn lists of names, concepts, ideas or other facts. You will find this process much easier if you can link these facts with particular visual patterns or images.

Most media students tend to have very good visual imaginations and this can be used to your advantage. Linking facts or names to specific mental images can make those elements much easier to recall. The names of the major studios in the Hollywood studio system, for instance, can easily be linked to appropriate imagery:

☐ MGM – a lion (studio logo)
☐ Paramount – a mountain (studio logo)
☐ Twentieth Century Fox – a fox
☐ Warner Brothers – a rabbit (Bugs Bunny, studio character)
☐ RKO – a monkey (King Kong, studio character).

Hopefully, the mental picture of the gathering of these four animals on a mountain will act as the trigger for the recall of the studios.

By using your imagination to place the images into familiar surroundings, it can also help you to remember them in order or priority. Think about sitting in your bedroom and looking from the left of the room to the right. Now pick out five significant objects in your room which are always in the same location. If you can link the imagery you have chosen for the studios to each of those objects, you should now be able to remember them in a particular order.

For example, if you wanted to learn the studios in order of respective size, picture a lion sitting on your bed, a mountain in the background of a family photo, a fox coming out of a wardrobe, a rabbit playing with the alarm clock and a monkey climbing over a chest of drawers.

MNEMONICS

A mnemonic is another shorthand way of remembering key facts or points. It prompts you to remember by the use of the first letter of a series of words to form a memorable word or a nonsense phrase which will prompt more detailed information.

For example in advertising, the acronym **AIDA** (the name of an opera by Guiseppe Verdi, incidentally) is used as a way of remembering the important aim of any advert:

☐ **A**ttention – the target should notice the advert
☐ **I**nterest – the advert should create interest in the product
☐ **D**esire – the target should desire the product
☐ **A**ction – the target will be prompted to buy the product.

BE ARTISTIC

Just as with the mind maps we discussed earlier, turning linear notes into diagrams, patterns or pictures can make them much easier to learn and remember. Create A3 or A2 posters based on different aspects of your notes. The more colourful and image based these can be the more that you are likely to recall. Display the posters around your bedroom in the weeks before the exam and test yourself on the contents regularly.

PLAN AHEAD – FIGHT NOT FLIGHT!

The day of your exam will come, ready or not, and the knowledge of such dates brings out either our primal flight or fight mechanism. Which one is it to be?

- ☐ Draw up a revision timetable; make a wall planner and put it in front of you where you work.
- ☐ Cross out any holidays and special days that you clearly won't spend on revision and work out how many days per subject you can devote to revision.
- ☐ Set realistic targets for how much you can do each day and try to cover the different areas of the course systematically.
- ☐ Spend more time working on those topic areas in which you feel uncertain or confused.
- ☐ Try to vary your revision, using different types of exercise each day.
- ☐ It is very important that you write some practice essays under timed conditions, so that you can see how much material you are able to include in your answers.

Examiners' tips

In the exam

- Write as neatly as possible in the exam. Your own tutor might be used to your style and might be used to trying to decipher your work. However, whether you like it or not, to an examiner, you are just a name and a number, so what you write is the only evidence of what you know.
- So, if it can't be read, it won't get a mark. Develop a style that is quick to write and legible.
- Don't make a mess of your answer paper with lots of crossings out and doodles, it suggests that you have little interest in, or respect for, what you are writing.
- It sounds obvious, but **answer the question** – not the one you prepared for in your head, not the past paper you tried a few weeks ago. It doesn't directly address the question, you can't

get credit for it, no matter how knowledgeable your answer is, otherwise, there would be no such thing as exam questions, and you could set your own questions (one day maybe)?

- Never leave a question out as you automatically score no marks. It's better to have a go and pick up even a few marks than leave one unanswered.
- Time your answers carefully and look at the amount of marks given for an answer; don't spend more time on it than it deserves.
- Don't waste time writing out the exam questions – your time is precious.
- Always leave a bit of time at the end for reading through your answers – a last chance to make changes or add a few points.

FINALLY ...

Don't try to cram too much on the night before the exam; have a flick through your revision notes or cards. Relax as much as is possible, check that you have pens and any other equipment that you need, particularly notes if you are allowed them in the exam. Check the time of the exam and arrive early; try to be calm and focused before the exam, don't get 'stressed' by standing near noisy or hysterical people!

At the risk of sounding too parental, have a good night's sleep. Make sure that you eat breakfast or lunch before you sit the exam, even if you are feeling nervous. Going without it will cause your blood sugar levels to drop and this will lead to poor concentration and a lack of energy. Likewise, have plenty of water, especially if it is a hot day, as dehydration will also adversely affect concentration. Don't let your mind wander in the exam room, focus on the task in hand.

Good luck!

Appendix

Bibliography and recommended reading

Following the **General titles** section, books for further reading have been listed alphabetically under the main media forms, plus sections on: Audience Research, Advertising, Cultural Studies, Media Production, Media Industries/Politics. Some of the titles anticipate the kinds of research and topics students are likely to encounter in the second year of an Advanced Level course or on an undergraduate media course.

Student guidance contains some reference books on media-related courses in higher education and careers-related titles.

STUDENT TEXTBOOKS

Burton G. 2001: *More Than Meets the Eye*. Arnold.

Clark V and Harvey R eds. 2002: *GCSE Media Studies*. Longman.

Downes B and Miller S. 1998: *Teach Yourself Media Studies*. Hodder & Stoughton.

Harvey R, Jones T and McDougall J. 2001: *AS Media Studies for OCR*. Hodder & Stoughton.

Joyce M, Rivers D and Bell A. 2001: *Advanced Level Media*, 2nd edn. Hodder & Stoughton.

O'Sullivan T, Dutton B and Rayner P. 1998: *Studying the Media*. Arnold.

Price S. 1997: *The Complete A–Z Media and Communication Handbook*. Hodder & Stoughton.

Rayner P, Wall P and Kruger S. 2001: *Media Studies: The Essential Introduction*. Routledge.

Stafford R and Branston G. 1999: *The Media Studies Students' Book*, 2nd edn. Routledge.

Stewart C, Lavelle M and Kowaltzke A. 2001: *Media and Meaning: An Introduction*. BFI.

Wall P, Beck A and Bennett P. 2001: *Communication Studies: The Essential Introduction*. Routledge.

Watson J and Hill A. 1999: *Dictionary of Media and Communication Studies*. Arnold.

GENERAL TITLES

Barthes R. 1975: *S/Z*. Cape.
Dyja, E ed. Annual: *BFI Film and Television Handbook*. BFI.
Ellis J. 1988: *Visible Fictions*. Routledge.
Gauntlett D. 2002: *Media, Gender and Identity*. Routledge.
Lacey N. 1998: *Key Concepts in Media Studies: Image and Representation*. Macmillan.
Lacey N. 2000: *Key Concepts in Media Studies: Narrative and Genre*. Macmillan.
Lacey N. 2002: *Key Concepts in Media Studies: Media Institutions and Audiences*. Palgrave.
Levi-Strauss C. 1964: *The Raw and the Cooked*. Penguin.
Peak S and Fisher P eds. Annual: *Guardian Media Guide*. Guardian Books/Fourth Estate.
Propp V. 1968: *Morphology of the Folktale*. University of Texas.
Todorov T. 1977: *The Poetics of Prose*. Blackwell.

Publications

Sight & Sound magazine (published monthly by the British Film Institute) is an excellent resource of reviews and news, mainly on film, but with reference to television and DVD/video releases as well and it is available for a reduced subscription price for students.

Sight & Sound/BFI Education publish the termly *Media Briefing: The Industry*, especially for Media Studies students, available from BFI Education Resources, 0870 241 3763.

Media Magazine (published termly by the English and Media Centre) is an excellent magazine for students, teachers, examiners and media professionals (contact: 020 7359 8080, e-mail: guido@englishandmedia. co.uk)

Advertising

Berger J. 1972: *Ways of Seeing*. BBC.
Brierley S. 1995: *The Advertising Handbook*. Routledge.
Fiske J. 1989: *Understanding Popular Culture*. Routledge.
Goddard A. 1998: *The Language of Advertising*. Routledge.
O'Sullivan T. 2002: *Studying Advertising*. Arnold.
Robinson M. 2000: *100 Greatest TV Ads*. HarperCollins.
Williamson J. 1992: *Decoding Advertisements*. Marion Boyars.

AUDIENCE RESEARCH

Ang I. 1991: *Desperately Seeking the Audience*. Routledge.

Buckingham D. 1987: *Public Secrets: EastEnders and its Audience.* BFI.

Morley D. 1980: *The Nationwide Audience.* BFI.

CULTURAL STUDIES

Brown, M.E. 1987: The politics of soaps: pleasure and feminine empowerment. *Australian Journal of Cultural Studies,* Vol. 4, No. 2.

Maslow A. 1970: *Motivation and Personality.* Harper & Row.

McRobbie A and MacCabe T. 1981: *Feminism for Girls.* RKP.

McQuail, D ed. 1972: *Sociology of the Mass Media.* Penguin.

FILM

Abrams N, Bell I and Udris J. 2001: *Studying Film.* Arnold.

Altman R. 1999: *Film/Genre.* BFI.

Arroyo J. 2000: *Action/Spectacle Cinema: A Sight & Sound Reader.* BFI.

Blandford S, Grant Barry K and Hillier J. 2001: *The Film Studies Dictionary.* Arnold.

Bordwell D and Thompson K. 2001: *Film Art: An Introduction.* McGraw-Hill.

Buckland W. 1998: *Teach Yourself Film Studies.* Hodder & Stoughton.

Bunten P. 2000: *York Film Notes* (series on individual films). York Notes/Longman re-published in 2001 as *The Ultimate Film Guides.* York Notes/Longman.

Buscombe E. 1970: The idea of genre in the American cinema. *Screen,* Vol. 11, no. 2, March/April.

Collins J, Radner H and Preacher Collins A eds. 1993: *Film Theory Goes to the Movies.* Routledge.

Cook P and Bernink M eds. 1999: *The Cinema Book,* BFI.

Derry C. 1988: *The Suspense Thriller. Films in the Shadow of Alfred Hitchcock.* Jefferson McFarland.

Hayward S. 1990: *Key Concepts in Cinema Studies.* Routledge.

Kitses J. 1969: *Horizons West.* Thames & Hudson.

McArthur C. 1972: *Underworld USA.* Secker & Warburg/BFI.

Neale S. 1980: *Genre.* BFI.

Neale S. 2000: *Genre and Hollywood.* Routledge.

Nelmes J. 1996: *An Introduction to Film Studies.* Routledge.

Phillips P. 2000: *Understanding Film Texts,* BFI.

Roberts G and Wallis H. 2001, *Introducing Film.* Arnold.

Roberts G and Wallis H. 2001: *Key Film Texts.* Arnold.

Ryall T. 1978: *Teachers' Study Guide no 2: The Gangster Film.* BFI Education.

White R ed. *BFI Film Classics.* BFI – a series on individual films.

White R ed. *BFI Modern Classics.* BFI – a series on individual films.

Wollen P. 1972: *Signs and Meanings in the Cinema.* Secker & Warburg.

MAGAZINES

Beetham M. 1996: *A Magazine of her Own?* Routledge.
Hermes J. 1995: *Reading Women's Magazines: an Analysis of Everyday Media Use.* Polity.
McKay J. 2000: *The Magazines Handbook.* Routledge.
McLoughlin L. 2000: *The Language of Magazines.* Routledge.
McRobbie A. 2000: *Feminism and Youth Culture.* Macmillan.
Winship J. 1992: *Inside Women's Magazines.* Pandora.

MEDIA INDUSTRIES/POLITICS

Balnaves M, Donald J and Hemelryk Donald S. 2001: *The Global Media Atlas.* BFI.
Curran J. 1999: *Media Organisations in Society.* Arnold.
Curran J and Gurevitch M. 2000: *Mass Media and Society.* Arnold.
Curran J and Seaton J. 1997: *Power Without Responsibility.* Routledge.

MEDIA PRODUCTION

Bernstein S. 1994: *Film Production.* Focal Press.
Dimbleby N, Dimbleby R and Whittington K. 1994: *Practical Media.* Hodder & Stoughton.
Jones C and Jolliffe G. 1996: *The Guerilla Film Maker's Handbook.* Cassell.
Lewis P. 1981: *Radio Drama.* Longman.
McLeish R. 1997: *Radio Production.* Focal Press.
Orlebar J. 2001: *Digital Television Production: A Handbook.* Arnold.
Thompson R. 1997: *The Grammar of The Edit.* Focal Press.

MUSIC

Goodwin A. 1992: *Dancing in the Distraction Factory.* Routledge.
Toynbee J. 2000: *Making Popular Music: Musicians, Creativity and Institutions.* Arnold.
Wall T. 2002: *Studying Popular Music Culture.* Arnold.

NEW MEDIA

Gauntlett D. 2000: *Web.studies.* Arnold.
Levinson P. 1998: *The Soft Edge.* Routledge.

NEWS (NEWSPAPERS AND TELEVISION)

Cohen S and Young J eds. 1981: *The Manufacture of News*. Constable.

Galtung and Ruge. 1981: Structuring and selecting news. In: Cohen, S. and Young, J. (eds). *The Manufacture of News*. Constable.

Hall, S. 1981: The determination of news photographs. In: Cohen, S. and Young, J. (eds). *The Manufacture of News*. Constable.

Hartley J. 1982: *Understanding News*. Routledge.

Keeble R. 1994: *The Newspapers Handbook*. Routledge.

Reah, D. 1998: *The Language of Newspapers*. Routledge.

Yorke I. 1995: *Television News*. Focal Press.

Grahame J. 1995: *News Pack*. English and Media Centre.

RADIO

Barnard S. 2000: *Studying Radio*. Arnold.

Crisell A. 1986: *Understanding Radio*. Routledge.

Shingler M and Wieringa C. 1998: *On Air: Methods and Meanings of Radio*. Arnold.

Wilby P and Conroy A. 1994: *The Radio Handbook*. Routledge.

TELEVISION

Burton G. 2000: *Talking Television*. Arnold.

Creeber G. 2001: *The Television Genre Book*. BFI.

Fiske J. 1994: *Television Culture:* Routledge

Geraghty C. 1991: *Women and Soap Opera*. Polity.

Goodwin A and Whannel G. 1990: *Understanding Television*. Routledge.

Holland P. 1997: *The Television Handbook*. Routledge.

Kilborn R and IZOD J. 1997: *An Introduction To Television Documentary;* Manchester University Press.

Martin R. 2000: *Television for A Level Media Studies*. Hodder & Stoughton.

McCrum M. 2000: *Castaway – The Full Inside Story of the Major BBC Series*. Ebury Press.

McQueen D. 1998: *Television: A Media Student's Guide*. Arnold.

Strinati D and Wagg S eds. 1992: *Come on Down? Popular Media Culture in Post-War Britain*. Routledge.

Winston B. 1999: *Fires Were Started*. BFI.

Useful websites

Every media company and regulatory body now has its own website. They are subject to frequent change, but the addresses can be found in the annual *Guardian Media Guide* and *BFI Film & TV Handbook* (listed above) or at www.mediauk.com – a free directory of media organizations and companies in UK.

Here are a few recommended sites:

☐ www.bfi.org.uk – The British Film Institute.
☐ www.imdb.com – Internet Movie Database.
☐ www.newmediastudies.com/ – David Gauntlett's site at Leeds University plus new media site.
☐ www.mediaguardian.co.uk – *The Guardian* newspaper's excellent website on media news.
☐ www.mirror.co.uk - *The Mirror*'s website.
☐ www.nmpft.org.uk – National Museum of Photography, Film and Television, Bradford.
☐ www.screenstudies.com – a website with a section for students of Media and Film Studies.
☐ www.theory.org.uk – David Gauntlett's other site.

Student guidance

BOOKS

Dyja E Ed. *Annual: BFI Film and Television Handbook 2003*, BFI. It provides the answers to many of the questions that the BFI receives each day from politicians, journalists, industry executives, researchers and film and television enthusiasts. This edition brings together a unique range of statistics spanning 20 years and more on the state of cinema, television and video/DVD. This includes the *Handbook*'s groundbreaking categorization of British films, details of major awards and festivals, as well as the comprehensive directory of industry contacts.

Elsey E. and Kelly A. 2002: *In Short: A Guide to Short Film-making in the Digital Age*. BFI. This book traces the history of the short film and its current role. Focusing on short-film producers and directors, it looks at the short film as a training opportunity for new talent. It covers issues of distribution, funding (including the lottery boom), exhibition, festivals, training and publications.

Jolliffe G. and Jones C. 2000: *The Guerilla Film Maker's Handbook: with CD*. Continuum International Publishing Group.

Langham J. 1997: *Lights, Camera, Action! Careers in Film, Television and Video*. BFI. Now updated and revised, this new edition of *Lights, Camera, Action!* is the essential guide to the competitive world of the media. It offers sound advice on career opportunities, educational qualifications required, training provision, the National Vocational Qualification system, new technical developments affecting employment and how to take the first step along a career path.

Orton L. Annual: *Media Courses UK*. BFI (available online at www.bfi.org.uk/mediacourses).

WEBSITES

http://www.bfi.org.uk/education/study/skillset/index.php – this is a comprehensive database for all short and long post-16 media/related courses, as well as HNDs, degree and post-graduate courses.

www.bfi.org.uk/education/study/careers/index.html – this page gives details of publications by BFI on media training and careers.

www.skillset.org – information from the main media training organization.

http://shootingpeople.org – a service for filmmakers and TV production personnel, with an e-mail alert subscription service if you're looking for various jobs or projects, including initial work experience as a runner.

Resources and contacts for tutors

BOOKS ON MEDIA EDUCATION

Buckingham D, Grahame J and Sefton-Green J. 1995: *Making Media: Practical Production in Media Education*. The English and Media Centre.
Buckingham D. 1990: *Watching Media Learning*. Falmer.

USEFUL CONTACTS

The following organizations can provide details of useful publications, newsletters/magazines, websites, classroom resources and in-service training:

☐ AMES (Association for Media Education in Scotland) and Media Education Journal (MEJ), Robert Preece (Treasurer), c/o Scottish Screen, 249 West, George Street, Glasgow G2 4QE – www.ames.org.uk
☐ Auteur Publishing – www.auteur.co.uk – publishes a range of excellent classroom resources for teachers, ideal for A-level.
☐ British Film Institute Education Projects, 21 Stephen Street, London W1P 2LN, Tel: 020 7255 1444 – www.bfi.org.uk. BFI Education Projects publish excellent resources and provide INSET via a national network of Associate Tutors (see website) and also run two distance-learning MA level professional development qualifications for teachers and annual A-level Media Studies conferences in London and Bradford.
☐ The English & Media Centre, 18 Compton Terrace, Islington, London N1 2UN, Tel: 020 7359 8080 – www.englishandmedia.co.uk – produce excellent classroom resources, a regular magazine and provide a comprehensive INSET programme.

☐ Film Education, Alhambra House, 27–31 Charing Cross Road, London WC2H 0AV, Tel: 020 7976 2297 – www.filmeducation.org – produce a wide range of free industry and educational resources on film.

☐ In the picture, 36 Hospital Road, Riddlesden, Keighley BD20 5EU, Tel: 01535 663737 – www.itpmag.demon.co.uk – produce an excellent magazine and educational resources.

☐ Keynote Educational – provider of INSET for Film and Media Studies teachers – www.keynote.org.uk

☐ www.mediaed.org.uk – is a website for media teachers which offers a national networking facility, forum and links to resources.

☐ Media Education Wales – Tom Barrance (Director), Media Education Wales, UWIC, Cyncoed Road, Cardiff CF23 6XD – www.mediaedwales. org.uk

☐ Media Matters – an educational consultancy, which supports media education in Scottish schools and colleges – www.netcomuk.co.uk/ ~mediamatters.html

☐ NIMEA – Northern Ireland Media Education Association, c/o David McCartney, Belvoir Park Primary School, Belvoir Drive, Belfast BT8 7DZ.

AWARDING BODY CONTACTS

OCR (Oxford & Cambridge RSA Examinations). www.ocr.org.uk. Main tel: 01223 552552 (for INSET programme ask for Customer Training & Support). In addition, there are two OCR Media Studies support websites: http://ital-dev.ucles-red.cam.ac.uk/ocrmediastudies – the original site; http://ital-dev.ucles-red.cam.ac.uk/listsupport/ ocr-mediastudies-a – an experimental site. OCR Media Studies e-community – subscribe to exchange good practice with colleagues: http://lists.ucles.org.uk/lists/listinfo/Ocr-mediastudies-a

WJEC (Welsh Joint Examinations Committee), www.wjec.co.uk. Main tel: 029 2026 5000. Contact Subject Officer for details of specification support and INSET programme.

AQA (Assessment & Qualifications Alliance), www.aqa.org.uk. Main tel: 0161 953 1180 (Manchester), 01483 506505 (Guildford). Contact Subject Officer for details of specification support and INSET programme.

QCA (Qualifications & Curriculum Authority), www.qca.org.uk. Main tel: 020 7509 5555. Useful for curriculum development press releases and information regarding Key Skills.

Glossary

Alternative in a media context, this is used to classify a text whose form or content differs from the mainstream equivalent.

Anchor in media terms, the process through which one element of a text confirms or supports the intention of another element, e.g. a caption for a newspaper photograph.

Archetype a stock character, which is frequently copied in literature, television, radio, film, etc. The hero, for example.

Asynchronous a term adapted from computer jargon, which indicates that behaviour is no longer restricted by traditional notions of time and order.

Atmos short for 'atmosphere', ambient sound that derives from the location itself.

Boom mic an external microphone on a long pole which can be held above or below the line of shooting to record sound at source.

Browser a web browser is a piece of software used to locate and display web pages. The two most popular browsers are Microsoft's *Internet Explorer* and Netscape's *Netscape Navigator*.

Call-sheet This sets out locations, equipment and the people required and when they are needed. It includes contact numbers for the crew, and the actors, in case you need to chase them up.

Chiaroscuro low-key lighting which produces strong contrasts between light and darkness and creates stylised shadows which are often mysterious and menacing. This style of lighting is a convention of *film noir*.

Closed texts media products whose form and content are arranged so that only a limited number of interpretations or readings are possible by the audience.

Compression digital information can be 'squeezed' so that more of it can be stored in existing spaces. Compression can result in a loss of quality in the information. But it increases the possibilities for two-way communication, allowing more interactivity between institution and audience.

Conglomerate a large corporation or company whose continued growth is achieved by buying or merging with other companies, who can support one another's business interests.

Consumers an alternative term for *audience*, often used when discussing the media as a business or institution to reinforce the role of profit and finance in the development of media forms and products.

Content analysis a way of analysing media texts which involves drawing conclusions from looking at the text as a whole or looking at a large number of similar texts.

Continuity editing the system of editing which is dominant in fiction TV and Hollywood cinema. It has been developed in order to provide the audience with a fluid and seamless experience of the text.

Convention an element whose repeated use in any form of media has become habitual or unavoidable.

Data transfer the movement of information (text, sound or video) electronically from one source to another. Conventional modems, connected to analogue telephone lines, allow this transfer to happen at a relative low rate of 56,000 (56k) bits per second (bps). New broadband technologies will increase the transfer rate tremendously.

Digital decoder the hardware required to transform a digital signal into its analogue equivalent so that the signal can be viewed by a conventional television set. Normally, this is a box through which the aerial or satellite dish connects to the television. Also known as a digibox.

Digital any electronic system which stores information in binary form. In this form, information is easily copied, transferred, compressed, combined with other sorts of information and rendered interactive.

Digitalization the process through which analogue media are turned into their digital equivalents.

Docusoap a form of documentary, normally focusing on 'ordinary' people and their lives or occupations, in which a soap-opera-style approach is taken. In this, multiple characters and 'storylines' are interwoven with one another to create the impression of real-life unfolding before us, examples include *Paddington Green* (BBC) and *Airport* (BBC).

Dominant groups those social groups who seem to have attained power or status within society, generally at the expense of other related groups. The dominance of particular groups is often achieved by the process of making their own viewpoints and values seem normal or 'common sense', whilst the values of others are marginalized, made to seem abnormal, unimportant or disruptive.

Film noir used to refer to a particular genre of thriller, made between 1941 and 1958. Protagonists usually include an ambiguous male hero and a desirable but dangerous woman (a femme fatale).

Flow a concept first used by Raymond Williams to describe the experience of watching television. In this and related media, products are not consumed as separate or discrete items, but as a continuous progression of sounds and images.

Found images Images found from existing sources, such as the internet or magazines.

Gun mic an external mic on a short stick which can be held by a recordist or mounted on the top of the camera.

Hardware the physical technology which stores and displays information.

House style the style of layout and language of a particular publication or the style of a particular institution.

Ideology often referred to as the system of **ideas, values** and **beliefs** which an individual, group or society holds to be true or important; these are shared by a culture/society, or groups therein, about how individuals/society should function.

Instant messaging a communications service allowing you to 'talk' privately with another individual online. Usually, the system will alert the user when somebody from their private list is also online. There are several different systems available and no agreed standard between systems.

Internet service providers companies which provide access to the internet. Normally these companies provide the user with a software package and a password. You can then browse the World Wide Web and send and receive e-mail.

Mainstream a term used to describe those areas of the media which tend to be highly commercialized. Mainstream media products reach large audiences and tend to make big profits for their institutions.

Mediation the process through which the real world is reconstructed in order to make it understandable to the audience of a media text.

Mode an umbrella term, used in Media Studies to describe the combination of genre, form, style and content adopted by a media text and in particular, the way in which it addresses an audience.

Mogul a term used to describe various powerful individuals who run or finance media companies.

Multiplexing is the process of simultaneously broadcasting a number of different signals through a single path of transmission (in this case a digital satellite frequency).

Narrowcasting the opposite of broadcasting. When a television channel broadcasts, it generally tries to attract as wide an audience as possible from those watching during any given period. A narrowcast channel targets a much smaller group of viewers, usually connected by a shared interest in a particular topic or genre, or a shared set of values. This type of audience is sometimes called a **niche audience**, as opposed to the **mass audience** which is targeted by mainstream channels.

Naturalization a form of realism in which the real world is presented as closely as possible to the ways in which we experience it on a daily basis.

Near video on demand film channels which repeatedly show a particular movie so that it can be ordered to start at specific timed intervals. Again, this is offered at an additional cost.

Neo-*noir* a 'new' *film noir*; one produced after 1958.

NVLA The National Viewers and Listeners Association is an organization which campaigns for stricter controls for material broadcast on television and radio. It is most strongly associated with its former president, Mary Whitehouse, who was prominent in the 1970s.

Open texts media products whose form and content (though particularly the former) allow a large degree of interpretative freedom to the audience. This kind of text produces many different readings or meanings, none of which are seen to be more legitimate than the others, for example, art films, alternative forms of music or television, radical magazines

Pay-per-view certain one-off televised events, such as boxing and football matches or a Robbie Williams concert, for example, are offered to viewers at an additional cost to their standard subscription.

Protagonist the leading character in a text.

Radio mic a cordless external mic.

Realism a combination of elements of form, style and content which has been constructed in order to create a particular sense of the real for the text's audience.

Reality TV either (a) a format in which documentary footage is used for entertainment purposes, for example *Police, Camera, Action* (ITV1), *America's Dumbest Criminals* (Sky One) or (b) a format in which real people are placed into an artificially created situation for entertainment purposes, examples include *Shipwrecked* (Channel 4), *Big Brother* (Channel 4) and *Faking It* (Channel 4).

Representation the process of making meaning in still or moving images and words/sounds. In its simplest form, it means to present/ show someone or something. However, as a concept for debate, it is used to describe the processes by which an image etc. may be used to represent/stand for someone or something, for example a place or an idea.

Rifle mic like a gun mic.

Rule of thirds conventional *mise-en-scène* of film and television relies on the screen being divided into three equal sections, both horizontally and vertically. Using these as guides, the framing appears 'natural' and avoids being overly symmetrical and artificial.

Scheduling the process of placing shows on the appropriate channel and at the appropriate time to gain the largest or most suitable audience.

Script the written text of a film, play or broadcast

Serial a television programme whose narrative or narratives continue from one episode to the next.

Series a television programme whose episodes tend to be self-contained narratives, which can often be viewed in any order.

Set-up the position of the camera/s and lighting in relation to the subject being filmed.

Shooting schedule this is a way of organizing the order in which you will take the shots, by writing them down in a sequential form.

Software the data or information to be stored by the hardware.

Storyboard this is a series of drawn camera shots in a camera sequence.

Stereotype an assumption about a person, place or issue that does not allow for flexibility or detail.

Subordinate used to describe groups who find themselves in less powerful positions than dominant groups.

Subsidiary a company wholly owned by a larger and more powerful parent company.

Synopsis a brief outline of about 200 words, give a brief outline of the plot or subject matter of a film, television programme, novel or radio play.

T-Commerce the activities of buying and selling through your television set.

Technological determinism the commonly held view that technology shapes, or determines, the kind of society in which we live.

Textual analysis a way of analysing media texts which involves drawing conclusions from a close examination of individual elements or small parts of a particular text.

Transnational a corporation whose various elements are no longer based in a single country but spread around the world in order to create a global operation.

Transparency in media terms, used to describe a text which does not draw attention to its own construction.

Vertical integration the extension of a firm's activities into earlier (backward integration) or later (forward integration) stages of production of its goods or services.

Walled garden this refers to a browsing environment that controls the information and websites that the user is able to navigate. Typically this approach is used to direct users to favoured content or to protect users from unsuitable material.

Watermark an encryption technique which ensures that broadcast material can be viewed live by subscribers, but cannot be recorded or copied for later viewing. The name derives from the *watermarking* of paper currency as a measure to prevent counterfeiting.

Whip pans a very fast pan between two or more characters or points of interest. It gives the impression that the camera has been 'surprised' by activity and is used in the place of a more conventional cut or shot/reverse shot.

Index

180° rule 152, 153

A Bout de Souffle 21
Absolutely Fabulous 85
Access 44
Action adventure films 25–30
    gender representation 25–26, 27
Action comedy (actcom) 79
Action match 21, 152
Actors 136, 164
Added value on DVDs 48–51
Adventure films 25–30
Advertising 7, 31
Advertorial 30
Aerial shot 19
Alien 26
Ally McBeal 23
Alternative genre 114
Althusser, Louis 35
Ambient lighting 24
Ambient sound 22
America Online 116
Analogue cameras pre-roll 147
Analogue editing 150–151
Analogue technology 44
Analysis 11, *see also* Content analysis,
        Documentaries, Textual analysis
Anchor 64
Angle shots 19–20
Animation 22
AOL, *see* America Online
AOL Time Warner 116–121
Archetypes 16, 26, 27
Artificial lighting 24

As If 69
Asimov, Issac 93
Assessment objectives 10
Asynchronous approach 102
Atmos 22, 144
Attachment 44
Audience 6
    digital television benefits 100–107
    expectation 16, 32
    mass 31
    needs 33, 34, 41–42
    niche 31
        vs mass 99
    pleasure 16
    research 133, 183–184
    response 128, 129
    sit-com 81–82
    soap opera 86–88
    see also Target audience
Audio
    editing 166–167
    production 159–160, 164–166
        post-production 166
Audio-visual media 15
    forms 1
    language analysis 18

Back light 24, 149
Back projection 22
Bandwidth 96
Banner 30
    advertisement 44
Barthes, Roland 53, 57
Batman 25

Beliefs 8
Bibliography 185
Big Brother series 51, 59, 63–64
Binary oppositions 28
Bird's-eye shot 19
Blade Runner 148
Bogart, Humphrey 23, 148
Bond films 25
Bookmark 44
Boom mic 144
Brainstorming ideas 132
Brand
    differentiation 40
    identity, newspapers 30, 32, 38–40
    image 107
Breaking news 47
    September 11 2001 48
Brief 127, 130–132
Broadband 96
Broadsheet newspapers 38
Brookside 89, 90
Broomfield, Nick 63
Brown, Mary Ellen 86, 89
Browser 44, 117
BSkyB 99
Buck Rogers 25
Buddy sit-coms 84
Byline 30

Call sheet 142
Camera care 143
Camerawork 18–20, 146–147
    in film 20, 29
    in television documentary 20
Captions 22, 30, 38
Casablanca 23
Cast 128
Castaway 66
    documentary text analysis 72–74
CD-ROM 44
Celebrity
        documentaries 63
        tabloid press and 41–42, 43–44
Channel loyalty 102
Characters, building 163
Charity advertisements 7
Chiaroscuro lighting 148

Chicken Run 139
Chromakey 22
Chronique d'un Eté (*Chronicle of a
        Summer*) 61
Cinema 75, 93–94
Ciné-vérité 20, 64, 146
Circulation 30, 42
Classic realism 68–69
Clear and Present Danger 25, 26
Cliff-hanger 16
Closed texts 88
Close-up 18
Codes
    moving image 16, 24
    narrative 57
Colour 168–169
Commodity 41
Communication Studies 2
Communication, forms of 1–2
Companionship 34
Composition 20
Compression 96
Computer software, *see* Software
Computer-generated images (CGI) 22
Concept, definition of 4
Conglomerate 110
Connor, Sarah in *Terminator* series 27
Connotation of text 53
Consumers 93
Content analysis 77
Contents page 158
Contingency 133–134
Continuity 145
Continuity editing 21, 69
Conventions 6, 69, 129
    ICT-based media 46, 167
    magazines 31
    moving image 16, 18, 24
    newspapers 38
Convergence 97, 105–106
Cookie 44
Copy 30
Coronation Street 88, 90, 91
Costume 24
Cover lines 30, 32, 37
Cover price 31
Covers, magazines 32, 154

Crane shot 19, 20
Crimewatch 64, 66
Critical language 4
Cropping 30
Crosscuts 73
Cross-cutting action 21
Crossing the line, *see* 180° rule
Crossroads 87
Crouching Tiger, Hidden Dragon 57
Cultural imperialism 98
Cultural rules and soap operas 88
Cut 20
Cut and paste 159
Cutaway 20
Cutaways 152
Cutting on movement 152

DAT (digital audio tape) recorder 160
Data transfer 119
Death of a Princess 66
Decoding meaning 53
Deconstruction 11, 55
Default settings in computers 45
Denotation of text 53
Depth of field 20
Design 24, 37
Dialogue 22
Diegetic sound 21
Digital broadcasting 48
Digital Cable Television (DCT) 99
Digital camera 45
Digital data 45
Digital decoders 100, 101
Digital editing
    audio 166–167
    video 150, 151
Digital Satellite Television (DST) 99,
        107–108
Digital technology 93, 99
    audience benefits 100–107
    quality 100–101
    value to its institutions 107–108
Digital Terrestrial Television (DTT) 99
Digitalization 96
Dineen, Molly 63
Direct address 22
Direct cinema 64

Direction 146
Disney Enterprises 110
Display advertisement 39, 40
Dissolve 21
Diversion 34
Documentaries 59–60
    brief history of 60
    celebrity 'access all areas' genre 63
    editing 69–70
    form and style 68
        timeline 61
    modes of 63–66
    narrative 70–72
        credibility 73
    realism in 66–68
    text analysis 72–74
Documentary 'look' in fictional work 69
Docusoaps 63, 65, 72
Dolly shot 20
Domestic comedy (domcom) 79
Dominant groups: 77
Drama-comedy (dramedy) 80
Drama-documentary 66, 67
DTP (desktop publishing) program 159
DVD (Digital versatile discs) 48
    added value features 45, 49–51

EastEnders 87, 90, 91, 92
Eastmancolor 93–94
Editing 20–21, 129, 150–152
    decision list (EDL) 150
    documentaries 69–70
    television 21
Editorial 30
EDL (edit display list) 166–167
Electronic programme guide (EPG)
        103–104
Ellen 85
E-mail 45
Emergency 999: 64, 66
Emmerdale 90, 91
Encoding meaning 53
Equipment 133, 142–143
    audio production 160
    ICT-based production 167
    print production 154
    video production 134

ER 87
Errol Flynn 25
Essay writing 179
   planning 180
Evaluating work 126
Evaluation questionnaires 128
Evaluative skills 13
Exam preparation 186
Exam questions
   analysing 179
   answering 181
   planning for 180–182, 189
Exclusive 30
Expository documentary 63–64
Eyeline match 152

Fade 20–21, 54, 152
Fairbanks, Douglas 25
Family, portrayal
   in sit-coms 80–81
   in soap operas 87, 90–91
Fawlty Towers 83
Feature 30
Femininity 77, 78
Fictional texts, documentary
     techniques in 69
File 45
Fill light 24, 149
Film 135
Film noir 23, 148
Films
   camerawork 20
   editing 21
   lighting 23
   promotion language 5
   sound 22
   special effects 22
   'swashbuckling' pirate 25
First-person documentary 65–66
Fiske, John 88
Flaherty, Robert 60, 68
Flash 45
Flash Gordon 25
Flow 75
Fly-on-the-wall documentaries 65
Fonts 37, 40, 43, 156
Ford, Harrison 26, 28–29

Forms 6, 8
   documentary 68
   ICT-based media language 46
   magazines 31
   moving image 18, 24
   newspapers 38
Found images 125, 157–158
Framing 20
Frasier, representation of men 83–84
Free gifts 32
Friends 79, 81–82
Front covers of magazines 32

Gatekeeping 38
Gels 148
Gender 78
   representation
      action adventure films 25–26, 27
      television 77, 78–79
Genre 15, 17, 24, 129, 131
   identifying 16, 17
   magazines 33
   theory 16
GIF 45
Gimme, Gimme, Gimme 24
Gladiator 25
Globalization 119
Godard, Jean-Luc 55
Gossip, use in soap operas 89–90
Grace Under Fire 85
Graef, Roger 61
Graphics 22, 30
Grierson, John 60–61, 62
Group work 125
Gun mic 144
Gutter 30

Hall, Stuart 53
Hamilton, Linda 26
Hammocking 102
Hand-held camera effect 20
Hard copy 45
Hard disk 45
Hardware 93, *see also* ICT
Headline 30, 39, 43
Hegemonic model 113
Heroes 25, 26, 27

High angle shot 19–20
Hillsborough
  drama-documentary 66, 67
  media coverage 113–114
Hit 45
Hollyoaks 87
Home Box Office (HBO) channel
    117
Homepage 45, 171
Hook 32
House style 31, 154
HTML (hypertext markup language) 45
Hybrid magazines 31
Hybrids 15–16, 31
Hyperlinks 45, 168
Hypertext 45

I Love Lucy 84–85
Iconography 16–17
ICT (Information and computer technology)-
    based media 15
  forms 1
  language
    analysis of 44–52
    forms and conventions 46
ICT production 167, 170
    pre-production planning 167–169
    post-production 171–172
Ideology 8
Images 157–158, 170
Incidental music 22
Independence Day 55–56, 57
Indiana Jones trilogy 26–27, 28–29,
    see also Raiders of the Lost Ark
Instant messaging service 116
Institutional models 111–113
Institutions 6, 109–110, 127, 136
Interactive services 99–100, 104–105
Interactive television 51
Internet 45
Internet Service Providers (ISPs) 116
Interpellation 35
Inter-personal communication 1
  main forms of 2
Interviews 137, 162
Inverting, accepted sit-com
    representations 85

ISP (internet service provider) 45, 171
ITVDigital 99

Jazz Singer, The 93
Jewel of The Nile, The 26
Jolie, Angelina 26
JPEG 45
Jump cut 21, 152

Key light 24, 149
King Solomon's Mines 25, 26

Lara Croft: Tomb Raider 22, 25, 26
Layout 31, 38, 156, 159
Lethal Weapon series 25, 26
Levinson, Paul 94
Lévi-Strauss, Claude 28
Lifestyle magazines 42
Lighting 24, 148–150
  film 23
  set-ups 148–149
Listings magazines 31
Location 24
Log sheet 146
Logging 145–150
Logo 38–40
Long shot 18
Long take 21
Low angle shot 19–20, 29
Low-key effect 149
Lucas, George 26, see also *Star Wars*
Lumière Brothers 60
Lure 31, 39, 40

Magazines 155
  audiences 31
  forms and conventions 31
  front covers 32
  genres 33
  see also Print
Mainstream 114
'Making of' documentaries 49–50
Malcolm in the Middle 85
Male heroes 25
Maltese Falcon, The 148
Manipulative model 111–112
Market model 112

Mary Tyler Moore Show, The 84–85
Masculinity 77, 78
Maslow, Abraham 33
 hierarchy of needs 33
Mass audience 99
Mass market 31
Master shot 18
Mastheads 31, 32, 37, 38, 39, 40, 154
Matriarchs 87, 88–89
Matrix, The 49–50
Meaning, encoding and decoding 53
Media–audience relationship 6–8
Media communication, main
 forms of 3
Media forms 1–2, 6
Media language 4–6
Media ownership 109–110
Media production skills 13
Media products 7
Media Studies 3–4, 11–12
Media text 4
 ways of studying 11
 moving image 178
Media theories 3
Mediation 68, *see* also Media language
Men Behaving Badly 84
Men, representation of
 in sit-com 82–84
 in soap opera 90–92
Microphones 160–161
Mind maps 177
Mise-en-scène 24, 145–146
 documentaries 68–69
 TV sit-com 24
Mission Impossible 27
Mix 21, 151–152
Mnemonics 188
Moana 60
Mock-up 157, 169
Mode 64
Mode of address 22, 31, 32, 35, 37,
 156, 161, 168
Models 23
Mogul 117
Moods 156, *see also* Lighting
Morin, Edgar 61
Moulin Rouge 51

Moving image media texts, taking
 notes from 178
MP3: 45
Multi-diegetic plot 16
Multiplexing 101
Multi-strand plots 16
Murdoch, Elisabeth 106
Music 166
Music industry 110, 114–115
Music radio show 165
MusicNet 115
My Family 24, 85

Nag 38
Nanook of the North 60, 62, 68, 74
Napster 114–115
Narrative 24
 documentaries 70–72
 form, deconstructing 55
 linking 54
 sequences 55–57
 displacing 55
 structures 58
 model of 71
 theory 57
Narrator, use in documentaries 63–64, 70
Narrowcasting 99, 102
National Viewers and Listeners
 Association (NVLA) 76
Natural light 149–150
Naturalization 77
Near video on demand 99
Neo-*noir* 148
New media 45, 92–98
 interaction with society 94–95
 value to companies and institutions
 107–108
News photographs 41
News values 31, 38, 40
Newsgathering 38
Newspapers 38
 analysing 38
 audiences 31
 brand identity 38–40
 language 41
 new audiences 47
 online 46–48

photographs 41
see also Print, Tabloid newspapers
Nib 38
Niche audience 99
Niche product/audience 31
Night Mail 61, 62
Noddies 20
Non-diegetic sound 21
Note-making 174–178
NYPD Blue 69

Observational documentary 64–65
Old media, persistence of 94, 96, 97
Only Fools and Horses 83
Open texts 88

Pan shot 20
Parallel action 21
Patriarchs 90
Pay-per-view 99
Peer-to-peer networking 115
Pennebaker, D.A. 61
Personal identity 34
Personal relationships 34
Photographs 158
Planning for exams 189
Plots 16
Plug-in 45
Pluralist model 112
Point of view shot 20
Points of interaction 16
Pop Idol 51
Popstars 59
Portal 45
Pre-production planning 130
Presenters 164
Primary media 75
Primary research 183–184
Print
    analysing 30–31
    -based media 15
    language 30–32
    media forms 1
    production 153, 157–159
        post-production 159
        pre-production planning 154–157
    see also Newspapers, Magazines

Printing 159
Production
    construction 129
    design 24
    evaluation 129–130
    organization 128
    processes 133–134
    see also specific types of media production
Program 45
Props (Properties) 24, 128
Protagonist 26
Puff 38
Pulp Fiction 54, 109–110
Pyrotechnics 23

Qualitative research 184
Quantitative research 183
Quatermain, Allan 26, 28
QuickTime 45

Radio 75, 96, 133, 161
    drama 165
    mic 144
    scripting 163
        improvised programmes 162
    show, music 165
    using variety 163–164
    see also entries under Audio *and* Sound
Raiders of the Lost Ark 26–27, 28–29
Rambo 25
Reaction shot 20
Reading 53, *see also* Research
Realism 66–68
    classic 68–69
Reality TV 63, *see also* Documentaries
Recces (reconnaissance) 128, 141
Reconnoitring, *see* Recces
Record keeping 125
Redefinition 16
Reel-to-reel editing 166
References 185
Reflexive documentary 65
Relationships in soap operas 87–88, *see also* Family, Gender
Repetition and difference in genre 16
Representation 3, 8, 76
    television 76–77

Research 127, 133, 135, 157, 161, 162, 182–185
  audiences 133, 183–184
  interviews 183
  media texts 136, 183
Reverse zoom shot 20
Rhoda 85
Rifle mic 144
Roles 128
Romancing the Stone 26
Roseanne 85
Rouch, Jean 61
Rule of thirds 69

Sam Spade 148
Sans-serif font 31, 37, 40, 43
Saturday afternoon serials 25
Saussure, Ferdinand de 52
Scanner 45
Scheduling 102
Scott, Ridley 148
Screen grabs 12
Scrim 149
Script 137
Scripting 138
  improvised programmes 162
  radio drama 163
Se7en 49
Search engine 46, 172
Secondary media 75
Secondary research 184–185
Seinfeld 84
Self-representation 10
Semiotics 52–53
September 11 2001 terrorist attack, breaking news 48
Sequencing narrative 57
Serial 79
Series 79
Serif font 31, 40
Server 46
Set-up: 142
Sex 78
Shooting procedure 144–145
Shooting
  ratio 69–70
  schedule 142

Shots in camerawork 18–20, 29
Signifier vs signified in text 52
Situation comedy (Sit-com) 79–81
  audiences 81–82
  character types 82
  men in 82–84
  women in 84–85
SkyDigital 99, 103, 104, 105, 107–108
Sky Television, *see* BSkyB
Slow motion 21
Soap operas 86
  audiences 86–88
  characteristics 86
  men in 90–92
  relationships in 87–88
  women in 87, 88–90
Social groups, constituents of 77
Society, effect of new technologies 94–95, 98
Software 93, 115, 116, 123–124, *see also* ICT
Sound 21–22
  editing 20–21
  effects 128, 131, 164
  mixer 166
  role
    in film 22, 28
    in television documentary 22
  video production 143–144
Soundtrack 21, 152
Spaced 79, 80
Space–time relationships 18
Special effects 22–23
  films 22
  sound 22
  television drama 23
Specialist audience 31
Spielberg, Steven 28, *see also Indiana Jones* series
Splash 38, 39, 43
Standfirst 31
Star Wars 26
Steadicam 20
Stereotypes 26, 27
Stock characters 16
Storyboard ideas 12
Storyboarding 138–140

Strapline 31, 32, 38–40, 43
Studio/set design 24
Stunts 23
Style, documentary 68
Subject matter 168
Subordinate groups 77
Subsidiary 116
Subverting, accepted sit-com representations 85
Suddenly Susan 85
Sugar magazine 35, 36, 37
Sun, The 111–112, 113–114
Superimpose 21
Surveillance 34
Swashbuckling films 25
Symbolic oppositions 28
Synopsis 137

Tabloid newspapers 33, 38
    celebrity coverage 41–42, 43–44
    textual analysis 43
    viewpoints 111–112
Taflinger, Richard 79–80
Talking heads mode 64
Tarantino, Quintin 55
Target audience 31, 127, 128, 161, 168
T-Commerce 108
Technical language 4
Technical support 133
Technicolor 93–94
Technological determinism 93
Technology, using 128
Technophile 97–98
Technophobes 98
Teenage lifestyle magazines 31, 35, 36, 37
Television 75–76
    advertisements 21
    documentary
        camerawork 20
        sound in 22
    editing in 21
    gender representations 76, 77, 78–79
    representations 76–77, 87
    see also Situation comedy, Soap operas
Terminator series 25, 26
Terrestrial television channels 99
Tests 128

Text effects 156
Texts, decoding by audience 53
Textual analysis 14, 77, 130
    theoretical approaches 52–55
The Blue Planet 22
The Naked Chef: Happy Days 21
Themes 21, 28
Third Rock from the Sun 85
This Life 69
Three-dimensional (3D) film 93–94, 95
Tilt camera movement 20
Timeshift 102
Time Warner 117–118
Todorov, Tzvetan 57
Topic areas 127
Touchstone 110
Tracking shots 20, 29
Transnational corporations 119
Transparency 69
Tune 22
Turner, Ted 117, 119
TV situation comedy, *see* Situation comedy
TV soap opera, *see* Soap opera
Two-shot 18
Typeface 31
Typography 156

URL (Uniform Resource Locator) 46, 172
Uses and gratifications theory 34

Values 8
Verisimilitude 68
Vertical integration 121
Video covers 9
Video diaries 65–66, 74
Video editing 150–152
Video equipment 134
Video production 134, 143–150
    post-production 150–153
    pre-production 135–143
    roles 137, 138
Video shooting procedure 145
VideoNation 65–66
Villains 25, 26, 27
    soap opera 92
Visual style 154
Visualization 187–188

Vladimir Propp 58
Voice-of-God mode 63–64, 73
Voice-overs 22, 63–64

Walking with Beasts 22
Walled garden 117
Watermark 108
Watkins, Paul 63
Weaver, Sigourney 26
Web site, constructing pages 170
Webmaster 46
Webpage 46
Websites 46
   addresses 38, 39
   for films 132
   new audiences through 47
   publishing your 171–172
   television programmes and 51
   newspapers and 46–48
   see also ICT production

Webzine 46
Whip pans 69
Wide shot 18
Wildtrack 22
Wipe 21, 152
Wiseman, Frederick 61
Women, representation of
   in action adventure films 25, 27
   in sit-com 84–85
   in soap operas 88–90
Word limits 127
World Wide Web 46, *see also* ICT,
   Websites
Writing articles 158–159
WYSIWYG 46

Youth audience 133

Zoom shot 20
Zorro 25